OUR LOVABLE BULLY TO THE SOUTH

There is a reason for this book. Over the years, your faithful servant, Dr. Foth, has repeatedly been called upon to examine the burning issues of our time. The next logical step seemed to be Washington. These past two years on the Potomac have been a cultural exchange with only one proviso: while my wisdom is offered free to the White House, the current resident retains the right to ignore it. It is a friendly truce. This book is not intended to be the definitive X ray of the United States. No castles will fall, nor embassies rumble. But I will have removed a lot of things from my chest. There is a reason for everything. That's why Dr. Foth goes to Washington.

Seal Books by Allan Fotheringham

MALICE IN BLUNDERLAND
CAPITOL OFFENCES

Allan Fotheringham

CAPITOL OFFENCES

Dr. Foth Meets Uncle Sam

SEAL BOOKS
McClelland-Bantam, Inc.
Toronto

For Brady,
the bravest man I know

*This low-priced Seal Book
has been completely reset in a typeface
designed for easy reading, and was printed
from new plates. It contains the complete
text of the original hardcover edition.*
NOT ONE WORD HAS BEEN OMITTED

CAPITOL OFFENCES
*A Seal Book / published by arrangement with
Key Porter Books Limited*

PRINTING HISTORY
*Key Porter Books edition published September 1986
Seal edition / October 1987*

ISBN 0-7704-2198-9

*Seal Books are published by McClelland-Bantam Inc. Its trade-
mark, consisting of the words "Seal Books" and the portrayal of
a seal, is the property of McClelland-Bantam Inc., 60 St. Clair
Avenue East, Suite 601, Toronto, Ontario M4T 1N5, Canada.
This trademark has been duly registered in the Trademarks
Office of Canada. The trademark consisting of the words "Bantam Books" and the portrayal of a rooster is the property of and
is used with the consent of Bantam Books, Inc., 666 Fifth
Avenue, New York, New York 10103. This trademark has been duly
registered in the Trademarks Office of Canada and elsewhere.*

PRINTED IN CANADA

COVER PRINTED IN U.S.A.

U   0 9 8 7 6 5 4 3 2 1

Contents

Our American Cousins

IN AN EMERGENCY, CANADA WILL GIVE YOU ALL AID
SHORT OF HELP—BOBBY KENNEDY

There is a reason for this book. As there is for everything.
Over the years, your faithful servant, Dr. Foth, has repeatedly
been called upon to examine the burning issues of our time.
Vancouver has been rescued from the developer-mind, from
those who wanted to pave Stanley Park and uglify the town
with freeways. Similarly, Victoria—God's waiting room—received
the healing powers of your agent and is a better backwater
because of it.

Next, I directed my ministrations east to Ennui-on-the-
Rideau, home of the Gliberals, the Regressive Convertibles,
and the Few Democrats. After the application of mouth-to-
mouth gossipication, Ottawa was brought giggling and protesting
into something vaguely resembling the twentieth century.

The next logical step, previous jurisdictions having been
soothed and pacified, seemed to be Washington, especially
since it calls itself the most important city in the world. It is
the New Rome, full of black boxes and red buttoms, all the
switches and knobs that can blow us to smithereens. One
might as well get close to the furnace if we all are going to
fry.

Besides, that land was obviously badly in need of advice
and guidance. Canada had been saved. Could we withhold
the healing powers from our supposed best friends? It is

1

expected that they will greatly appreciate them, being the most tolerant of all nationalities.

The author came of age, as did several generations of Canadians, under the spell of America, especially the silver screen of Hollywood, Our view of the world and the United States was shaped most of all by what we saw on Saturday afternoons at the movies. It is appropriate, therefore, that the most influential country in history, which covers us like a benevolent smothering blanket, is now run by a man who was part of that very system—a man who became rich and famous and then immensely powerful because he was apprenticed in myth, raised in fantasy, trained in transparency. He is the product of a culture that captivated the rest of the world with its unreal dreams, and he has transferred that crazy view of reality to the White House, where popcorn is served in silver bowls most every night, and the myth glides on.

The current Canadian regime of the Jaw That Walks Like a Man is attempting to cuddle up to the Reaganauts. The consequences are as yet unknown, though probably perilous. Ottawa is shaking and shingling in anticipation, while Washington barely notices. This situation is a symptom of a condition discussed herein: the usual casual disdain with which most American presidents have regarded the Great White North. If you are a Canadian prime minister, as will be shown, the chances are that you will be sworn at by a president—either to your face or behind your back. It goes with the territory. Only big boys should go into politics.

Over the years, I have tracked the spoor of the shifty politician, in Vancouver, London, and Ottawa. I have examined the mating habits of those who hang about the political trough, their tongues adrool in anticipation of some tiny reward, some pat on the forehead.

In previous incarnations, I was sentenced for several decades to cover the intellectual perambulations of one Pierre Trudeau, whose thought processes and flexible vocabulary dominated the Canadian scene for almost too long. One could not understand Canada during his hegemony without understanding Trudeau. One cannot understand the United States of the 1980s without understanding Ronald Reagan.

The boy who types this is, therefore, now using Washington for the finishing touches on his scepticism. These past two years on the Potomac have been a cultural exchange with only one proviso: while my wisdom is offered free to the

White House, the current resident retains the right to ignore it. It is a friendly truce.

This book is not intended to be the definitive X-ray of the United States, our lovably bully to the south. Esteemed academics do more thorough jobs. Retired diplomats offer austere and more dispassionate critiques. All it is is a truthful tracing of one Canadian's views of our relationship with our amusing neighbours—along the route that started in Hearne, Saskatchewan, and ended in Georgetown.

It also roams about American, after it disengages itself from Mr. Reagan's cranium. Washington, like Ottawa, regards itself as the centre of the universe but is regarded with suspicion by those who live in the hinterland. The hinterland, from Peoria to Georgia to San Francisco, is explored.

It includes the usual respectful view of the White House and the inevitable dissection of the Gotliebs and a lot of wild prejudices and crazy insights. No castles will fall, nor embassies tumble. But I will have removed a lot of things from my chest. There is a reason for everything. That's why Dr. Foth goes to Washington.

1

Canadian Graffiti

In which Dr. Foth as a tad is introduced to the wonders of the U.S.A. and how he grew up in a town that is in the Bible and Shakespeare and why he didn't make it to the Olympics and how he almost was seduced by America and how he got in the RCMP security file and how New York was shaken by his boycott.

> *My generation of Canadians grew up be-*
> *lieving that, if we were very good or very*
> *smart, or both, we would someday graduate*
> *from Canada.*—ROBERT FULFORD

I can remember exactly where I was the day that Franklin Delano Roosevelt died. I was outside Pearson's General Store in Sardis, British Columbia. It was late afternoon and I can still see the shocked, stilled expressions on adult faces as the word went around. They had lost someone who had seemed close to them. It was one of those frozen moments that stick with you forever, like the exact time you heard about John Kennedy's assassination in Dallas or you learned that the Challenger shuttle had blown up. I was thirteen, and that incident made me aware of the power American figures had over Canadians.

The next year I met my first American, Golden Boy. (Ronald Reagan had just finished making *This Is the Army*, in which he played Johnny Jones, and which starred George Murphy, Kate Smith, and Joe Louis, and was preparing for *Stallion Road*, with Alexis Smith and Zachary Scott.) Golden Boy was perhaps seventeen, and he and his family were vacationing at Cultus Lake, a pool of wickedness some seventy miles east of Vancouver. It was considered wicked because it had an outdoor roller-skating rink where you picked up the girls who came in on the weekends from Vancouver. Sardis was three miles from Cultus Lake, and my mother always said, "I wish we lived a thousand miles from that den of iniquity."

Golden Boy was from Tulare, the same small town in California as Bob Mathias, the seventeen-year-old phenom who had won the Olympic Games decathlon gold medal. Anyone who had even passed within shouting distance of

Mathias' birthplace was automatically held in awe by this here fourteen-year-old (then headed in his dreams for the Canadian Olympic track team). Golden Boy seems so different from any Canadian teenager. He was everything that California was famous for. His hair was sun-bleached. His jeans were properly faded. His T-shirts were always spotlessly clean. He had a year-round tan and a square jaw; he was effortlessly athletic, modest, slow to speak (and, now that I think about it, probably quite dumb). He came back to Cultus Lake for several summers and I worshipped him. He is today, I would suspect, a salesman for IBM.

The high school was in nearby Chilliwack, and there appeared one day a new boy. He attracted immediate attention because he was from Arkansas, which none of us had ever heard of. His name was Charlie. He was short and broad-shouldered, and had a deep tan and an open, honest face. Most of all, he had this accent. He was incomprehensible. It would not have occurred to us that perhaps our early McKenzie brothers' accent might have been incomprehensible to him; it is always other people who have the accents. (Ronald Reagan was then making *The Girl from Jones Beach*, with Virginia Mayo and Eddie Bracken, who in the filming accidentally tripped Reagan, causing him to fall and break his coccyx.)

Charlie had played football, naturally—a game not then played in Fraser Valley high schools. One could see that, with his squat, low-to-the-ground build, he would be the prototype halfback or fullback. He came out for our track team and was an immediate sensation—quite the most spectacular sprinter we had ever seen. It was his intensity and drive that were so impressive. Flailing out of the starting blocks, all energy and little style, he seemed like a whirlwind on the way to the finish line. It appeared as if he would run through a brick wall to win. He was intimidated neither by the new surroundings nor the new school nor the unfamiliar equipment. Those of us who were the hotshot sprinters felt we would die in his shadow. He seemed to embody all the qualities Canadians lacked—confidence, energy, ambition.

In the end, the bowling ball from Arkansas did not dominate. He did not make it to the top echelon (meaning those of us headed for the Olympics). It was his head-long style and will to win that had made him seem so overwhelmingly impressive. He subsided and those with more natural talent and greater speed prevailed. It was an early lesson about Canadian-American relations—transferable to films and books, TV and journalism, theatre and radio: I eventually learned that the Great White North had no need to be intimidated. Anyone who has ever watched *This Hour Has Seven Days* or *the fifth estate* has no reason to be dazzled by *60 Minutes*. Anyone who has heard Jack Webster has no excuse for being overwhelmed by Ted Koppel. Does anyone doubt that the protean energies of Pierre Berton would not have gained him the same success (with more money) in the Excited States of America?

Charlie taught me that being American is no guarantee of excellence. At the same post-puberty level, I was learning most of my geography lessons from American sources. Growing up, Canadians of my generation were prisoners of Tin Pan Alley at a time when half the hit parade seemed to come from the Rand-McNally road map of America. If it wasn't "Chattanooga Choo-Choo," it was "I've Got a Gal in Kalamazoo." One of the reasons Canadians can't take the Nicaraguan threat seriously is that they still can't get out of their heads that old Andrews Sisters number, "Managua, Nicaragua" ("*is a wonderful spot*"). I once drove a half-day out of my way just so I could dateline my column from Kokomo, Indiana, the name of another hit.

Kokomo in reality is about as romantic as Hamilton but when I was young the United States existed only as a vast, undecipherable space filled with places exciting enough to be the subject of songs. No one wrote about Swift Current or the joys of the Bay of Fundy. It was all about "Down on the Bayou" or "Across the Alley from the Alamo" or the "Banks of the Wabash" (the Wabash, a river, would not make a healthy creek farther north). The fact that the names for these songs were probably chosen by throwing a dart at a map in the office of some North American song writer didn't matter. The reality was that the radio waves were full of swallows coming back to Capistrano and "Deep in the Heart of Texas" and "Oklahoma!" and "Moonlight in Vermont" and "Stars Fell on Alabama" and "Mississippi Mud" and "Sioux City Sue" and "My Old Kentucky Home" and "Nothing Could Be Finer Than To Be in Carolina in the Morning." We didn't know where they were, but we sang them, captives of someone else's geography. Harmless brainwashing, but effective.

Years later, decades later, I drove through Kalamazoo and

Chattanooga and Tallahassee and all those places writ large in Tin Pan Alley's geography phase, and I decided that the view from a distance was better. (You not only can't go home again, you can't go away.) I realized, belatedly, that Canadian place names, although they may not ring bells, do have historic meaning. Two in particular—ones that shaped me—are Hearne and Sardis. Both are proud names—well, one of them at least. Hearne, Saskatchewan, which during my stay (Ronald Reagan was then making *The Cowboy from Brooklyn*, with Pat O'Brien, Dick Powell, and Ann Sheridan) consisted of one church, a store, a blacksmith shop, a garage, two grain elevators, one (1) tree, thirty residents, and four children (myself, a brother, and two sisters), was of course named after Samuel Hearne, the famous English explorer who roamed the territory west for the Hudson's Bay Company. The United States, although no more than an hour's drive south from Hearne, did not exist. Its only presence was a summer treat in a Saturday night drive to the town of Avonlea (home of the four famous Campbell brothers, who used to win the world curling title) where in the town hall they would hold a movie night—Disney, if I recall correctly—the showing interrupted as they rewound the reels.

When I was eight, I left the one-room school house for a two-year stay in Regina, then it was west to Sardis. The town, which had one church, a butcher shop, and perhaps two hundred inhabitants, derived its name from a more interesting source. Sardis is in both the Bible and Shakespeare. You could look it up. It is in Revelation (betcha didn't know that Philadelphia is also in the Bible), and in *Julius Caesar*. Shakespeare set most of scenes two and three of the fourth act at a battle in Sardis.

The original Sardis was the capital of Lydia in what was called Asia Minor. Its ruins still sit there, in what is now Turkey. It was quite a joint in its day. Compared to Sardis, Sodom and Gomorrah were an IODE picnic. Athenaeus, a papyrus-stained wretch, wrote in the second century A.D. that the Lydians came to such a pitch of wantonness that their king, one Adramytes, was the first to sterilize women and use them instead of male eunuchs. (They didn't do much of this in my Sardis.) If you don't believe me, you can look up Xenophanes. Herodotus, no mean scribe, informs us that the Sardis girls normally earned their dowries by prostitution, a practice that carried no reproach (also not, as far as I know, true of my Sardis).

The Lydians claimed to have invented all the games that became common to the Greeks—dice, knucklebones and ball. The Lydians invented coined money, made of an alloy of gold and silver, bearing nothing but the lion's head which was the royal emblem of Sardis. The gold for the coins was obtained by laying sheepskins in a shallow goldbearing stream that flowed through Sardis—which is the basis of the legend of the Golden Fleece. Croesus was the last Lydian king and introduced coins of pure gold—hence his reputation.

In Revelation, Sardis is one of the Seven Churches of Asia. It was destroyed by the great earthquake of A.D. 17, rebuilt by the generosity of Tiberius, but was sacked by Tamerlane in 1401, which was only right and proper since our friend Athenaeus (a good rewrite man quoting Xanthus) recounts how Cambles, a king of Lydia, who was quite a heavy drinker, one night slaughtered his wife and ate her. When he found her hand in his mouth the next morning, he killed himself, since the murder, no surprise, had become common knowledge. I digress.

The point is that one cannot be raised in such heady historic surroundings—Sardis, not to mention the ineluctable Hearne—without being infected by a smidgen of hubris. It's called roots.

Is New York in the Bible? Is Tokyo in Shakespeare? Of course not. Tell me another town that has the twin billing of both the New Testament and Willy Shakespeare. I rest my case.

Along with the American songs, we grew up on American movies and a regular Saturday afternoon infusion of values *à la* Hopalong Cassidy. He was the standard fare at the Strand Theatre in Chilliwack, and he taught us that retribution always followed the crime and that no sin went unpunished. Hopalong, with his big white hat that was never tattletale grey or spotted with mud despite endless high-speed chases, helped by Gene Autry on Champion, and Roy Rogers on Trigger, made sure that the bad guys always paid for their sins. These cowboy heroes were, one can see, simple precursors of Rambo, who takes it upon himself to avenge the slights that a mere state, with its cumbersome government, cannot attempt to correct. Hopalong strode into a saloon.

Rambo goes into a jungle. Ronald Reagan flies down on Libya. The bad guys must be seen to pay.

Henry Kissinger has not been taken quite as seriously around the world since the shrewd Italian journalist Oriana Fallaci stroked his ego and he confessed into her tape recorder that he viewed himself in the finest American tradition: the lone cowboy on a big white horse riding into town to put down trouble. That the most powerful diplomat in the world at the time could view the subtleties and minefields of shuttle diplomacy so simplistically was one thing. Even better was the realization that this short dumpy little man—whose dream of becoming president was thwarted, however unfairly, by the law requiring presidents to be born on American soil—really envisaged himself in the classic American mould of the tall and lean Gary Cooper, drawling "yup" and quieting the natives. Fallaci gelded Kissinger.

Along with Hopalong came the wartime comics—incendiary bombs shipped north over the border, engraved with POW! and BAM! and OOPH! It is claimed that we are not as violent as the Americans and are more subservient to authority because we did not have a Wild West—law-enforcement authorities kept our frontier regions relatively peaceful—and because we did not form a country out of revolution and bullets as they did. Perhaps. But the youth of Canada enjoyed the gleeful violence purveyed by America's comic books, movies and TV just as much as American kids did. The Americans also assume we are a naturally docile bunch. John Kennedy did not believe it when John Diefenbaker told him that there were more Canadian soldiers killed in the First World War than Americans and that, on a percentage basis, our casualties in the Second World War were about equal. That didn't fit our image, and images never change.

My early experiences with Golden Boy and Charlie aside, my first impression of Americans—at least our brand of American neighbours—was that they were Paul Bunyan types who went to church and were rather stolid and dull. I formed this opinion based on the inhabitants of the State of Washington, which was only twenty miles away from Sardis.

Washington ranks very close to being the dullest of the fifty American states, having been settled by stolid Scandinavians, puritanical Dutch, and other strong silent types who can fell the north woods. Even today, as we type, there is a Seattle entrepreneur who is becoming rich by running tour buses from his city to Portland, Oregon, where the attraction is table dancing (a.k.a. girlies who are allowed to drop their knickers and cavort on saloon tables where the boys are drinking), an advance in culture denied by law in Seattle. You get the idea of what growing up next to this state was like.

When you think about it, practically every American state bordering on Canada is exceedingly dull. Even that portion of New York State that touches Lake Ontario is as mundane as most of Minnesota or North Dakota or Idaho. New York Mayor Ed Koch, while running against Mario Cuomo for governor of New York State, unwisely remarked that rural life in upstate New York was "a joke." Since Albany, the capital, happens to be in upstate New York, he was naturally defeated, while being correct.

There is a reason, one supposes, that Canada has had the bad luck to be situated beside the most boring of all fifty states. (Hawaii, we will concede, is absolved.) But moving from left to right, it is really an abysmal scene. Washington State is terminal dullsville. Idaho? What can one say about Idaho? Or Montana. There is then North Dakota. Its only claim to fame is that the Bronfmans used to smuggle their whisky there, which was considerate of them because it is a desolate oasis that badly needed some cachet.

There is Minnesota, which abuts Manitoba, the dullest of all our provinces, if you can except Prince Edward Island, which is not really a province, but a duchy. It would do well to declare itself as such and anoint Mike Duffy as king. The best way to illustrate the purse-mouthed relationship between Minnesota and Manitoba is to talk of Bud Grant, who was an All-American at both football and basketball at the University of Minnesota and passed up the National Football League to sign instead with the Winnipeg Blue Bombers, where he became an all-star pass-catching end and eventually the coach of the club.

Bud Grant does not smoke, a wise and abstemious man. (We're now into basic border dullness.) Grant, on the way home from football practice, used to offer rides to assistant coaches and players. If any one of them lit up a cigarette, Grant never said a word. But that chap never rode in his car again. An avid hunter and fisher (*Minnesota*, remember?), he once invited some of the gang on a deer-shooting expedition. Dick Thornton, an antic defensive back, remembers it well. A heavy storm descended, the group had to take shelter for hours in a cave. After some time had passed, Grant reached into his jacket and took out several chocolate bars. He munched on them, saying nothing, his glances indicating he could not understand how his companions, obviously idiots, could venture out in the wilderness without provisions. I mean, that's Minnesota.

Since Wisconsin, Michigan, Ohio, and the teensy portion of Pennsylvania and upper New York State are separated from Canada by the Great Lakes, they have effectively been protected from any discernible impact on their Canadian cousins. Lakes, to paraphrase Robert Frost, make great neighbours.

So that leaves us the tight-assed buddies up against the underbelly of Quebec and New Brunswick: New Hampshire, Vermont, and Maine, the grim-faced Yankees whose eloquence can best be described as constipated. In all, from Pacific to Atlantic, you could not choose a duller lot.

There is a reason, one presumes. Those of dour disposition and hardy nature tended to drift north. It really would not work, logically, if immigrants from Norway and Sweden drifted to New Mexico and Alabama. They went the route their roots inclined them. They hugged the border to the north. That's okay. We're stuck with them. They're dull, but they're all we've got.

My impression of Americans as a dull lot was reinforced by my high-school and university experiences. In high school, we played basketball against pristine schools in Washington where the girls were not allowed to let lipstick touch their lips, let alone cigarettes or cheap likker. It was there we met Slippery Joe Cipriano, who crossed his eyes to confuse you before he dribbled through your legs. He went on to become an All-American at the University of Washington and then a coach at the University of Nebraska.

Later I enrolled at the University of British Columbia, which, pristine in *its* own interpretation of what was important about life, had no sporting intercourse with institutions its own size, such as the University of Washington or the University of Oregon. Instead, with the excuse that it did not offer athletic scholarships (harrumph, harrumph), it played pitty-pat with tiny little colleges in Washington called Whitworth, Gonzaga, Central Washington, and so forth.

The result was that, once every autumn, we entered into a home-and-home football rivalry with the Western Washington

College of Education, which was located in Bellingham, an innocent little town some fifty miles across the border. UBC in those days was probably the third-best university in Canada, behind the University of Toronto and McGill (its academic credibility has been going down steadily, starting from the day that Dr. Foth graduated), and it towered intellectually over the little teachers' college across the world's most boring border. UBC had a law faculty, architecture, those despicable engineers, and other graduate schools. The entire enrolment had a black belt in drinking. Loosing such a horde on the unsuspecting, milk-fed co-eds of Western Washington and the completely blameless little centre of Bellingham was not unlike allowing the Visigoths and the Huns to range down upon the helpless inhabitants of northern Italy.

What happened, annually, was a precursor of the Grey Cup weekend, the Grand National Drunk, when horrified hotels in Toronto or Vancouver or wherever stockpile their lobby furniture and hire extra security guards. The Leopold Hotel in Bellingham could have written the manual. The town was a sedate retreat for well-to-do farmers' wives who came into "the city" on weekends for shopping and a decent meal. Once every October they found instead of mob of out-of-control Canucks who turned on fire hoses in the corridors, did unspeakable things in bathtubs, and convinced every resident of Bellingham that anyone who lived north of the border was just one step removed from swinging from the trees. It was disgraceful, but it was fun. If we couldn't beat them on the football field, we could destroy a hotel much faster than a bulldozer could.

By contrast, when the Western Washington campus newspaper staff paid us an exchange visit, they were astounded at the beer we drank and the dirty words we allowed in print. To this day, we remain the only Canadians any Americans have ever been interested in.

Improbable as it sounds, I almost ended up in the American ambience. My high-school track coach had arranged an athletic scholarship to the University of Washington in Seattle. The university's other attraction at the time (a horrible vision to contemplate today) was its journalism school—one of the worst inventions ever devised. The university was huge, beautifully situated on Lake Washington in a leafy and affluent section of Seattle. (We used to drive there to watch Bob Houbregs with his world's longest hook shot lead the Washington Huskies against the likes of Wilt Chamberlain and the University of Kansas.)

Fortunately, as it turned out, a knee injury suffered in an illegal basketball tournament ended my Olympic dreams. As captain, defying the high-school principal's orders, I led our prize hoop squad to an Easter holidays tourney against some Alberta teams. The event was held in the far-off fastness of Trail in the Kootenay Mountains, closer to the Rockies than to the Pacific. Trail is the home of the world's largest zinc and copper smelter and, you'll recall, the celebrated Trail Smoke Eaters, the last Canadian hockey team to win the world championship, in 1961.

The father of one of our players owned a funeral home; we commandeered a nine-passenger mortuary limousine and, bodies piled on bodies, drove the long, tortuous trip to Trail. In those days, mountain roads through British Columbia were so bad that it was quicker to detour through the longer—but faster and safer—route down through Washington. (That was another early imprint: American roads were good, Canadian roads were lousy. Americans were advanced, we were primitive.)

We made it safely to Trail, but I wrecked my knee in the tournament. My knee and I were jammed in among the writhing bodies in the funeral car and driven back the tired route to a doctor and a cast. By then, the knee was thoroughly gone. The track scholarship disappeared, and to my good fortune I was forced to scrabble in other ways while the University of Washington struggled to get along without me. (Ronald Reagan that year was making *John Loves Mary*, with Jack Carson, Patricia Neal, Edward Arnold, and Paul Harvey.)

The near-miss illustrates the north-south pull that makes keeping together an east-west Canada so difficult. Other Canadians have found the pull south to be stronger than ties that would keep them in Canada. Marjorie Nichols, the tough-minded, intelligent *Vancouver Sun* columnist, grew up in Red Deer, Alberta. The only journalism school in Canada in those days was at the University of Western Ontario in London, a long way from Red Deer. Instead, she hopped across the border to the university at Missoula, Montana. The NDP's Dave Barrett graduated from his Vancouver high school without the language credits required by the University of British Columbia. He looked south instead, went to Seattle University, and did his graduate work at St. Louis University.

(Franklin Delano Roosevelt to this day is his political hero, not Laurier, not Macdonald.) When Barrett became premier of British Columbia in 1972 at the age of forty-three, he had never been to Montreal.

At the University of British Columbia, I was editor of *The Ubyssey*, the campus newspaper that over the years had produced Earle Birney, Eric Nicol, Pierre Berton, Ron Haggart, Joe Schlesinger, Pat Carney, Helen Hutchinson, and a sports editor by the name of John Turner. My time at the paper was in the early 1950s, during the McCarthy Red Scare. One of McCarthy's targets was diplomat Herbert Norman, Canada's ambassador to Egypt, who was an old friend of Lester Pearson's. The jingoistic *Chicago Tribune* and its owner, Colonel Bertie McCormick, then went after Pearson, Canada's most distinguished foreign-service officer, on the usual soft-on-communism charges. (When a U.S. Senate subcommittee later revived the allegations against Norman, he leaped to his death from the Swedish Embassy in Cairo). At *The Ubyssey* we felt it was our responsibility, naturally, to set the world aright, and this meant disciplining Colonel McCormick. We staged a highly publicized effigy burning of the American tycoon, complete with such so-clever protest signs as DON'T MOLEST LESTER and PEARSON'S NO PINKO. Among the usual coeds and beer guzzlers in the crowd around the bonfire were detected the world's oldest graduate students—several of the fuzz in their trench coats.

Sometime later, after we had all been pushed out into the real world to earn pay cheques, a reporter friend with RCMP connections was shown a file with the dreaded name Fotheringham therein, accompanied by the comment that here was a "potential subversive." I have never felt so important since.

One cannot escape the pervasive American influence anywhere. In 1957 I was living on the Costa del Sol in Spain, in a little village called Carvajal, just along from Torremolinos, not writing the great Canadian novel. One day, the proprietor, a Dutchman named Willy (who spoke no English) came running up to me very excited, pointing to the sky and barking. After much body language and multi-lingual charades, it was determined that the Russians had put into space a Sputnik bearing a small dog. It was a moment in history. (Ronald Reagan was then making *Hellcats of the Navy*, with one Nancy Davis.)

Later, when the chagrined and embarrassed Americans had finally caught up enough to prepare their first space launch at Cape Canaveral, I was working at Reuters, the international news agency, on Fleet Street in London. The general newsroom was huge, so long that during winter days when the worst of the famed London smog hit and seeped in through the cracks, you could not see the occupants at the far end of the room. I worked with a dozen other "foreigners"—Yanks and Canadians—on the North American desk, our job being to make sure that in the copy headed to New York for distribution to American and Canadian newspapers *petrol* had safely been translated into *gasoline, boot* into *trunk, lorry* into *truck,* and other such vital considerations.

The tense moments of the countdown on the Florida coast came over the common loudspeaker. The entire room fell silent in expectation. There was a pause, then the announcement that the spacecraft had exploded and fallen off the launch pad. At that, the entire room burst into laughter and jeers and turned in sarcastic resentment toward the North American desk—symbol of all that a tired and fading Britain disliked.

For the first time, a Canadian reporter who always absentmindedly thought of himself as more British than American, more drawn across the ocean than across the border to the south, recognized his *North American* ties and sympathies. The Brits, who had lost an empire and resented the new world power, took pleasure in the American accident and found small consolation that the smartass Yanks had had their comeuppance. It was the first time (not the last) that I felt sorry for the United States of America. Given the choice between the supercilious superiority of the Brits and the naïve aggressiveness of the Americans, a colonial finds himself siding more and more with the latter.

However much I might have sided with the Americans, I never expected to be mistaken for one. That is what happened on my first day in London, which I used as a base for three years of wandering the Continent. I had gone to Hyde Park, it being a Sunday, to Speaker's Corner. There, standing on soapboxes were all the anarchists and witty eccentrics and certifiable lunatics who make that city the most interesting in the world. I headed for a chocolate-bar stand but, apparently, did not notice the patient and disciplined queue—the device that makes the English so civilized (and so accepting of inefficiency and sloth). A sharpish man, who obviously had devils to exhume from his own soul, whirled on me with the bitter, "You're not in America now." Implicit was all the penis-envy, love/hate relationship between British and the Yanks.

I was mortified. It was the first time in my life anyone had ever taken me for an *American*, or suggested I even looked like one or—worse—that I acted like one. I resented, as most Canadians abroad do,. being lumped in, just a part of an amorphous North America.

Thereafter, in travels throughout Europe, I brandished a small Canadian flag on some appurtenance, or tried to make, early on in conversations, some reference to "In Canada, we . . ."

Once, on a New Year's Eve in London, a group of us burst into an English party, full of shouts and high spirits and the usual party nonsense. An Englishman seated there, full of the usual lassitude, said, "They're Canadians, obviously—or Australians. You can, tell by the energy." There sat a defeated country, a spent race. (There is the celebrated wartime story of the English housewife who was asked if she had met any Canadians. "Have I met Canadians?" she replied incredulously. "I'm on me way back from the pub with a bucket of beer for hubby, this Canadian solider jumps me, ups me skirt, ins me, outs me, drinks the beer, pisses in the bucket, and you ask me if I know Canadians?")

I may digress, but the point is that the Brits think of Canadians as more vigorous, younger, and more aggressive. The Americans (since they are really all those things) think of Canadians as watered-down versions of the essential snob whom they cannot stand. (Someone once said that the average American, deep down inside, believes that if you woke up an Englishman in the middle of the night with a start, he would speak *American*! The accent's really all a put-on.)

A feeling common to most Canadians is that Americans, when met individually, can be so likable, while the country as a whole is not. The American I liked best in my travels about Europe was the young man I encountered one day at the Acropolis as tourists scrambled to record that crowning achievement high above smoggy Athens. He was standing outside the Parthenon, offering to operate the cameras carried by an endless series of puffing couples in pastels and pinks. He had grown so ashamed of the gaucheness and vulgarity of his fellow Americans throughout Europe that he decided the

Parthenon—the site of the photograph of a lifetime for Madge and Henry—was the spot for revenge. He took all their pictures for them—while carefully cutting off their heads or including only their feet. He cackled as he imagined all those tourists, safely back home in Iowa or Louisiana, finding out when the drugstore returned their Kodak prints that a saboteur with the same passport had betrayed them.

I once drove from Toronto to Vancouver—by the scenic route. That means heading straight south, through Ohio, Kentucky, Tennessee, and Alabama, until you make it over to New Orleans on the Gulf of Mexico. Take a right, across Louisiana, Texas, New Mexico, Arizona, and California, until you come to the little community of La Jolla outside San Diego, which is the single most pleasant spot in the entire country. Take another right, drive up the length of California, through Oregon and Washington, and you hit Vancouver. Simple.

One thing you will find is the finest rib-eye steak in the world in a little spot on the highway just outside Lyndon Johnson's Texas ranch. Also, the educational information—in those tense civil-rights days—that anyone found in Selma, Alabama, with strange licence plates was considered only one of two things: an FBI agent or a civil-rights worker. The solution? Sugar in your gas tank. A most educational experience.

It was that American propensity for violence that turned me off the country for a time. After living for three years in Europe, I can back through New York and was appalled by the filth, the rudeness, and the frenetic pace. When friends who lived just off Central Park, in an otherwise thoroughly decent section of town, advised one night that I should never stand on the park side of the street while looking for a taxi—for fear someone in the bushes might grab me—I decided that New York could do without me for a while.

My boycott lasted ten years and, you will note, the city suffered tremendously, going through its near-bankruptcy phase until it pulled itself back with the "I Love New York" campaign. The place quivered visibly through my absence.

A Canadian cannot, in reality, escape the weight of the United States, boycotting it or not. Its economic and cultural sway is too heavy, its citizens everywhere around the world when you travel. You can't get away from Americans. You can only cope with them.

2

Damn Yankees

In which a young sportswriter makes it to the home of Ruth and DiMaggio and why Canadian sports pages are ashamed of their own and why all the great political columnists come from the sports pages.

Canada has never had a major civil war.
After hockey, Canadians would probably
have found it dull.—JIM BROSNAN

As a young jock who turned to sportswriting and eventually
to the hard-hitting game of political journalism, I found that,
no matter what the field, Americans always intruded. The
dominant players in the dominant sports (save hockey) were
always Americans. The very finest sportswriters were Americans. And, eventually, the really heavy hitters in politics were
Americans. The drag, the osmotic pull, was always across the
border—leading, one supposes, to this scribe's current stay
on the Potomac.

Growing up, we learned a lot about American sports from
the movies. Alistair Cooke, the brilliant correspondent who
has been broadcasting his *Letter from America* radio show
from New York for the BBC for forty years now, says as a young
reporter he gained a more realistic view of American life from
minor films than glossy "A" films. Similarly, I knew the greats
of American sports from the movies. The first time I ever
entered Yankee Stadium, to see Mickey Mantle in the 1950s,
I was already familiar with every angle of the place. A dying
Lou Gehrig (a.k.a. Gary Cooper) standing at home plate in
The Pride of the Yankees saying goodbye to his fans, telling
them he felt "like the luckiest man on earth"—that seared
Yankee Stadium in my memory. Gehrig and Ruth were gone,
even DiMaggio was gone, and I had to ride a filthy subway
through hostile Harlem to get there, but it wasn't just Mantle
I went to see, it was Yankee Stadium. It was the star, as it had
been in so many movies.

In moving from Canadian teenager to Canadian sportswriter, I simply moved from American hit parades and American

film stars to American football players dominating Canadian
teams. Spaghetti-legged Jackie Parker, beetle-browed Johnny
Bright. Mercurial Rollie Miles. Hal Patterson from Kansas,
and Sam Etcheverry with the Alouettes. Bernie Faloney in
Hamilton. Frank Tripucka from Notre Dame with the
Saskatchewan Roughriders, along with Bobby Marlow from
Alabama. Buddy Tinsley and Leo Lewis in Winnipeg. Al
Pollard and Arnie Galiffa and Paul Cameron with the B.C.
Lions, along with Willie Fleming, who in the felicitous
phrase of a *Toronto Star* writer "ran the way Max Bentley
used to skate," and whose one-year mark of a 9.9-yards-per-carry
is still the record in any pro league.

Foreigners were the stars in a Canadian game. In those
days, before television made football into a new American
religion (with Howard Cosell as the pope), the Canadian
Football League could afford to compete with the U.S. flesh
merchants. Billy Vessels of Oklahoma, the Heisman Memorial Trophy winner as the outstanding college player, went
straight to the Edmonton Eskimos. Parker, Patterson, Faloney,
Cameron, Galiffa, and the like were legitimate All-Americans.

So foreigners were the stars in a Canadian game (Fritzie
Hanson of the Winnipeg Blue Bombers being the first of
them). And Canadian sports pages reacted in a most peculiar
way. They developed a nomenclature that included "non-
imports" when describing team rosters. Russ Jackson was the
best quarterback in Canada and Don Getty, now premier of
Alberta, quarterbacked Edmonton to a Grey Cup victory, but
on the sports pages they were "non-imports." Know what a
"non-import" is? A *Canadian*! Canada must be the only
country in the world that is ashamed to use its own nationali-
ty in its newspapers. A "non-import"—by its negative
connotation—teaches every young Canadian that somehow
they can't be as good as imports. Except that imports are
never called imports; they're called Americans.

Canadian sports pages then and now are examples of
sweaty imperialism. Aside from the American presence in
Canadian sports, there is the presence of so much American
sports in Canadian newspapers. Why? Because it's easier (and
cheaper) to print irrelevant material that pours over the
teletype from the United States than to cover Canadian
sports. It always puzzled and annoyed me that Canadian
papers allowed so much space to be devoted to the doings of
obscure colleges and obscure linebackers from another coun-

try. It still puzzles me that the injury to a defensive back of West Ucatah State and the firing of an offensive line coach at Bowling Green State Universiy are given space in Canadian sports pages. The reason, of course, is that the trivial and inconsequential stuff pours over the wires every day from the American Associated Press juggernaut. Every small detail of every small athletic happening in the United States is recorded in exquisite detail.

Canadian papers use these reports to fill their vacant corners. Since there is no liberally funded, well-staffed sports-information office at, say, the University of Calgary to flood the local Canadian Press office with the hot news of injuries to its defensive backs and the sacking of its line coaches, Canadian papers run the hot news from West Ucatah State. In no other part of the paper does so much news appear about *irrelevant* foreigners. It's lazy journalism. It's also cheap journalism. The wire machine is the salvation of the accountants.

Ah, but then there were the columnists. As a young sportswriter, my hero was Red Smith, the finest sports columnist in the world, then with the New York *Herald Tribune* and syndicated wherever an intelligent sports editor could be found to buy his material. It was Smith who said that writing a column was easy: all you had to do was to sit down in front of a typewriter "until little beads of blood appeared on your forehead."

He also mocked those sportswriters (this author among them) who claimed that they could have been star athletes themselves. "I too," he wrote, "could have been a great athlete except for the fact that I was small, weak, uncoordinated— and cowardly."

I first met him in the press box at the 1976 Montreal Olympic Games on a dull day when we were both covering the equestrian events opened by Queen Elizabeth and the Duke of Edinburgh at Bromont, in the Eastern Townships south of Montreal, a kickback site that later figured prominently in the scandals arising out of the Drapeau Games. He was as polite and gentlemanly as he was talented.

For me he was also a link back to the legendary Grantland Rice and Frank Graham. The three of them used to hang out together on their road trips. Early one morning, after they had stayed up all night with a bottle and a lot of raucous stories, as they often did, their train pulled through the New

York suburbs on the way to Grand Central Station. They watched through the train window as the streets filled with people rushing out of their houses. "Look at the poor suckers," Smith said, "having to go to work."

The last time I saw Smith was at Secretariat's last race, at the Woodbine Track in Toronto, where the great red horse, the finest since Count Fleet and Whirlaway, ran away from the field with consummate ease. The race was barely over when a tremendous thunderstorm hit and the *Toronto Star*'s Milt Dunnell, the kindest man in Canadian sports-writing, managed to arrange for me a ride to the airport on the back of a pick-up truck, where I was accompanied by Robyn Smyth, who at thirty-five was one of the leading American female jockeys, that sex having just been allowed into major races. I was greatly taken with her, and shortly after she married Fred Astaire, who was then eighty-one. They lived happily ever after.

One of Smith's other sports-writing pals was Stanley Woodward of the sadly dead *Herald Tribune,* whose credo I have always tried to follow. A colleague described him thusly: "He was unfailingly kind to his subordinates, barely tolerated his equals and was openly contemptuous of his superiors."

In 1976 Smith received the Pulitzer Prize for Distinguished Criticism, the first sportswriter in the history of the award to be honoured with it. He loathed hockey and basketball (he coined the memorable line "how high the goon") and could write wonderful stuff on events like the Westminster Dog Show. Of one judge, he said: "He had splendid conformation—broad shoulders, white hair and an erect carriage—and he was beautifully turned out in an ensemble of brown. One was inclined to hope that he would, in the end, award first prize to himself."

Red Smith, who obviously had the capability to do so, was never tempted to "go global" like the other great ones who started in sport: Heywood Broun, who was the founder of the American Newspaper Guild; Paul Gallico, the novelist whose famous "Farewell to Sport" is still the best explanation for leaving the toy world; Bob Considine, later a world star for Hearst; Westbrook Pegler, the celebrated polemicist; Herbert Bayard Swope, the war correspondent; and James "Scotty" Reston, who is now the dean of American political columnists for the *New York Times* and was once, if you can believe it, the press secretary of the Cincinnati Reds, who, if you believe it, were renamed the Cincinnati Redlegs during the

Commie scare of the Senator Joe McCarthy era. The Reds, who are now safely the Reds again, were the first team ever to use relief pitchers and the first team to travel by plane. You could look it up.

There was Jimmy Cannon on the New York beat and Melvin Durslag and Jim Murray in Los Angeles and the delightfully named Shirley Povich of the *Washington Post*, a very tough guy. Murray of the *Los Angeles Times,* the best guy now writing, is so good despite near-blindness that he approaches the level of some of the droll British sporting writers. (The finest opening sentence in sports history appeared in *The Guardian* in 1966 on the day before soccer's World Cup was played in Wembley Stadium between England and West Germany. "If on the morrow," it went, "the Germans should beat us at our national game, let us remember that we have beaten them twice at theirs.")

One of the things that happens to you if you are a sportswriter is that your day gets turned upside down. After going to yet another fascinating hockey game, or lacrosse game, or football game, and going back to the office to put down your Olympian prose into a typewriter (there were such things then) you need time to wind down. You can't drop off immediately into the sack, any more than an actor or a ballet dancer can after a performance. So you end up in some Chinese food emporium at three o'clock in the morning, retelling old lies, or occasionally wander into the nether world of the nightclub circuit.

Vancouver, this being the paleolithic fifties, had a very heavy nightclub scene, which provided for this innocent another insight into the Americans. One of the reasons the Palomar Club and the Cave and such were so popular was that black American entertainers were still not fully accepted in their own country. The equivalents of Bill Cosby and Richard Pryor and Flip Wilson and Whoopi Goldberg were not worthy of top billing. So black stars of astonishing ability would year after year come up to Canadian clubs, where they were very popular hits.

So, as luck would have it, in 1952 a rival Vancouver sportswriter named Al Hartin and your agent were sitting in a Montreal nightclub. We had spent the day covering the first east-west university football battle, the University of British Columbia visiting dear old James McGill U. on the slopes of Mount Royal, later made famous by René Lévesque as the home of the Westmount Rhodesians. (Ronald Reagan then was making *She's Working Her Way Through College,* with Gene Nelson, Don DeFore, and Virginia Mayo.) Hartin and I had watched the nightclub act, called the Will Mastin Trio, and Hartin asked if I would like to buy a drink for the star. He snapped his fingers to a waiter and out trotted a slim young man called Sammy Davis, Jr., who had long been grateful for Hartin's kindness to him over the years in Vancouver clubs.

As Americans' attitudes to blacks changed, Sammy, of course, became a big star in his own country, too big for the Vancouver clubs to afford, and so he disappeared from our town. (The attitudes didn't change all that fast, actually; a black man, Robert Parker, who was mâtre d' of the Senate dining room in a Capitol Hill career that lasted thirty years, who chauffered Lyndon Johnson around and did many a task for him, was regularly referred to as "nigger" or "boy"—in the 1950s and 1960s—by the Texan who as Majorty leader in the Senate was for years one of the two or three most powerful figures in Washington and, of course, became president on the death of John Kennedy.)

Davis, who had barely survived a bad auto accident and was converted to Judaism, used to reply to those who asked on the first tee of a golf course what his handicap was, "My handicap? I'm a one-eyed black Jew." He went on to become part of Frank Sinatra's Rat Pack, was invited to the White House, and, on his fiftieth year in show business, appeared wih Dr. Robert Schuller, the famed evangelist shouter, on a Sunday morning network show explaining how "his faith" had carried him through. (Linda Lovelace, who described some of his other activities in her book, might disagree.)

My days as a sportswriter ended in the mid-sixties when I turned my attention to the politics of the nation, a field badly in need of someone's ministrations. It's amazing, really, how many political commentators have come from the sports pages. The reason is that they have simply moved up to another game. It is a more serious game, with more serious consequences, but it essentially is a game. It is even dirtier than hockey or football. There is boarding, there is slashing, there is highsticking, there are offences that haven't yet been written into the penalty book.

The sportswriter learns to sit in the press box and view the spectacle. When he moves on to politics, he finds himself in a similar situation. He is given an aisle seat at the best theatre in town. What he has before him, with the star players, is the most important spectacle of all, the political game. Practically all politicians (although not all) are actors; certainly, the most successful are the best actors.

It's almost become a cliché by now to observe that Ronald Rambo succeeded in politics because he was an actor first. He is no deep thinker, he hates detail, gets facts mixed up, falls asleep in front of the Pope, contradicts himself—but, whambo! when the lights go up and he has to project leadership (as after the Challenger explosion, or following the Libya bombing) he struts the footlights and gets a standing ovation.

All the great ones were actors. The aristocrat Franklin Roosevelt won them over with his fireside chats and his dog Fala. Churchill, with his siren suits and cigar and his V-for-Victory signs and his mesmerizing British bulldog growl, was a supreme actor, a politican who had developed a persona for himself that made Chamberlain and Attlee and the rest seem like mere ciphers. It came out recently that his famed "blood, toil, tears and sweat" speech—delivered in the House of Commons—was read for the radio by an actor since Churchill was too busy. It didn't really matter (aside from the fact that no one noticed) because the myth of the man had already been established.

John Kennedy knew the whole thing was an act, and that the audience wanted spectacle. He once described himself as the man who had accompanied Jackie Kennedy to Europe; he knew what the photographers really coveted. Pierre Trudeau was a superb actor, at times petulant, at times imperious, sometimes profane, always mysterious: a game player. Bob Stanfield and Joe Clark were not successes because they could not fake it: they could only be themselves. And that wasn't quite enough. Jimmy Carter couldn't act, he could only grin. Gerald Ford could do neither.

Margaret Thatcher, the grocer's daughter playing it as the Iron Maiden, was a great act until it grew boring. One of the reasons Richard Hatfield has survived so long is that the residents of his not-wealthy, not-sophisticated province secretly liked the idea of their bon vivant bachelor flitting off to Morocco retreats and New York weekends. They were voyeurs at the voting box, much as Canadians as a whole were for years with Trudeau. They really didn't like him much, but

quietly liked the fact that he was romancing Barbra Streisand
and skiing in Switzerland and taking out mysterious blondes
in London and, especially, giving his finger to the nasty
press.

Moving from the press box to a seat on the aisle is simple
stuff. Ralph Allen, arguably the best journalist Canada has
produced, did it effortlessly. Scott Young, from downtown
Manitoba, used to move in the *Globe and Mail* from sports
page to editorial page with no diminution in his audience.
(First rule of journalism: there is no such thing as a dull
subject, there are only dull writers.) The wittiest Canadian
columnist at the moment is Allen Abel, who moves from
covering sports to covering China and back again. A prede-
cessor was the antic John Fraser, who went from ballet critic
to China correspondent, thus proving the above first rule.

When I moved from sports to politics, I found many
similarities between the two fields. In both, the bigger
figures were always the Americans. I missed covering the
Camelot years, but in 1968 I found myself chasing Bobby
Kennedy in his final chance to avenge his dead brother. His
eleventh-hour decision to run for the presidency attracted
that same slice of America that thought neither Kennedy was
really of politics (when both were brutal practitioners of it)
but somehow high and clean and above it all.

Like most Canadians, like most liberal-leaning reporters, I
had never really liked Bobby or had the same respect for him
as for his brother. He was a little too voracious, a little too
mean. That aura of a young aide to Senator Joe McCarthy was
still with him. He was still the touch football player who
would do anything to win. He didn't have the sense of
humour that was his brother Jack's saving grace, nor the easy
charm of the too-charming Teddy. He seemed too vicious, too
much the family hit man for his own good.

One night out on the flat wheat-growing plain of eastern
Oregon, in a town called Bend, the little hit man on a
high-school stage seemed most vulnerable, most likable. It
was the penultimate primary, with just California to go.
Bobby had just come from a tour of Idaho Indian reserva-
tions, where the rate of teenage suicides had reached crisis
proportions, a signal of the despair of a race thrown on the
junk heap. He had been mobbed, yet another example of the
fact that the millionaire Kennedys were somehow seen—even
then—as the champions of the underclasses.

He obviously had been moved by the experience and, on the ninth or tenth frenetic campaign stop of the day, was totally exhausted, as are most politicans, in most campaigns, most of the time. On that stage he was just the soft younger brother, asking for help, requesting that he be allowed to carry on the torch that these younger, better-educated followers felt was deserved by no other politician. He seemed a different Bobby Kennedy and I liked him.

He won the Oregon primary, narrowly, in what was regarded as an astonishing upset for a candidate starting so late, but there was still California to go if he was to have any chance of pulling off enough support among delegates to win the Democratic presidential primary. I wrote an analytical piece for the *Vancouver Sun* editorial pages, explaining that it was a great try but unfortunately too late. California was too late. I concluded the article with "he's dead."

My wise editor read the article and told me that he knew what I meant—that RFK was *politically* dead—but, considering what had gone before in the family, perhaps I'd like to change the wording. I stubbornly declined, insisting that he stick with my ending.

A week later, in Vancouver, I watched with the mother of my children Kennedy's wrap-up speech from the Los Angeles Ambassador Hotel as the results of the California primary rolled in. She started upstairs to bed and I asked if she wasn't going to wait for the results. "Nope," she said. "The Americans are crazy. They'll kill him, just as they killed his brother and just as they'll kill Teddy." An hour later, after Sirhan Sirhan had done his business, I went upstairs to tell her she was right. As was my wise editor.

3

Dr. Foth Goes to Washington

*In which it is laid out why Washington is so much
prettier than Ottawa and why the French planner
died in poverty and why they drink less on the
Potomac than they do on the Rideau and why there
are so many potholes and why the planes fly so low
over your barbecued steak.*

*If you want a friend in Washington, buy a
dog.—ANONYMOUS*

With Brian Mulroney and his goofy Tories safely elected, and
the hated Trudeaucrats banished to oblivion for a spell, it
seemed the good doctor's offices could be safely removed
from the banks of the Rideau Canal. There remained one
band of heathens to be saved. And so, in 1984, I left the little
town on the Rideau, built on a swamp and infested with
mosquitoes, for a bigger town on the Potomac, built on a
swamp and infested with cockroaches. It seemed a fair trade.
In Ottawa, they worry about tuna. In Washington, MX missiles. Washington's main enemy is the "evil empire" of the
Soviet Union. Ottawa's main enemy is the three o'clock traffic
rush. Both towns are run by Irishmen who live on a quip and
a prayer. It's useful to go from a town where you're a
somebody to a town where you're a nobody. It's good for the
soul.

On arrival in Washington, there was the small problem of
Dr. Foth and his White House pass. A journalist in this
security-tight town cannot, as would be imagined, operate
without the proper credentials. My very proper employers,
supported by a letter from the very proper Ambassador Allan
Gotlieb, made the proper application to the White House.
More than the usual bureaucratic time elapsed while the
usual security check into my activities in Hearne, Saskatchewan,
went on. More time went by, as I cooled my lonely heels on
the fringes of polite society, my nose pressed forlornly against
the White House fence.

Finally, word came down. The White House did not wish
to grant credentials to Dr. Foth. The excuse was that the
resident Southam News correspondent in Washington, Brian

Butters, had a pass, and the White House decided that they didn't want to grant one to your poor agent. More months went by, me a forlorn leper at the National Press Club, scorned by all, pitied by few, unable to set foot on the sacred White House lawn where Sam Donaldson and Joe Schlesinger and all the great ones did their stand-up thirty-second clips for the evening news.

Impassioned letters flowed forth. Southam News General Manager Nicholas Hills, from Ottawa, wrote an inflamed tome to White House spokesman Larry Speakes, suggesting that not only would Canadian-American relations be strained if Dr. Foth did not get his pass, but possibly the survival of democracy was at stake. Faced with Hills' prose, the minions of the president of the United States blinked and gave in. I was duly fingerprinted, photographed, and sternly ordered to make sure my official application did not vary a whit from my passport. I obediently followed the strict instructions, giving my name, as it appears on my passport, as "Murray Allan Fotheringham," with the *Allan* carefully underlined. And so I was eventually summoned, six months after arriving in Washington, and handed the precious White House press pass, plasticized and bearing the name of that well-known Canadian journalist—Murray Fotheringham.

The city of Washington is the precursor of the "planned city"—the dreamy concept that has led to such sterile disasters as Canberra in Australia and Brasilia in Brazil. I was going to add Ottawa, but that would be a mistake, since it was selected only as an artificial site, not a new city—which is the reason it ended up a failure as both.

Queen Victoria, who had never seen the spot (obviously), picked the swamp-and-mosquito juncture of two rivers, the Ottawa and the Rideau, solely to offset the rivalry between Toronto and Montreal. Canberra, a dismal retreat where there are more journalists than there are policemen, was plunked in an isolated tract of bushland between the competing centres of Sydney and Melbourne. It was named the capital in 1913 but, because of the rivalry between the two cities, Parliament did not move there until 1927 and government departments not until 1948. Every other large city in Australia is situated on the coast. There is a good reason for this: Australia resembles a large, overdone pizza, with almost all the population huddled in a narrow strip around the crust. The only exception is unfortunate Canberra. It is even more isolated than Ottawa, if that is possible, and suffers from the same ingrown-toenail mentality.

Like Ottawa, Washington was located on a swamp, presumably because no one else wanted the marshland on the Potomac that, in summer months, is fit for neither politician nor beast, only for tourists. In early days, diplomats who were forced to endure the summer in the capital received hardship pay from their home offices. The best description of it remains that of Jack Kennedy, who said the city combined Northern charm with Southern efficiency.

Its only consolation is its beauty. Washington is so beautiful—the most spectacularly laid out capital in the world, as opposed to the cozy warmth of London or Paris or Rome—mainly because Americans didn't trust an American to louse it up. They chose a Frenchman instead, the French being experts on other people's business.

The Americans owed their independence to the intervention of the French against the hated British, and by 1791 France was at a peak of popularity in the United States. All things French were favoured. And so Captain Pierre Charles L'Enfant was chosen that year as the planner of the new capital on a bare landscape. He was an artist and military engineer whose revolutionary spirit inspired him to offer his services to the army of the young American republic. He had been in the country for fourteen years and had made a name for himself as an architect in New York.

The site of the capital, like Ottawa, like Canberra, was chosen because of a compromise. Over dinner in New York one summer night in 1790, Secretary of State Thomas Jefferson agreed to deliver crucial Virginia votes for assumption of the debts of the states; in return, Secretary of the Treasury Alexander Hamilton agreed to deliver northern votes for a southern capital. President George Washington wanted most of all to make sure the capital did not get moved to New York.

Washington got what he wanted. He selected a ten-mile-square site on the Potomac—which just happened to be convenient to his own landholdings in Mount Vernon on the river. The excuse for choosing the low marshy land and the humid climate was that a higher and cooler site farther up the Potomac would have ruled out navigation, and the founders of this great new city saw it as a future emporium of trade and dominant urban centre of the nation. Unfortunately, New York, Philadelphia, Boston, and even nearby Baltimore had a bit of a head start; Washington never became more than the home of swivel servants.

Although the founders' grand dreams of another Paris or London didn't pan out, the physical layout they planned did become a reality. L'Enfant was raised in Paris, a city whose influence on the formal Washington design is most apparent. He drew up an elaborate scheme of grid streets (designated by numbers and letters of the alphabet), which were interrupted by elegant diagonal avenues, squares, and circles.

Being a military man as well as an architect, he reasoned that an invading army—on encountering this plan—would find it very difficult to find its way to the centre of the city. How true. Today, the invading army is rush-hour traffic and, thanks to L'Enfant, in Washington you can't get there from here. You need a Sherpa guide to find your way around, as streets disappear behind spacious boulevards, and circles send you spinning off in the wrong direction.

George Washington found L'Enfant "extravagant, over-optimistic, egocentric and prickly," which seems a pretty good description of an architect. L'Enfant also fought with some of the land speculators, and he battled continuously with the new city's bureaucrats. After less than a year on the job he was fired and in his rage burned all his drawings on the city plan. But his concept was so spectacular that one of his surveyors, a free Negro by name of Benjamin Banneker, redrew the plan from memory and the beauty of the capital was retained. When L'Enfant died in 1825, his estate was worth forty-five dollars and he was buried in an unmarked grave in the garden of friends.

L'Enfant's plan divided Washington into four quadrants—radiating from the mighty white dome of the Capitol. But the real centre of the city is the magnificent green sweep of the Mall, as impressive in its vista as the Champs Elysées. In perfect symmetry, it runs west from the Capitol, lined by some of the world's finest art galleries and the Smithsonian museums, the White House off to one side, the Jefferson Memorial off to the other. There is the Washington Monument, then the Reflecting Pool and the Lincoln Memorial, the most superbly mounted monument these eyes have ever seen.

The Mall is the perfect stage for the great American dramas. Martin Luther King gave his "I have a dream" speech there before two hundred thousand civil-rights march-ers in 1963. It was also the rallying point for the endless thousands of anti-war protestors during the Vietnam struggle.

Now, down on the Mall beneath the Lincoln Memorial is the newest and simplest monument of all. The tributes to Washington, Jerfferson; and Lincoln tower over everything in the city. It is stunning, therefore, that the most emotional monument is buried in the ground.

Visitors from all over the United States are drawn to the Vietnam Veterans Memorial, almost hidden in the green beneath the awesome dimensions of the Lincoln marble. In a brilliant concept disguised by its diffidence, the tribute to the dead of Vietnam is tucked below the level surface into the green grass of the Mall. It consists, simply, of a wall of black granite into which have been cut the names of every one of the fifty-six thousand soldiers who died in that foreign war, a war that split the nation and set two generations against one another.

Every day, Americans prowl the black granite in silence, their faces contorted in grief, their fingers tracing the cold surface over the names of their dead ones. It is a dreadful, moving thing to watch. The marble monuments to Washington and Jefferson celebrate the men who fought the British and created this great country. The one to Lincoln thanks him for saving the republic. Vietnam, on the other hand, still confuses Americans. That is why the Vietnam Memorial, hidden in the side of a hill, so mesmerizes them with its honesty.

On the tenth anniversary of the retreat from Saigon, the country was obsessed with reminders of its greatest humiliation. The TV screens played over and over again the familiar sight of desperate Vietnamese trying to cling to the struts of the helicopters carrying the last of the Americans from the grounds of the U.S. embassy as that dismal non-war ground to a halt. The *New York Times* devoted its entire Sunday magazine to an agonizing autopsy. The *Washington Post* devoted exhaustive amounts of newsprint to a ten-part series. The networks dispatched to Saigon, for morning-show instant nostalgia, hosts who were in high school when the shooting took place.

What a foreigner cannot share is the American torment that crippled a generation, drove many of them north to Canada, and still troubles the soul of a country that does not like to lose and is still split over the rightness or wrongness of being in a war it could never win. They walk that sad incline below the Lincoln Memorial, looking at the names of the boys who were sent overseas into a senseless battle their leaders stumbled into.

When it comes to beautiful cities in the world, there are two categories. There is Paris, and then there are all the others. Washington reminds me more than a bit of Paris because of two factors. The most striking is the height restriction on all construction. No building is permitted to be taller than the Washington Monument—in effect, thirteen storeys. The result is that the monuments, rather than look-alike glass-and-steel towers, dominate. Almost anywhere you are in the city, you can see the beautiful slim spire of the Washington Monument and the gleaming white dome of the Capitol.

The uniform building height, so unlike the picket-fence appearance of other cities, has a calming and soothing effect that is pleasing to the soul. Ottawa, tragically, has let the copper-domed complex on Parliament Hill become lost in a forest of square boxes. The Americans, by contrast, view all Washington as an exhibit, a planned city that has conformed to the plan. The Memorial Bridge, which stretches from the Lincoln Memorial across the Potomac in a precise architectural line to John Kennedy's grave in Arlington National Cemetery, is so graceful and beautifully designed that it is worthy of the highest praise of all: it would not look out of place crossing the Seine in Paris.

The second feature reminiscent of Paris is the trees. Washington, while a lousy place for a hay-fever sufferer, is filled with trees that add to the feeling that you're living in a horizontal city instead of a vertical one. The west side of the city is divided by an ample ravine containing Rock Creek, which runs from the Maryland border all the way south until it joins the Potomac at Georgetown. Rock Creek Park, as the ravine is called, is like a forest that bisects the city. Ottawa, despite its parks, has nothing to compare.

The essential difference between Ottawa and Washington is that Ottawa thinks it is important; Washington is important. Ottawa thinks it is a pretty city; Washington is a pretty city. The reason is that Americans, with their gung-ho patriotism, people who had to fight a war to establish a nation, revere their capital and hold it up as an icon, a symbol of their pride and independence. Ottawa is viewed by most Canadians as a sump hole of tax dollars.

Washington was a planned city and its authorities have adhered to the magnificent plan, guarding carefully against any intrusion upon it. Ottawa just growed, and a weak city authority and confused federal governments have allowed what little grandeur there is—Parliament Hill—to be overwhelmed by a nest of office towers that could be in Calgary (which is easily the most "non-planned" downtown core in the country).

Washington, on the other hand, has a sweep and a majesty. The grandeur of the corridor from Capitol Hill through the Washington Monument to the Lincoln Memorial rivals that of the great sections of London, Paris, and Rome. Ottawa, desperately attempting to preserve Wellington Street (before it dissolves into that dreadful claustrophobic tunnel past the Chateau Laurier), really has little left to work with. The great god Mammon has pinned the parliamentarians into a very spare corner of grass. They no longer have even the succor of the Rideau Club across the street to sustain them; it burned down and its successor is in some anonymous tower. The only refuge left is the National Press Club, 150 Wellington Street, where never is heard a succoring word.

An American does not really feel he has paid his dues as a real American until he has visited Washington. The citizen approaches the capital as one approaches the famous statue of Christ and the Virgin Mary in St. Peter's Cathedral in Rome, where a marble toe is almost worn away from the number of tourists who have kissed it over the centuries. Americans revere Washington in much the same way. This is their Holy Grail, their touchstone, the home of the spirit of Washington and Lincoln and Jefferson and Kennedy. They take their endless snapshots, they feel renewed, they show their kids what their capital looks like and represents—and go home to Iowa and Louisiana and Nebraska and feel *better* for it. Aside from a momentary twinge on the back of the neck at first seeing the Peace Tower from Wellington Street, Canadians simply are not capable of those same emotions. They don't come from the same space. Washington attracts the largest number of tourists of any city in the world. They come from all over the globe, of course, but the main contingent is composed of Americans, proud of their capital (every single museum in town is free, no charge), jealous of their capital, and determined to see their capital. Canadians with some leisure time are more likely to head to Florida or Hawaii. There is no gut feeling dragging them to Ottawa.

The inhabitants of the two capitals behave differently as well. One of the more surprising differences I have discovered is that there is less drinking in Washington than in Ottawa. At embassy parties, if the invitations state seven o'clock, at the dot of seven the doorbell rings and the ladies in their little bland dresses and the men in their pinstripes from Brooks Brothers are there. Within ten minutes they all flood in. Promptly at ten o'clock, they all leave. The only one left standing around the fireplace sucking on a Scotch is a stray Canadian, or perhaps a Brit, looking for some action.

The reason is the Washingtonians are much more serious about government than residents of Ottawa are. In Washington, the social life is simply an extension of the office. It, too, is work. That's the reason why Allan and Sondra Gotlieb became so successful. It's why you never see anyone from Thailand at a Gotlieb party, or from Belgium. Their residence on Rock Creek Drive is filled with Type-A Americans—leavened perhaps by an occasional Canadian scribbler, if he has not blotted his copybook with an indiscretion that particular week.

The National Press Club, sitting on the top floor of the thirteen-storey National Press Building, is beautifully done in marble and brass. It contains restaurants, lounges, a luncheon theatre where a major political figure goes live on CNN television every noon hour when the coffee is finished, a health club, private meeting rooms, and the H.L. Mencken Research Library. By two o'clock in the afternoon, the bar is practically deserted. In Ottawa, at the National Press Club, the boys are just getting into the brandy and there's part of a good afternoon left.

The reason the Washington crowd takes life more seriously is that half of them are there to learn, and the other half to gain future rewards. Under the American system of political appointments, each president on coming to office can bring 1,286,825 new bodies with him. From ambassadors on down to the office help, the whole complexion of the town changes with each new administration.

At the lower end are all the bright and shining young men and women out of the nation's best law schools and universities, who find a few years working as an assistant to a senator or a congressman an invaluable lesson in the mechanics of government. The experience will give them a head start when they go back to the law firm in Denver or New Orleans.

At the top end are the corporate types who accept high administration posts at relatively modest salaries in the knowledge they won't be on the Potomac long and that their value in the marketplace will be greatly increased because of their Washington profile and connections. Paul Volcker, head of the Federal Reserve Board and as such the most powerful man in the world in economic terms, makes just $75,000 a year.

In Ottawa? There are obvious advantages to the parliamentary tradition of a career civil service, which is supposedly loyal to whatever party is in power, but there are too many "lifers" in Ottawa. All the way through the system, from Parliament itself to the swivel servants through the press and to the lobbyists, there is not the renewal and change that is apparent in Washington. That's why they drink more in Ottawa.

I am reminded daily of another difference between the United States and Canada. Every morning, I drive from my home in Georgetown to my office, which is one block the other side of the White House. It is a simple route, since it starts at one end of the world-renowned Pennsylvania Avenue and ends just where the avenue does a quick jog around the president's home, and before it sweeps up to the majestic marble dome of Capitol Hill, where Congress sits. In all, my route extends some fifteen blocks—an easy commute compared to the distance most people drive to work.

Having said that, it must be confessed that it is like driving through Beirut bunkers. The pavement dips and dives and descends into craters. The surface undulates; it is patched with steel plates that tear your tires; it sinks into gullies and raises horrendous bumps. As I pass the manicured lawns of the White House, the most famous presidential residence in the world (careful of the huge post-Lebanon concrete barriers), my car doodles like a dodge-em car at a country fair.

The reason for the disrepair is that there is no tax base in Washington. The affluent whites flee to the suburbs, leaving a population that is 80 percent black and mostly poor. As a result, the city budget is so bare that the street system is a joke. This fact will come as no surprise to anyone who has been to New York, where the flood of yellow taxis, threats in themselves, bounce through the potholes of Fifth Avenue in a manner guaranteed to leave the visitor in a thoroughly jangled state, nerves atingle and arthritis alerted. The same ailment (tax base, not bone deterioration) afflicts Philadelphia and Chicago and Detroit and the other cities that are dominated by a poor black population in the downtown cores. (Detroit, which now stages a world-class Grand Prix race through its downtown streets each summer, has to *upgrade* its pavements before the daredevils of the sport will even start their motors.)

Each time I return to Vancouver, blissful Vancouver, I suffer a shot of culture shock on the way in from the airport. The taxi rolls smoothly, there are no jolts to the spine, it is actually possible to read the newspaper, the wheels glide over the serene asphalt. Canadians take such municipal amenities for granted. The White House, if you must know the truth, probably does the same. The resident would never know. He wafts aloft from his lawn in a helicopter.

The spine-jarring jolts are some of the prices you pay for residence in the city, centre of the known world.

Georgetown itself, the best address in town, is only ten blocks square. With its narrow streets and intense street life, it resembles a small slice of London. High up on the Potomac bluff, on one side of Georgetown, is the Roman Catholic university of the same name. Founded as a seminary in 1789, it is famous for its basketball team and is a safe haven for any government official who wishes to teach and thereby become an official "expert."

Georgetown began as a river port, antedating Washington, and was the base for a canal that was going to bring produce from the Ohio Valley. The railway made the canal obsolete, but it still cuts through Georgetown, and in summers a mule pulls along it a canal boat full of tourists while a gal in calico and a bored chap in wool trousers play the banjo and try to evoke something.

By the 1920s, its canal and port dreams gone, Georgetown became a black slum until the 1930s when New Dealers bought houses there for practically nothing and renovated them. Then a young bachelor senator by name of John Kennedy moved in, and the area became the place for the swinging set. Restaurants and boutiques followed as night the day.

Containing mostly tiny lots, Georgetown now includes

some of the most expensive residential real estate in the world. It feels it is so special that it even voted against having a stop on Washington's excellent (and clean) subway system. It wouldn't, well, fit in.

You can hardly expect to be rising star at the *Washington Post* unless you have a Georgetown address. Chairman Katharine Graham lives at the top of the Georgetown hill, editor Brad Bradlee is in the neighbourhood in a $2.5 million mansion, Bob Woodward of Watergate fame is down the street opposite Sarah's, a mom-and-pop grocery store, and the neighbourhood is speckled with senators, high mandarins, socialities, and poseurs. The notice board in the delicatessen on P Street is heavy with offers to walk your dog for pay. Dogs are very prominent in Georgetown, as are BMWS. There is even a "Pet-Net of Georgetown," a "non-profit community service" that tries to put people and their pets back in touch. Lost a cat? Found a dog? Seen a stray? Your information will be "recorded in our files." Sondra Gotlieb, the Canadian ambassador's wife, entered her Tibetan terrier, Sweet Pea, in the annual celebrity dog contest. (My favourite piece of American trivia, as a matter of fact, was reserved for a Texas poodle by the name of Leo. He was playing with eleven-year-old Sean Callahan of Hunt, Texas, in 1984 when he saw a six-foot rattlesnake poised to strike. Leo jumped in front of the boy, took six snake bites, but eventually recovered and regained sight in his injured left eye. In 1986 Leo was inducted into the Texas Veterinary Medical Association's Pet Hall of Fame.)

One of the distinctive things about Georgetown is that you can't talk outdoors, only indoors. Any conversation outdoors is sure to be interrupted by the low-flying jetliners that are constantly overhead, either on takeoff or landing patterns. Because there are no skyscrapers in the city, no buildings more than thirteen storeys in height, Washington enjoys the handiest airport in the world, just ten minutes from downtown.

Washington National Airport is right on the Potomac, alongside the Pentagon, and the huge jets glide in low over the city, so low you can read the markings and tell immediately whether the pilot is wearing sideburns. Georgetown is directly in line with the runways. This causes, particularly when you're on your patio or in your garden, awkward pauses in your conversation—usually just when you're into the punch line. In fact, the speech patterns of everyone in Georgetown resemble those of Robert Stanfield. Dinner parties consume four hours, seven courses, and perhaps six sentences. True conversationalists die in this town, which is why so many of them move to New York.

No one is Georgetown owns an alarm clock, since the entire community is awakened at the same time, seven o'clock, when the first wave of jets takes off. The airlines are not allowed to land or take off after ten at night because of the noise, but at seven every morning the sky is black with them. The house shudders and you can't talk through breakfast. Which is why the *Washington Post* is so fat and prosperous.

Those who want to escape the District of Columbia height restriction go across the river to Arlington, Virginia, with the result that office workers in the new U.S.A. Today tower filed an official complaint when they began seeing jets *below* their windows as they swooped in over the Potomac.

The cosy location of an airport right in the centre of a city was brought home to the rest of the continent, of course, when that ice-encumbered Florida Air plane hit a bridge on the Potomac. A bit farther over and it could have smacked the Lincoln Memorial, the John F. Kennedy Center for the Performing Arts, or the White House.

There is a solution, naturally, to the constant complaints from Georgetown clientele about the noise and the warnings about air safety. It is called Dulles International Airport—America's answer to Mirabel. The terminal, designed by Eero Saarinen, looks like a graceful kite about to take off. Situated out in the green countryside of Virginia, halfway to St. Louis, it is so far away from downtown Washington (a forty-dollar cab ride, thank you very much) that it is as deserted as the disaster called Mirabel.

The pressure on the airlines to move from dangerous National to remote Dulles is steadily resisted by politicians and their aides, who love having an airport ten minutes from the office. There is even a special parking lot at National reserved for Supreme Court justices. The airport operators know who to dangle the carrots in front of.

Me? I confess I also like having an airport ten minutes away. You see, I regard myself as possibly the only living example of the Andy Warhol theorem that everyone should be famous for fifteen minutes. I can accomplish that. On days when I'm feeling down and put-upon, I nip over to National Airport where, since I am nobody, I am pushed, kneed, stepped upon, and jostled. I take the USAir flight to Toronto, get off at beautiful Terminal 1, and am assaulted by little old ladies who demand autographs and little young ladies who want their underwear autographed. After a quick ego fix, I get on the plane and return to Washington.

It's a frustrating city to live in, and a fascinating one. There are fifteen thousand journalists in Washington and thirty thousand lobbyists—about six for every congressman. You need a shoehorn to belly your way up to the bar. The town is wall-to-wall expense account. It also has just one month of winter, which makes it Paradise Island for this scribe, who has put in his term in the penitentiary of Ottawa winters. I'm not saying it's a good place for Dr. Foth to die, but the Geritol goes down very smoothly here, mixed with branch water.

4

Dressed for the Hill

In which our hero explains why everyone in Washington dresses so bland and the ladies march to success on sneakered feet and why there is so much flesh on the Fourth of July and why yellow paper ties are now surpassed by red power ties and does anyone care. Yes.

*The key to success in Washington is suck
above, kick below.*—SONDRA GOTLIEB

Clothes not only make the man (and, as we will see, the
woman), they make the city. Montreal is a symphony on the
streets, everyone on display and giving off subtle vibrations.
In Ottawa, people are either bundled up all winter or, in the
brief steamy interlude that is called summer, practically
naked as they roam the streets. Vancouver people just *ooze*
about, rapping to their inner rhythms, a sort of water-logged
California. Toronto people can't decide if they're from New
York or Guelph. The native costumes reflect this.

Washington? Washington dresses basic government: don't
dare anything different, don't attract attention, dress like
your neighbour. He didn't get fired for the way he looks, did
he? All government towns confirm, of course. In Ottawa all
the swivel servants wear parkas and Wallabies. So do the
lobbyists. In Washington, it being a government town, everyone wears a beige raincoat. Why beige? Because that is the
blandest colour of all. And since this is a city with only one
month of winter, a raincoat is a safe, year-round investment.
Since you don't want to stand out, you wear beige, which
blends well with the sidewalk, the building fronts, and the
personalities.

Under the raincoat, every male once wore a button-down
shirt and a yellow tie. Yellow ties were very popular—signifying
anyone up and coming—until they invented the red "power
tie." "Power lunches" once denoted those midday meals at
which one made incredibly crucial decisions over *nouvelle
cuisine*, but they became too nakedly vulgar and so the city
moved on to power breakfasts. In the same way, red surpassed
yellow as the town's new power tie.

It is connected, of course, to the fact that red is Nancy Reagan's favourite colour. White House reporters at the rare presidential press conferences even dress in red—the women in red frocks or sweaters or scarves, the men in red ties—in an attempt to catch the president's eye. In·1986, Reagan told the White House Correspondents' annual dinner, "I think it's ridiculous when people put on a red dress just to catch my eye. Nice try, Sam"—Sam being, of course, the designated shouter from ABC television, Sam Donaldson.

One night at a Washington party, gazing across the sea of black and beige, I spotted an unusual sight. There, at the other end of the room, her back to me, was a woman in a colourful frock. It was all red and yellow and green in wild patterns! *Colour!* Like a dying man in the desert, I walked up behind her and whispered in her ear that she was the best-dressed woman in the whole gathering. She turned around: it was Maureen Forrester, the celebrated Canadian singer, whom I had never met before.

Colour at a Washington party is somewhat like verbosity in Erik Neilsen. If not forbidden, it is rationed. The early Jackie Kennedy is partly to blame. She once told some prying fashion writer that with a little black dress and a strand of pearls a woman can go anywhere. Unfortunately, too many people heard her. When I moved to Washington I thought I had arrived at a wall-to-wall 1950s sorority party. Every woman's dress was safe. Every woman's wardrobe was cautious. Every woman looked the same.

It was no accident that the vivacious Maureen Forrester, whose personality resembles her garb, stood out at that cocktail party. She didn't know the Washington rules. The rules are: if in doubt, go bland. Bland never lost your husband his job. Bland never attracted attention. The bland leading the bland, as we used to say about Eisenhower's leadership in America.

In Ottawa, most women in the ruling circles dress badly simply because they lack taste. In Washington, they lack courage. (As a matter of fact, Ottawa is saved because of the French element. You can spot a Quebec woman at fifty cigarette lengths; in a room filled with dull men in dull grey suits, she is the one with élan, the one dressed to her fingernails.) At one Washington party, a blonde in a sparkling blue dress stood out like a peacock at a convention of sparrows. Ever a man for research, I quickly confirmed my suspicions: she was Gayle Wilson, the wife of Senator Pete Wilson of California, formerly mayor of San Diego. They were relatively new in town and she hadn't yet been beaten into beige.

The problem is that most women in Washington are not women at all. They are attachments. Sondra Gotlieb, whose husband, Allan, is the Canadian ambassador, made her reputation in the town with her columns in the *Washington Post* mocking the official pecking order. Her husband was Ambassador; she was merely Wife Of—as are all the other diplomatic wives and the wives of the eager, ambitious politicians and the eager, ambitious silly servants (who are waiting either to start a lucrative PR firm, *à la* Michael Deaver, or to sign a million-dollar advance for a kiss-and-tell book, *à la* David Stockman). Margaret Trudeau made the same point as Sondra—though in a different way—when she said she was tired of being a rose in someone else's lapel.

There are two strata among Washington females. At one level are the women of the capital whom Sondra writes about, and to. They do not dress for success. They dress to blend into the woodwork. That is their job. To be innocuous. To be Wife Of. (It is why Sondra went up and down the social ladder so noisily: she made fun of the whole spectacle, observing how ludicrous it was.)

At the other level are the cream of the nation's universities, eager to get a few years' experience near the height of power. They are the lawyers and executive assistants and rising bureaucrats who help and assist their almost entirely male political masters to the top. (Fifty-three percent of the U.S. population is female. There are only two women in the hundred-member Senate. There are only twenty-three women in the 435-member House of Representatives. Of all the state legislators, only 14.8 percent are women. By contrast, there are twenty-seven women in the 282-seat House of Commons. Three of the most powerful ministers in the Mulroney cabinet, Pat Carney, Barbara McDougall, and Flora MacDonald, are female. There is one woman, Elizabeth Dole, wife of Senate Majority leader Bob Dole, in the Reagan cabinet.)

The women lawyers and assistants are young (in their thirties), terribly determined and, in the new feminist age, terribly independent, and they have an eye on the top. They belong to the dress-for-success school. For some reason, whoever invented that creed determined that to succeed in a man's world women must dress like men, in severely tailored suits and floppy silk ties that are the closest the designers can come to the most-hated part of a man's attire: the necktie. Why women would want to wear the most uncomfortable item in the male wardrobe is incomprehensible. Do they feel that to succeed in a man's world they must suffer the same discomforts? Like male executives, do they want to die until five o'clock when they can rip the damn things off and get into T-shirts?

Far be it from this male observer to figure out the attraction, but the bars around Capitol Hill after work reflect the triumph of unisex among the upper classes. Since both sexes come armed with expensive, embossed briefcases, blue suits, blow-dried hair, and silk chokers around their necks, constricting the breathing but not impairing the ingestion of gin, there's very little difference. Take away the pantyhose and you've got a draw.

Indeed, those of us involved in the desultory game of woman-watching (the only alternative, man-watching, leaving something to be desired) have put up with a lot over the eons. There was the sack, that apparition foisted on the female by Paris, a fashion breakthrough that actually turned out to be the world's most successful birth-control method. There was the miniskirt, causing whiplash injuries to half the male population. We will not discuss the beehive hairdo or harem pants or other such assaults on the eyeball. Let it remain said that we have been patient over the years. Even the success suit and necktie were met with calm resignation.

What has caused us to snap, however, is the creeping trend, the blight of the sidewalks. It is called Adidas-in-nylons. The most horrifying sight in Washington today is the spectacle of an immaculately dressed young woman marching off to the office wearing jogging shoes. Beneath the dress-for-success outfit, beneath the gold-embossed briefcase and all the eyeliner topping off the impressive package is a pair of scuffed sneakers. To get the message across, they are usually accompanied by white gym socks.

The overall impact is like being hit in the mush with a soggy dishrag. Here is the finest product of centuries of civilization—the successful, educated, emancipated, liberated, sexually freed woman—and she's wearing running shoes at nine o'clock in the morning. Lord be with us.

The trend started several years ago in New York, birthplace of the dreaded Yuppie, during a transit strike. The young ladies who marched the rotted sidewalks of that burg in search of success, men, and materialism hit upon the method of saving their Italian-designed high heels on the way to work. The excuse, understandable at the time, was comfort: sneakers on the street, heels in the office. The trend has now spread to Washington, where there is no transit strike and where a morning drive to the office is like viewing a running-shoe contest. Recently it has even been seen in Ottawa, the town that fun forgot.

As all fads go, success breeds excess. If a man so much as hints criticism of this nonsense, he is accused of being against upward mobility, the executive stream, planned parenthood, and proper carriage. All he is asking for is a sense of aesthetics, of what looks right to the eye, of balance, of proportion, and—does one dare say it?—of beauty.

Consider the high-placed executive who awakes to prepare himself for his arduous profession as chief assistant deputy associate minister to the vice-president in charge of corporate communications. He puts on his Italian silk jockey shorts, his striped shirt from Harvie & Hudson of Jermyn Street, London S.W.1, his Brooks Brothers pinstripe, tie by Pierre Balmain, and his shoes, from Betty's of Montreal, with the two cute little tassels. Striding off to work, he tops it all off with a scuffed baseball cap. Would his secretary scream? Would his mistress yelp? Is the Pope Polish?

What we have here, you see, is not so much a plea for comfort as a subtle protest movement. If comfort were the criterion, men decades ago would have junked the necktie. They retain it because they retain a sense of decorum, a feeling that rules are rules. Otherwise, we'd all come to work in our jogging suits—which would suit most of us fine.

What the young ladies are doing is establishing the fact that we must pay a penalty for their invasion of what was, supposedly, a male *sanctum sanctorum*—the marketplace. The Nikes and Reeboks treading down the sidewalks are their Yuppie version of *Lysistrata*—the Greek women who withdrew their sexual favours from their husbands until they stopped warring. The sidewalks of New York and Washington today are not a comfort zone for bunions; they are a combat zone, registering sexual angst. They are voting with their feet.

There have always been these wars of the sexes. The suffragettes threw themselves under the hooves of the horses at the Epsom Derby and chained themselves to the gates of Parliament at Westminister. Carrie Nation took her axe to the booze parlours to drive husbands back to their loved ones.

Men for years have used various methods to distance themselves from the "weaker sex." Women have had to retire when the brandy was brought out. Cigars have been a successful scam to drive them beyond shouting range. Men used sports to create a DMZ between the boys and the little woman. Dirty jokes used to be a useful buffer, but no more, as any office break can tell you, or a brief, startled glance at the supposed real-life experiences in *Playgirl*.

So now we have the revenge. First of all, we were made to reform our language. "Girls" was demeaning. "Ladies" was condescending and marginally sexist. "Women" was okay with "female" probably better. For a while there, "Hey you" seemed the safest bet.

With all that cleaned up, there was only one thing left. High heels. They know our weakness. The ankle bone connected to the thigh bone connected to the hip bone. You got it. In the morning, it's better than orange juice. They're inconsistent. They do it in the office but they don't do it in the street. They use the way they dress as a means of protest, just as another generation did to get back at their parents.

There was a time, not long ago, when youth had its own goofy uniforms and attires. The hippies of the 1960s affected long hair and rainbow hues, and the adults were properly appalled by the outrage of it all, sucking their teeth and shaking their neat heads in despair. Alas, the parents of the world did not continue this sensible approach of superiority to all the vulgar doings displayed before them. Instead, they have tried to emulate the acne crowd, dressing not like adults but like the children they deplored. It is not a good thing. We do not approve.

The ultimate display of this secret desire to play Ponce de Léon in cutoff jeans comes on the United States' birthday, when a half-million human beings restage Woodstock beneath the Washington Monument, across the street and a bit over from the White House. It is considered sacrilege, if not treason, for an American not to go to a picnic on the Fourth of July. In Washington, one can see enough bare flesh to drive one indoors for the rest of the year. It seems a basic rule now applies: the more obese the specimen, the more flesh must be exposed. Businessmen trying to look like their teenage sons parade in T-shirts that should have remained in junior high. Matrons better kept under a shroud insist on displaying their imperfections for all to see, monuments to cellulite, captives of a generation that fears age. The reason Americans are larger than Canadians is that they eat more.

A half-million people, composed in large part of adults who weren't at Woodstock and regret the omission, are not a pleasant sight when they are all cheeks to jowls, the beer mixing with the lost babies. It illustrates one factor of Americans' lives that differs from Canadians': they don't have much privacy and so ignore it. Any Canadian who travels a bit in the United States is struck by the obvious—there are ten times as many bodies down here. Wherever you go, there are people about. It's not as bad, overall, as Japan or Britain, those two clastrophobic islands of city dwellers, but a Canadian in the United States is suddenly aware of the space he enjoys at home.

Canadians always complain about how loudly Americans talk in restaurants, elevators, airplanes. The reason they do is that they have given up trying to keep things to themselves; there is always somebody around, so they shout their secrets to the wind.

Canadians—reticent, soft-spoken—insist on a certain "body space" enveloping them, a pocket of air separating them from their conversational mate. Europeans, if you'll notice, like to move within about six inches when carrying on a conversation, forcing the proper Canuck to have a continual list backward, as if the continental were suffering from a bad dose of garlic.

Brian Mulroney and John Turner are the most "American" politicans we have had in a long time, liking the rush they get from pressing the flesh. Turner, the self-proclaimed "tactile" man, loves to grab and squeeze people—like Lyndon Johnson, who didn't so much shake hands as massage his supporters, copping a feel on the way. (LBJ once explained his philosophy to an aide by announcing that "if you get the voters by the balls their minds will follow.") Pierre Trudeau always maintained his isolation with his intellectual cattle prod, and Mackenzie King kept his distance even when talking to his dog.

Americans, however, like to get down and wallow in familiarity. They invented the politician whose main attraction was his smile. (Eisenhower) and now seem stuck with that silly habit (Jimmy Carter, the man whose teeth were his trademark, and Ronnie Reagan, the president whose answer to almost everything is the aw-shucks grin of the second lead who didn't get the girl). Mondale's smile was the photogenic equivalent of a limp handshake, the kind that makes you feel unclean after you unentangle yourself.

It's why Canadian politics is now a battle of tactility: Sparkling Eyes vs. The Jaw That Walks Like a Man. We really haven't had such a struggle of equal personalities since Sir John A. was a pup who liked his cup. George Drew was a stiff product of Men's-Clubland who delighted in French-Canadian jokes and always looked as if he were going to cut his throat on his stiff collar. Louis St. Laurent looked as if cocoa wouldn't melt in his mouth. John Diefenbaker, all fire and brimstone, an evangelist who missed his calling, always made the neat and careful Lester Pearson appear the product of the Ottawa he was.

It was simply unfair billing when Trudeau of the trampoline went up against Bob Standstill, the classic product of Nova Scotia, which Michael Jackson will never visit. The unathletic Joe Clark stood no long-range chance against Trudeau even though he tried a serious counterattack by wearing a yellow cardigan. It is why Old Athlete Turner likes to be filmed on the tennis court, as a contrast to Mulroney, whose only serious exercise is lifting a telephone with each hand.

What we've got is a struggle for the flesh of the nation. Unless they hide in the root cellar, there is a good chance that three-quarters of the population of the country will be personally massaged by either Brian Turner or John Mulroney in the next few years. We have two incipient LBJs among us, the only guarantee being that neither will show us his gall-bladder scar or pick up a dog by the ears. Other than that, if you value your pinkies, keep them in your pockets or your purse. They're in danger.

The struggle for flesh, now that I mention it, is a new obsession of the conservative governments both north and south of the border. The sex police of the United States are led by Mr. Reagan's attorney general, Edwin Meese III, whose porn commission has convinced the 7-Eleven franchise stores to ban *Playboy* from their magazine racks. This is in line with John Crosbie, then justice minister, who proposed a new Canadian law that would define as pornography the depiction of everything, including dull old heterosexual coupling.

In the wake of the Meese commission report, the U.S. Supreme Court astonished the public by ruling that there is no constitutionally protected right to engage in homosexual conduct, even within the privacy of one's home. The case involved a Georgia policeman who, pursuing a parking-ticket complaint, came upon a homosexual bartender engaged in oral sex with his lover in his own bedroom. The man was charged with sodomy. Since there are still twenty-four states with anti-sodomy laws on their books, the court in effect was saying that happily married men and women would be breaking the law if they happened to prefer that form of satisfaction. Law professors and civil libertarians were appalled at the ruling. But luckily Canadians have nothing to fear. We have been told by John Merner, a fifty-nine-year-old Canada Customs official, that Canadians don't do that sort of thing. This statement was made after Merner, in his bureaucratic wisdom, decided to ban an issue of *Penthouse* magazine from entering our pristine borders because of twelve pages of naughty pictures. The Canadian public, he explained, speaking for all of us, "Is anti oral sex."

I don't know where Merner did his deep research into the Canadian public's preference in the bedroom, but he obviously had not been hanging around movie houses and bookstores. One of the greatest audience reactions in modern filmdom came in *Shampoo* when Julie Christie announced that she'd like to perform that specialized deed on Warren Beatty under the table at a political banquet. In the big hit move *Slap Shot* (now shown quite blithely on afternoon TV), Paul Newman spends what seems like half of the time talking about the same supposedly *verboten* subject, women to women, men to men. The movie was billed, in its time, as the comedy hit of the year.

Merner's pronunciamento came just after I had read in *Esquire* the funniest magazine article I have ever seen. Written by Helen Lawrenson, a woman then some seventy years of age, it dealt with a certain way of pleasing the male sex organ. Entitled "How Now, Fellatio? Why Dost Thou Tarry?" it was the first magazine article ever to deal with that tricky art. Lawrenson, somehow, by the ruse of artful innocence, managed to reduce the whole practice to high farce, to the extent that the reader was left, uh, limp with hilarity. The lesson that can be drawn from this is that there is now no aspect of sex that cannot be made fun of publicly.

What poor Merner doesn't realize is that real pornography is boring. After about ten minutes, the only way to stretch the interest is with humour.

The whole Canada Customs scandal reminded me of what James Thurber said in 1929 in explaining why he and his confrère at the *New Yorker*, E.B. White, had written a book called *Is Sex Necessary*? Thurber said that "the experts had got sex down and were twisting its arm, and someone had to restore the subject to the levity it so richly deserves." (How true. Truman Capote, then a copyboy at the *New Yorker*, had as one of his duties to escort Thurber, by then blind, to his noon-hour assignations with a lady in a nearby hotel—and help him dress. One day Thurber went home to his wife with different coloured socks; he claimed Capote did it on purpose and hated him ever after.)

The English gentleman who said long ago that sex is highly overrated explained that "the pleasure is purely temporary, the price is exorbitant and the position is absolutely ridiculous." The reason *Deep Throat* made $40 million on two days' filming and enabled Linda Lovelace to get into the enclosure at Ascot is that it was the first porno film made with tongue-in-cheek, as it were. The breakthroughs are being made not in technique—since nothing really new, beneath all the whipped cream and black whips, has been invented—but in the humorous ways of treating it.

Everybody thought a semi-underground book, Mason Hoffenberg and Terry Southern's *Candy*, had exhausted all the satiric aspects of eroticism until Gore Vidal gracefully swept up the bestseller heights with *Myra Breckenridge*. We assumed that Philip Roth with *Portnoy's Complaint* had left nothing more to deal with after making male masturbation funny. Now? He looks old-fashioned and humourless after Erica Jong.

Critic Robert Fulford has complained that Jong writes "pornography for people who have gone to college." Perhaps, but doesn't everyone have rights? Why discriminate against the poor deprived Ph.D.? Should he have to buy his own dirty raincoat to get his jollies? Ms. Jong, who taught women about zipless things in *Fear of Flying*, next soared to the best-seller lead with *How To Save Your Own Life*, which advanced women's liberation another hilarious step on the road to somewhere. She is of the school of raunchy old Henry Miller, who thought that sex was delicious but also very funny, and Erica has romped in print through lesbianism, group sex, aids such as champagne bottles, and other subjects too droll to dwell upon.

In this decade of liberation, when any self-respecting career girl can't make it through coffee break unless she knows all the words from *Slap Shot,* it is even more imperative for the male to have a sense of humour about the most ludicrous sport of all, since there are indications he is going the way of the wombat. Germaine Greer is now marching about the lecture halls of the globe advocating that women use a new birth-control method—abstinence—until male society is forced to devise a more acceptable contraceptive device than the Pill or the intrauterine contraptions.

Yet another folk hero of the feminist movement, Shere Hite, came up with a solution to the dearth of female orgasms: do it yourself. In *The Hite Report,* she took the Mr. Fix-It rage of the 1960s, when one could do one's own plumbing, to the ultimate extreme. It's the newest cottage industry. The male attachments became superfluous in the Hite world where any imaginative woman who owned a shower nozzle could get along without him very well. A man reading *The Hite Report* got the sort of queasy feeling a buggy-whip manufacturer must have felt when he saw the first quarterly sales figures on the Model T.

If Ottawa missed all this, it is hard to imagine how it will cope with the nuances of inflation and free trade. Just when sex was getting funnier, the government and Mr. Crosbie (since moved out of Justice) were taking it more seriously. Censorship is not the answer. Laughter is.

5

A Tale of Two Countries

*In which it is explained why the Americans have a
more democratic system than Canadians and why it
takes Canadians so long to make up their minds and
why Americans want to be liked and basically more,
more, more.*

Canada is a decaffeinated United States.
— ANONYMOUS

The simple fact, the incontrovertible fact, is that the American system of government is more democratic than the Canadian system. There are great subtleties and nuances, as God in Her Wisdom knows, to the parliamentary system, but they really do not flow down to the grubby citizen. Too much is dependent on the verities of "responsible government," on the way those in power answer the prying opposition in the House of Commons, a ritual that has become a stand-up farce, played out for the thirty-second clip and the front page of the *Globe and Mail*.

Americans are much more suspicious of power than Canadians are. It has a lot to do with the fact that they had to fight a colonial war to establish their country. Having thrown the tea into Boston harbour and defied an English king who resided on the other side of an ocean, they were very wary about setting up a system in which anyone had too much power. Hence their famed system of checks and balances, which sometimes seems to result only in government paralysis (whereas the Canadian system is so "efficient").

The creators of the American Constitution knew exactly what they were doing. Congress was there to keep a check on the president. The president could veto certain congressional initiatives. But, if he got out of hand, the Supreme Court could overrule the president. As it did, of course, in the historic decision on the Watergate tapes, ruling that Richard Nixon had to hand them over, thus sealing his doom. That unanimous court decision was led by Chief Justice Warren Burger, a man Nixon had appointed.

It's standard wisdom by now that in Canada a Watergate

would never have reached the public eye; it would have been kept from scrutiny by a majority government (such as the one Nixon enjoyed but could not control). A Pierre Trudeau or a Brian Mulroney or a Mackenzie King with a majority in the Commons is in effect an elected dictator for five years. The clout of party discipline, with the threat or reward of a cabinet appointment, or of being sent to Coventry, makes for a docile and obedient band of sheep in the back benches.

There is no real provision under the outmoded Canadian system (through Parliament is tentatively and nervously trying a variation thereof) for reforms that will allow politicians not obeisant to those in power to establish themselves as influential and respected figures. In Washington, a William Fulbright or a Mike Mansfield or a Teddy Kennedy, or even a weirdo like Jesse Helms, can, through the powerful committee system, establish himself as a national figure that the White House has to deal with.

In Ottawa, those who have not been favoured with cabinet appointments become docile wimps waiting for the nod; they dare not kick the traces. Under the American system, someone with a good mind and a strong personality like Canadian Jim McGrath (who was shut out of cabinet because of his icy relations with both John Crosbie and Brian Peckford) could become an influential figure on the national scene. Crosbie, whose maverick nature has been reduced to a cipher mentality under the discipline of a Mulroney cabinet, would be a far more useful national figure as a chairman of a powerful committee—as some of his American equivalents are.

The Canadian system keeps some very useful NDP members, like Ian Waddell and even the annoying (to most of his fellow MPs) Svend Robinson, from establishing more constructive Ottawa roles and national reputations. Instead, they are stuck in relentless and eventually relentlessly boring minor-party opposition roles. Who knows, Sheila (Sister Rat) Copps could put her pith-and-vinegar style to better use in committee-interrogating than she does in the House of Commons, where she embarrasses her old-school-tie leader, whose fraternity manner never taught him how to deal with 1980s-style broads. He clearly does not know how to deal with her, while Brian Mulroney exults in her excesses.

The main point is that Americans get on with it. The frenetic pace of their daily life—in the cities at least—may not be to everyone's taste, but at least they don't abide delay.

On January 28, 1986, the Challenger shuttle exploded off Florida, taking Christa McAuliffe and six other astronauts to their grisly deaths. Ronald Reagan immediately appointed a presidential commission to look into the disaster. In just 132 days, that commission had its report on his desk. Blame was apportioned; no feelings or reputations were spared. A number of high NASA officials took early retirement or disappeared. Guilty manufacturers were fingered and shuffled off their executives.

Could we compare that with the leisurely drift of a Canadian royal commission? The Le Dain Commission, set up by the Trudeau government to look into the use of marijuana, took four and a half years to hand down its conclusions, so long that the middle class had by the time the report came out moved on to cocaine and other designer drugs. In Canada, society moves faster than the dreamy government. In the United States, the two are more in tune.

It was the same with Donald Macdonald's royal commission, which was given the task of examining Canada's economic prospects. By the time the report came out, thirty-four months later, everyone had forgotten the question. It was a $20.6 million operation that did nothing but encourage the manufacture of paper.

In the summer of 1983 an Air Canada jet from Montreal, headed to Edmonton, made an emergency glider landing on an unused tarmac at Gimli, Manitoba, because the brilliant people fuelling the kite at Montreal's Dorval airport got all fouled up on metric measurements. An inquiry was ordered— as there always is when no one wants to assess blame—and it went on for eighteen months until, again, the public got bored with the result.

So it took a Canada commission four times as long to figure out the relatively simple question of why a plane ran out of gas as it did an American commission to resolve the complicated question of why the Challenger blew up. Therein lies the basic difference between the two countries: the one impatient for answers, the other relaxed and non-demanding. (Being non-demanding means that Canadians were shocked when the White House "unexpectedly" dumped a tariff on cedar shakes and shingles. Being non-demanding means that, during his eleven year reign as premier, Bill Bennett of British Columbia, the province most affected by U.S. restrictions on Canadian lumber imports, visited Washington only once.)

Part of the reason Americans are more demanding is that they think anything is possible. The belief runs from the Gipper—Ronald Reagan and Pat O'Brien a.k.a. George Gipp and Knute Rockne—pulling out a second-half comeback for old Notre Dame, right through to Rambo. If the proper authorities can't set things aright in the jungles of Southeast Asia, then Sylvester Stallone (a modern-day Charles Atlas with a Uzi as well as muscles) will do it on his own. Atlas taught the beach weakling not to let the bully kick sand in his face; Stallone demonstrates that people with yellow faces can't push Americans around.

When Reagan approved the name "Peacemaker" for the latest nuclear weapon, he was merely following in the great American tradition that sees guns as a way to solve problems and has since frontier days used them to "keep the peace." In America, most anyone can buy a gun at a corner store; even the First Lady once confessed to keeping a cute little pistol by her bed. The right to bear arms is guaranteed by the Constitution and, with their civil rights, has become a touch-stone of Americans' heritage: they used arms to free them-selves from the hated British overlords, arms to settle a bloody civil war, and arms to tame the wild west. Guns have become a projection of the country's exaggerated masculine self-reliance and Americans' patriotism.

Americans are big on patriotic symbols, and they have a lot of them, from the bald eagle to the Statue of Liberty. There is no country in the world that flies so many flags as the United States of America. A reporter who roams the land in his Hertzomatic continually comes upon lonely farmhouses in Iowa and isolated cottages in Georgia with the Stars and Stripes proudly displayed out front. No occasion, no reason: just pride. Approaching the Fourth of July, the country simply bursts into star-spangled patriotism. It's almost embarrassing for a foreigner to watch, somewhat like the uncomfortable feeling you have when the people in front of you at the movies are necking. Canadians don't go in for symbols in the same way. If anything, they are embarrassed by public displays of patriotism, and they treat their flag with a casual disregard that Americans find shocking.

What Canadians do have, and Americans lack, is royalty. Americans are really closet royalists. Having kicked out the wretched Brits and then fought a war of independence, they are still impressed by the trappings of king and queen. Witness their gaga response to the visit of Prince Charles and the Princess of Anorexia, Shy Di, to Washington. Leading matrons in the capital were stabbing one another with their swizzle sticks in the competition for invitations. When the time came for Randy Andy and the Fab Fergie to do their glass-coach effort for the tourist industry, Nancy Reagan not only went to the wedding to placate English criticism of the "cowardly" Americans who deserted London for fear of terrorists, the dignified *Washington Post* went gaga just like any Fleet Street tabloid.

In their lust for royalty, Americans anoint Hollywood film types and crown rock figures. Jackie and Jack Kennedy for a brief shining moment gave them their closest equivalent to their own monarchs.

Americans openly believe in the magic of a fairy tale, complete with the beautiful princess, wicked stepmother, and handsome prince rushing to the rescue on a prancing horse. They believe it is written into the Bill of Rights to expect a happy ending. They are probably the only remaining nation on earth to expect this—as when Reagan, borrowing from Lincoln, talks about America being "the last best hope of man on earth." It's a wonderful conceit, breathtaking in its arrogance.

Americans are such a wonderful combination of openness, naïveté, and toughness. You always know where you stand with them; they are like a whole nation of Sagittarians. It would be interesting to pick the sign of the zodiac for a country. If you had to choose one for the United States, it would be Sagittarius: the fire sign, full of energy, action, impulsiveness, honesty to the extreme, a healthy sense of tactlessness, a love of social occasion, speed, and sports. Canadians are probably fussy and rather boring Virgos.

Like Sagittarians, Americans are somewhat innocent and very insular, but their hearts are in the right place. They want to be liked, and they rather resent the responsibility that has been thrust upon them with the collapse of Britain and the other major European powers, bled by two wars.

The French don't care if no one likes them. The Brits are famed xenophobes (originators of the phrase, "The Wogs start at Calais"); they built an empire on the basis of being insensitive abroad. The Russians, a terribly insecure nation, don't trust anyone, mostly because they think no one trusts them. The Chinese, if you must know, are the happiest ones of all, serene in the belief that theirs is indeed the Middle Kingdom and that they were creating exotic civilizations when the rest of us were still swinging from trees. As an example, they regard the French—who think themselves the centre of world cuisine—as quite promising apprentices who have learned much from the Chinese and someday may amount to something.

The Americans, however, want to be liked and are hurt when their idealism is not returned. The American public greatly resented the fact that Washington was criticized by her allies after the raid on Libya, which, obviously aimed to rub out our friend Qaddafi, succeeded in killing one of his children, wounding several others, and happened to hit a few innocent targets.

America is truly the most generous nation in history and Americans cannot see why their virtue is not applauded. It is why Gordon Sinclair's celebrated radio broadcast on their kindness and good will was so widely repeated and appreciated in the United States; here at last was one foreigner who understood. Can anyone imagine the Brits or the French giving a damn what a foreign commentator thought about them? Forget it.

6
Lost in America

In which an attempt is made to explain why you can't get many television channels in the most important city in the world and how this is connected to the black population and why civil-rights leaders hid the truth and why pro basketball teams search so desperately for a player whose skin is white.

It is by the goodness of God that in our country we have those three unspeakably precious things: freedom of speech, freedom of conscience, and the prudence never to practise either of them.—MARK TWAIN

The American beast is a strange beast, wanting mostly to be left alone. Americans play games—American football and baseball—that almost no one in the rest of the world (Central America and Japan in the latter case being the exceptions) plays. And then declare their champions in those sports "world champions." Being impatient, they have invented junk food and fast food—the first not really food at all and the second a contradiction in terms.

They export most of their bad ideas (see two of them above) and import few of the good ideas from abroad. The American automobile industry was almost destroyed before Detroit noticed the obvious: that consumers wanted quality above all (a fact Japanese auto makers figured out years ago), and that you had to break up the monotony of Henry Ford's outmoded assembly line and put workers into self-sufficient and proud teams to counteract the drudgery of the workbench that produced so much American sloppiness and so many assembly-line errors (an innovation introduced by the Swedish long before).

In melding as astounding and successful nation out of immigrants—so many of them unwanted in their own lands—and creating a ferocious patriotism and nationalism, Americans have manufactured a land of conformity. There is much noise, but there is not a great range of dissent. There is no real "Left." The word "socialism" is thought a dirty word. Although the saintly, white-haired Norman Thomas ran as the socialist candidate for the presidency for decades, he was regarded as a kindly eccentric and as not only the leader but probably the only member of the Socialist Party of the United States of America.

Those who consider themselves of the "Left," including all the impassioned college students and "radicals" who were set to overthrow the establishment of the country in the 1960s, expressed themselves by voting for the Democratic party, which contains on its right wing millions of adherents who cannot be distinguished from millions of voters on the more tolerant wing of the Republican Party. In the United States, there ain't far you can go.

Their weaknesess—their uniformity in thought, their conformity, their suspicion of outside ideas—are of course what allows them to pull together in moment of need. Their weaknesses may also inspire their patriotism, their love of country, and their ferocious attitude toward anyone who dares challenge their mettle. The latter is not really a strength, but it's an illuminating trait to someone who comes from a country that shares almost none of the above.

Joe Rauh is a seventy-five-year-old lawyer, a legend in civil-rights circles, a man who wants to retire but vows never to do so until he can get some satisfaction out of the U.S. government (and the Canadian government) regarding the suit of nine Canadians who had their minds altered by CIA-financed brainwashing experiments at McGill University's Allan Institute. Rauh has been pursuing the case for six years through U.S. courts, has spent some $200,000 that his law firm will never recover from the aging and destitute Canadians who were turned into vegetables by the bizarre experiments conducted by a Dr. Ewan Cameron, and Ottawa would like the whole thing just to go away. Rauh writes long, reasoned letters to External Affairs Minister Joe Clark, and he writes to Brian Mulroney—and almost nothing happens.

The first of the nine died in Montreal early in 1986, and the others (including the wife of Winnipeg NDP MP David Orlikow) are elderly and aging. One wonders whether Ottawa (the previous Liberal government was even more shamefaced and secretive about the matter than this Conservative one) hopes to stonewall, since there was Canadian financing as well in the McGill caper, until there are no more witnesses alive. One feels ashamed to be a Canadian when one talks to Rauh. He says, in wonderment, "If the opposite had happened, if Americans had had their brains scrambled by the foreign government of Canada, I can tell you the Marines would be across the border in hours." In Canada, you can't induce passion. Passion is un-Canadian.

Another prospesity Canadians do not share with Americans is the use of violence—to settle disputes, to commit crimes, to let off steam. The United States has the highest rate of violence in the industrialized world. It has the highest proportion of people in prisons outside South Africa and the Soviet Union. The *Washington Post*, every Thursday, devotes an entire page tucked well inside to crimes in each Washington neighbourhood—muggings, robberies, rapes—so at a glance you can determine what is the prevailing crime to look for in your particular block.

On a Monday night a twenty-five-year-old woman was fatally stabbed in her southeast Washington house because of an argument over food preparation. Police say the fight started when the woman served "too many potatoes" on her sister's plate. So the sister got mad and stabbed her to death. A seventeen-year-old student was hit on the head and killed during a fight in a schoolyard, the second student to be killed in that schoolyard in recent months.

There is a lot of competition for the most horrible crime committed in Washington during my period of watching. London—and Britain in general—has always been famous for gruesome murders, the supposed excuse being that there are too many people enclosed in too small a space on the Tight Little Island and eventually they quietly go berserk and chop each other up and put the pieces in the sewer, or board the bodies up behind the walls in the house, or bury them in the back garden. Washington, perhaps because it is a government town, seems to have a similar penchant.

First, there was the Fuller case. Catherine Fuller was a tiny, ninety-nine-pound mother of six children. She was black. In late 1984, she was walking home from the grocery store when at least two dozen young people set upon her, robbed her of her change purse, dragged her into a garage, kicked and beat her, and thrust a steel pole up her rectum. Eleven young black men between the ages of sixteen and twenty-six—almost all neighbours of Fuller and some of them friends of her children—were found guilty of the murder.

They were school dropouts who spent their time smoking marijuana and PCP and hanging out at arcades. None of them could explain why a random robbery over a coin purse turned into a vicious killing.

Then there was the crime committed one January night in 1986. A thirty-year-old professional woman, returning to her car in a shopping plaza, was abducted by a man carrying a knife. He drove her to the Executive Motel, where he rented a room, bound, and gagged her, and raped her. Then, at 1:30 A.M., he drove her to the Rocky Gorge Bridge—still gagged with her hands bound behind her back—and dropped her thirty-five feet into the Patuxent River. The temperature was just below freezing. She swam on her back to shore and survived. Richard Baumgartner, a twenty-five-year-old, was later picked up because he was so bright as to leave his truck in the shopping-plaza parking lot.

Then there was the case, a few weeks later, when a nine-year-old was found in an apartment building decapitated, his ams chopped off, his torso disembowelled. His young mother, who had been on drugs, was taken away.

My choice for the most bizarre Washington crime occurred in February, during one of the infrequent light snowfalls in the capital. Cheryle Wallis, who manages a dentist's office, opened the door of her home to a messenger who carried a bouquet of roses and announced, "Flower delivery." When Wallis asked, "For whom?" the messenger began slashing at her with a kitchen knife.

Wallis fiancé, with whom she shared the house, was a U.S. government lawyer by name of Robert Hogue. He was in the shower upstairs when he heard the commotion. He raced down and, naked, ran two blocks through the falling snow before tackling the attacker, who wore a moustache, a green hat, and a parka. Hogue threw a few punches, the hat and moustache fell off, and he discovered he had nabbed Mary Prevost, an ex-girlfriend he had broken off with some three years earlier. Miss Prevost, a twenty-four-year-old described as a stunning beauty, was jailed. Bail was set at $100,000 and Prevost was ordered to undergo psychiatric tests. Mr. Hogue and Ms. Wallis have since broken up.

In 1985 there were, 1,384 murders in New York City, which is nowhere near the most dangerous American city. (The top six are Gary, Indiana; Detroit, Michigan; Miami, Florida; New Orleans, Louisiana; Richmond, Virginia; Oakland,

California.) The New York murder rate is 20.2 per 100,000 population. The rate in London is 2.2 per 100,000—which is why the Brits were so contemptuous of all the frightened Americans who cancelled their European trips in the summer of 1986 because of the terrorist threat. Better, perhaps, to avoid Portugal, which has Europe's highest rate of traffic fatalities—30.7 per 100,000, even worse than New York's murder rate. There are more murders a year in Detroit, 636, than in England and Wales combined, 616. In Greece and Spain, the supposedly passionate Mediterranean countries, the murder rates are only 1.7 per 100,000 and 1.1 per 100,000 respectively. That's even less violent than mild old Britain.

Americans are not nearly as horrified by their crime rates as the rest of the world is. They just buy more guns, put more locks on their doors, and place bars and bullet-proof glass between their public figures and the public itself.

When the ex-"B"-picture star returned to Los Angeles, several miles from Hollywood, it should have been a triumphant return. There he was, watched by the world, as he officially opened the 1984 Olympic Games. But to do it, even in his old town, he had to be encased in a bulletproof glass cage for fear of terrorists, and he was unable even to go down to the field and shake the hand of a live athlete.

Ironically, America, formed by people who fled older lands for a better living, feels a missionary need to teach other people how to run their business and conduct their lives. Thus, the sermonizing to South Africa on apartheid. (It was another celebrated sanctimonious sermonizer, John Diefenbaker, who initiated the move to kick South Africa out of the Commonwealth. It's not clear that that really caused any improvement in the situation.) The Americans, having made a preliminary and tentative start to reform their own record of dealing with their black minority, now feel capable of telling the South Africans how they should deal with their black majority.

Only two blocks from the White House, tourists might encounter a black man, standing on a street corner in alley-stained clothes, babbling and completely out of it. Visitors are often struck by the dichotomy. That again is both the weakness and the strength of this contradictory country: their idealism urges them to change the world while they still haven't had time to solve all their own problems. When the magnificent Lincoln Memorial was officially dedicated in 1922, erected in honour of the president who freed the slaves, there were separate stands set aside for the "colored" people.

Canadians, smug as only Canadians can be, cluck about America's treatment of her blacks. But Canada's rotten record with native people is just as bad as the United States' rotten record with native people. In both countries, the highest suicide rate in the population is among young male native Indians. That says it all.

Americans now have a national holiday in January to honour Martin Luther King, Jr. They have a national holiday in February on George Washington's birthday. They don't have a holiday on Abraham Lincoln's birthday. It might seem strange that Honest Abe, the Great Emancipator, has never been honoured with a national holiday, while King, the benfactor of his wisdom, does. The reason is that in order to save the union Lincoln freed the slaves, and there is still enough resentment among southern voters and southern congressmen to thwart any move to name a holiday after him.

It might seem puzzling to an outsider that such feelings still persist in 1986, but an example may illuminate matters. Washington is still a city of the South in many ways, with the old Confederate state of Virginia just across the Potomac. There is, on a popular Washington radio station, a morning disc jockey by name of Doug "The Greaseman" Tracht who specializes in racial insults. On the day of the Martin Luther King holiday in 1986, he told his eager listeners that if the assassination of one black leader was the cause for a day's holiday, then killing four more would result in the rest of the week off. Fun stuff, in a city that is 80 percent black.

The Greaseman has said that if Virginia highway officials want to blacktop state roads, they should steamroller some Negroes and throw in some Koreans to make the yellow lines. The Greaseman is particularly popular in suburbia, where most of the white folk who work in Washington live. That would be out beyond the Beltway, as the freeway system encircling the capital is known (also called, in local parlance, the Congo Line).

The Greaseman pulls in some 63,000 listeners every morning who delight in his stuff as they drive in to "Nigra City," as he calls it. He also has a contract worth one million dollars over five years, an indication of how much his sicky stuff is worth. The slick *Washingtonian* magazine, full of ads for the suburbanites, has for the past three years named the Greaseman as "Best Radio Deejay" in the area.

He is not unique in his field. Two other chaps of his ilk were exceedingly popular before him. One of them, Howard Stern, was fired only after he phoned Florida Airlines on the air—the day their jet hit a bridge on takeoff and sank in the Potomac, killing nearly a hundred people—and asked for the one-way fare to the Fourteenth Street Bridge. The Greaseman, however, sails merrily along, leavening his jokes about blacks with jokes about homosexuals, who are quite prevalent in Washington, as in most government towns.

Do the owners of his station, wwdc, care? Nope. He brings in those 63,000 faithful listeners every morning with breakfast. Does the Federal Communications Commission, which is supposed to regulate the publicly owned airwaves, care? In answer to a written complaint, the fcc said only this: "Unless the content of the program can be clearly shown to be obscene or indecent, there is no recourse at the federal level. . . . It has been our experience that most material complained of, as offensive as it may be, is not actionable."

There are strange standards in the city about what can be said on the air. One afternoon I heard on my car radio two deejays making their Academy Award predictions, including one "to a movie that's never been seen, because it was written by Ray Charles and Stevie Wonder." Both black musicians happen to be blind. A real thigh slapper.

We all recall the fuss when cabinet member Earl Butz was forced to resign his White House slot after he joked that the only things blacks wanted were "a tight pussy, loose shoes and a warm place to shit." (American newspapers, while highly publicizing the event, left readers in the dark by refusing to repeat the remark, leaving columnist Art Buchwald to explain that it was simply a desire of blacks to have comfortable shoes, a satisfactory sex life, and a well-heated toilet.) Public opinion forced his resignation after he told his "private" joke to a couple of the fellows on an airplane—and John Dean squealed. Now we have exceedingly well-paid radio jockeys spewing forth the same stuff on the air. Honest Abe, who probably wouldn't care about a holiday, might wonder whether any progress has been made after all.

This supposedly "advanced" nation is surprisingly behind in a number of things. On my television set, even with an aerial on the roof of the house, I can get three channels. As someone who became spoiled on the twelve channels available in Vancouver—which has the highest cable-TV penetration per residence on the globe—it came as somewhat of a shock to learn that the city of Washington has no cable television.

The reason is simple. A city that is 80 percent black simply doesn't have the economic base to support a cable-TV system. It is the same in most of the major cities in the United States. The same population that provides the cities with black mayors dictates that they don't have the TV choices available to most of the rest of the country.

Washington has a black mayor. So do Philadelphia, Atlanta, Detroit, Chicago, and Los Angeles. Of the largest cities in the country, New York is the only one that does not have a black mayor. A nation that is just 12 percent black has never yet come to grips with that ratio. A nation that endured a Civil War to free the slaves, a struggle that is not forgotten, still does not know how to cope with an unhappy and undereducated minority that cripples the economy of its largest cities.

While blacks are elected at the municipal level, the imbalance in the other political fields is still striking. Nearly 12 percent of the population of 260 million is black. But of the 500,000 elected and appointed public officials in the country, only about 6,000—slightly more than one percent—are black. In the 115 southern congressional districts stretching from Virginia, across the Potomac from Washington, to Texas, home to 53 percent of the nation's blacks, there is one black congressman. In all the rest of the United States, there are only nineteen black congressmen. There are no black senators, no black governors.

Two decades ago, a young assistant secretary of labor by name of Daniel Patrick Moynihan wrote a then-controversial report that warned: "The Negro family evidence, not final, but powerfully persuasive, is that the Negro family in the urban ghettos is crumbling." Civil-rights leaders attacked Moynihan and the report, claiming it would give whites ammunition to blame blacks for their own problems. Even Martin Luther King said, "It wasn't the right time."

Negros are now called blacks, Moynihan is now a veteran New York senator, and the problem he described has simply multiplied. When he wrote that report in 1965, one-quarter of all black births were out of wedlock. Today, 58 percent of all black babies born in the United States have unmarried mothers. America now has a subculture of thirty-year-old grandmothers.

In the most comprehensive survey of the wealth of Americans to date, the U.S. Census Bureau reports that the net worth of the typical white American household is twelve times as great as the figure for the typical black household. It found that nearly one-third of all black households had no assets and were in debt. Fewer than one in ten whites had no assets or were in debt. (The survey showed, no surprise, that 12 percent of American households held 38 percent of all personal wealth in the nation.)

Blacks in America, while just one-eighth of the population, are convicted of half of all rapes, robberies, and murders and a fourth of all burglaries, larcenies, and aggravated assaults. The most prevalent type of murder in the United States is one young black man killing another young black man. The incarceration rate in the District of Columbia itself is in fact higher than in South Africa.

It was in 1954 that the Supreme Court made the ruling that supposedly allowed blacks the same educational opportunities as white. Some educators warned at the time that three decades would have to pass before there could be rational public debate about how blacks were doing in the classroom.

Those thirty years are now up and it seems clear the self-imposed silence—in essence protecting blacks from the truth—has only done them harm. The unequal education opportunities for blacks are now a national disgrace. That's not the word of an outsider: that's the word of educators themselves. At a time when Americans are fulminating about South Africa and putting economic pressures on the Pretoria government, figures show that black students trail white students on all the scholastic tests.

It's obvious that millions of black kids have never seen a magazine, let alone a book, around the house. How many have ever been read to? Of course, the school gap between whites and blacks has its roots in family background and education, neighbourhood influence, cultural motivation, and all those factors so lovingly quoted by the sociologists. But the facts remain, by the year 2000, it is estimated one of every three Americans will be non-white, and yet the country is only now waking up to the implications of an undereducated increasing minority population. Part of the problem is that school authorities have repressed these figures—for fear of being accused of "racism," the currently popular buzzword in all the right liberal circles.

Chester Finn, Jr., an assistant secretary at the U.S. Department of Education, says, "Black leaders and civil rights leaders have not encouraged people to look at this"—"this" meaning the fact that blacks lag far behind whites on standarized test scores. "Why?" Finn went on. "Ask them. Only now are they willing to talk openly and seriously about out-of-wedlock birth and that has been a problem for a long time too." It's a simple fact that by as early as 1982, 49 percent of all black children in this country lived with one parent. It's conceded by almost everyone (except the White House) that the plight of the black community has become worse during the Reagan years.

One school district after another in the Washington area has now released figures—at first tentatively, a lttle nervously—showing that blacks trail whites by twenty to forty-eight percentile points on test scores. The reason school authorities have come out of the closet with their alarming figures is their growing concern about the drain that millions of undereducated citizens will have on unemployment and on Social Security benefits.

The suburban counties near Washington, in Maryland to the north and Virginia to the south, are now announcing million-dollar programs to reduce the size of classes, hire more teachers, provide tutors, and introduce a number of other rescue techniques. It's clear that it will be many more decades before any improvements can be measured, but at least the authorities are talking about it now, rather than keeping the depressing scholastic figures hidden in their files.

In the richest nation in history, unemployment among blacks is roughly twice that of whites. The median family income for blacks is about 55 percent that of whites. Unemployment among black teenagers is more than 40 percent—more than double the white teenage rate. One of every three blacks lives below the poverty level; nearly half of all blacks under eighteen exist in poverty

The first thing one sees when alighting at Washington National Airport is a large and beautiful colour picture of Washington adorned with these words: "Welcome to the most important city in the world." That it is, but it is still apparently powerless to do anything about the plight of American blacks.

The sense of despair is shown by the fact that fewer than 40 percent of Washington residents vote in elections, the lowest turnout of any major U.S. city. Across the country, unemployment rates for black men and women have increased steadily since 1965. By 1983, about one of every five blacks in the labour market was without work. The figures, naturally, are much higher for teenagers and young adults.

Those who do work have the low jobs. The postman who comes to my door in Georgetown (six days a week—thank you very much, Canada Post) is black. The man who reads the meter is black. The man who offers to shovel off the steps in the ever-so-rare dusting of snow is black. The man who delivers the cordwood for the fireplace, however, is white, since he comes from deep in Virginia across the river (with the Virginia hardwood, which, since it cast no sparks, makes superfluous the most despicable—and contradictory—beast of our time, the "fireplace screen"). Every attendant at every parking lot is black. Waiters are black. The people at the gas-station pumps are black. Anyone in a low-level service job is black. It's a given.

There's a sardonic joke in Washington. What do you call one white man surrounded by ten black men? A basketball coach. What do you call one white man surrounded by a thousand black men? A prison warden. What do you call one white man surrounded by a hundred thousand black men? The Postmaster General.

I took my teenage daughter, visiting from out of town, to a musical in Washington, in the theatre where Lincoln was shot. It was a send-up of a black gospel church, with a dancing pastor in a white rock 'n' roll Little Richard suit and full of magnificent, soaring voices. She could not take her eyes off the audience, their attire ranging from dripping mink and pearls to jeans and sneakers. We were the only people in the entire theatre who were white.

The subtleties of the American black-white dilemma are many. Doug Flutie is a football player. He is five foot nine and three-quarter inches tall, handsome, articulate, an honours student—and white. The colour of his skin is the main reason he became in 1985 the highest-paid athlete in the world, signing a contract worth $7 million over five years.

Flutie is a bit of a freak, a quarterback who does not fit the standard mould of a statuesque hunk reaching six-foot-three or more, in the line of a Dan Marino or a Joe Montana, who can throw over the 280-pound monsters who masquerade as defensive linemen. There are strong doubts whether Flutie can ever make it in professional football, but that's not why he's worth $7 million. He was worth it to his new owners because he was a good-looking white boy in a jock world short of white heroes. The case of Doug Flutie illustrates something so apparent to a foreigner: the reluctance of Americans to debate openly the continuing problem of the 88 percent of the country that is white to relate to the 12 percent of that is non-white. In private the owners of the professional sports franchises of the land take very seriously the problem of the predominantly black players. You can see it in their desperate search for white stars, so as to placate their overwhelmingly white customers.

St. John's University of New York came to Washington in 1985 and upset the then-reigning collegiate basketball champions, Georgetown University, which had a twenty-nine-game winning streak and, like most major college teams, had an entirely black line-up of players. The star player for St. John's was a tough New York Irish kid called Chris Mullin, who had the pro scouts drooling. He was good, but he went for several million more than he was athletically worth in the professional basketball draft because he was white. The only other white starting player on the St. John's team was seven-foot centre Bill Wennington, a member of Canada's Olympic team. In 1985 the only white starter on the highly ranked Duke Univerity team was Danny Meagher, another Canadian Olympian.

Two generations ago, the route out of the ghetto for black youth was to follow Joe Louis and Sugar Ray Robinson into the brutal boxing ring. Now, thanks to the bottomless wallet of TV, pro football, baseball, and basketball offer untold riches to gifted high-school students. Black youths in the ruined inner cities now spend endless hours in playgrounds, perfecting their free-form skills.

The Boston Celtics, which is the best team in basketball

and has all those Boston Irish fans, will do almost anything to capture white stars. In basketball, where athletes show a lot of skin—unlike those in football and baseball—skin colour is important and obvious. The Celtics plotted for years to snare Larry Bird ("the hick from French Lick," Indiana), the best player in the game today despite the playful taunt from his black mates that he suffers from "the white man's disease" (he can't jump).

Danny Ainge, who was an All-American in both basketball and baseball at Brigham Young University in Utah, chose baseball and the Toronto Blue Jays. The Celtics never let up on him and finally persuaded him to break his Toronto contract and come to them. He'll never be a first-rate star, but he's white. The Celtics are unique in pro basketball as a result. They can now have three white men as starters on the floor in a five-man sport: Bird, Ainge, and a good Irishman, Kevin McHale. In addition, their first substitute, Bill Walton, is white, as are two other subs, Scott Wedman and Jerry Sichting.

The problem no one talks about long ago took over the American Olympic track team (a fact that Europeans always comment on disparagingly) and professional baseball and football, where the only remaining star running back in the NFL who was white, the Washington Redskins' creaky veteran John Riggins, has been told to retire.

There is so much made of the bravery of Branch Rickey of the Brooklyn Dodgers in breaking the colour bar in major league baseball by introducing the brilliant second-baseman Jackie Robinson. In fact, just to test whether it would work, Rickey introduced him to professional baseball not in America but in Canada, the decaffeinated United States. Robinson thus played a season with the minor league Montreal Royals. Canada was the market research territory, Brooklyn and Rickey getting all the acclaim.

. Flutie took the $7 million from the New Jersey Generals of the maverick U.S. Football League without even waiting for a National Football League offer because his agent said he would make, in the New York endorsement market, even more money outside football than in it. He was the first winner of the Heisman Trophy in six years who was white.

Meanwhile, the lack of other opportunities for blacks is a nervous subject, and Ronald Reagan merely encourages the gap. In the 1984 election, he received 66 percent of the white votes, 10 percent of the black. As a right-wing columnist who supports the Republicans smugly told a Democratically inclined columnist before the election: "We've got the whites and you've got the blacks and we're going to win."

And Washington, 80 percent black, can continue to boast about how important it is around the world.

7

Close Encounters of the Worst Kind

In which it is detailed why Johnson swore at Pearson and why Kennedy hated Dief and why Mackenzie King read to Roosevelt in bed and how Calvin Coolidge couldn't figure out where Toronto was, not to mention the congressman who was surprised that a prime minister could speak English so good and why the presidents can never remember the names of the prime ministers.

> *The boundary between Canada and the*
> *U.S. is a typically human creation; it is*
> *physically invisible, geographically*
> *illogical, militarily indefensible, and*
> *emotionally inescapable.*
> —HUGH L. KEENLEYSIDE

American attitudes toward Canada have always swung from the poles of indifference to acquisitiveness. (The one constant is ignorance, which, to be honest, also characterizes the American attitude to Mexico, Central America, Britain, Japan, and most elsewhere.) It is therefore no accident that although the first visit by a prime minister to Washington was in 1871—four years after this country was stillborn—it took seventy-two years before anyone bothered to visit Canada's capital: Franklin Roosevelt in 1943 was the first American president to set foot in Ottawa.

It's more amusing than demeaning, but most of all it's educational. It puts things in perspective. We've always been the Great White North to Americans, even before the McKenzie Brothers invented the term. (Fleet Street improved on the phrase in the 1980s when, piqued by some cheekiness from the colonies, it dubbed Canada "The Great White Waste of Time." This is hardly an improvement on Voltaire's comment in 1759 that "Canada is a few acres of snow not worth a soldier's bones.")

Ulysses S. Grant was known to his detractors as Useless S. Grant. Shortly after our Confederation he decided this northern neighbour was ripe for swallowing. He wanted it, in fact, in time for his reelection in 1872. Britain owed the United States compensation for damages caused by the cruiser *Alabama*, which had been built in British shipyards for use by the

82

South in the Civil War. Grant suggested that London hand over Canada in fair exchange for the damages. Canada swapped for a boat? It seemed a reasonable idea at the time.

President Rutherford B. Hayes also very much liked the idea of swallowing Canada. President Grover Cleveland passed down an order boycotting all goods from north of the border. Teddy Roosevelt, a man not lacking in self-esteem, thought it was a shame—for Canadians, not Americans—that Canada wasn't part of the U.S.A. His classic quote, grand in its chutzpah, explained that, as Americans, these people "would hold positions incomparably more important, grander and more dignified than they can ever hope to reach." The people to whom he was referring were Canadians. The quote should be engraved over the front door of every Canadian school.

Teddy Roosevelt's successor in the White House, William Howard Taft, wanted a free-trade pact with Canada (hi there, Simon Reisman), which he insisted publicly had nothing to do with annexation—while writing privately that it did. The Canadian voters, suspicious even then of the real aims of presidents as they always should be, shot the idea down.

The Taft presidency, as author Lawrence Martin has perceptively pointed out, was the end of the first of four clearly delineated periods in the murky relationship between Ottawa and Washington. This first period, which lasted from 1867 to 1911, was a time of annexationist presidents. The second stage, from 1911 to 1932, was a time of aloof and indifferent presidents. The prospect of annexation was dead, and the White House, with its different occupants, yawned at the thought of Canada. President Calvin Coolidge, though born in the border state of Vermont, once wondered whether Toronto was near a lake. (He perhaps should not be blamed, since Toronto has only recently discovered that fact.)

Woodrow Wilson and Herbert Hoover were never interested in Canada, the former being too interested in establishing the League of Nations and the latter in putting a chicken in every pot. Both failed.

In between Wilson and Hoover was one president, Warren Harding, who did brave a trip to Canada, and his experience might explain why subsequent presidents avoided us and why Dwight Eisenhower—this was in the 1950s, remember—was only the second president ever to set foot in Ottawa. Canada is clearly not a safe place for the world's most powerful elected leader. Gremlins lurk and jinxes abound. Evil spirits hiding in the weeds keep an eye peeled for Yanks. Bad things have happened to them here.

President Harding made his ill-fated visit in 1923. He was on his way back from Alaska when he decided to stop off in Vancouver. The locals were ecstatic, since the twenty-ninth president was the first in American history to set foot on Canadian soil. Soldiers in pith helmets, arms swinging high, marched before Harding to the slow rhythm of kilted pipe bands—all the imperial display that Canada had inherited from England. The *Vancouver Sun* ran a huge Second-Coming banner headline trumpeting CITY FALLS TO HARDING and devoted its entire front page to four excruciatingly obsequious stories.

But it was July, there was a heat wave, and the enthusiastic hosts weren't too concerned for Harding's obviously fading health. He had to make five impromptu speeches before addressing a crowd of forty thousand in Stanley Park. He appeared worn and almost frail. Taken to play golf by his Vancouver hosts, he fell ill before he could complete the round and had to go back to his hotel for a rest.

At a banquet in his honour, he said, "I like that word—*neighbours*. I like the sort of neighbours who borrow eggs over the back fence."

He sailed out of Vancouver for San Francisco completely exhausted, not helped by the fact that a heavy fog had enveloped the harbour and the foghorns were wailing in the darkness. Just as his ship was edging into American waters, she struck amidships the destroyer U.S.S. *Zeilen*—one of thirteen destroyers sent to escort her. (The *Zeilen* suffered severe damage and eventually had to be beached, but Harding's ship suffered only minor damage.) An aide rushed to Harding's room and found the president lying on his bed, his face in his hands. Told that there had been a slight collision, Harding remained motionless. "I hope the boat sinks," he said softly. He died before he could see Washington again.

After his death, those shipboard words of the up-to-then popular president seemed prophetic. Shortly after he died, evidence came out that corruption and malfeasance had been widespread in Washington. The scandal most damaging to Harding's reputation was the Teapot Dome affair. (Teapot Dome was a naval oil reserve in Wyoming that, contrary to promises given to conservationists, was privately exploited.) As knowledge of Harding's own habits became public, his reputation went downhill. He had had a fifteen-year affair with the wife of a close friend and another affair with a damsel who was only sixteen. She subsequently published her memoirs, alleging that Harding had fathered her child. As one of his biographers pointed out, he was "by no means the first or last philanderer to be president, but he was the only one unfortunate enough to have one of his mistresses write memoirs." It also was revealed that he had openly consumed liquor in the White House during Prohibition.

Today Harding is held in very low esteem in America. Vancouver, however, was so impressed with him, that a Harding memorial—two bronze female figures representing Columbia and Canada, flanked by eagles—was erected in Stanley Park alongside the tea pavilion. In 1969, someone, obviously not a fan of America, sawed a hand off each lady and amputated the birds' beaks. Borrowing eggs, indeed.

The next era—the thirties and early forties—was unusual for the exceedingly chummy relationship that existed between Franklin Delano Roosevelt and William Lyon Mackenzie King. They met over the years a total of nineteen times, a situation that completely puzzled Eleanor Roosevelt, who found King boring. Perceptive Eleanor.

Roosevelt's association with Canada went back to the year after his birth in 1882, when his well-to-do parents bought a summer home on Campobello, a New Brunswick island some nine miles long in the Bay of Fundy. The family returned every summer and the young Roosevelt loved it there. Like his cousin Teddy, he was very athletic. A sailing instructor said that as a boy he "could sail like a man of fifty." He not only was an eager golfer, but acted as greens keeper on the island course.

In the summer of 1921, the rising political star, then undersecretary to the Navy, longed for a break from Washington pressures. He had just been through the grinder of a Senate committee investigating homosexuality in the Navy. He had been accused of willingly letting investigators—"fairy chasers" in the term of the day—act as agents provocateurs in their attempt to catch homosexuals.

In August, he left for a rest at Campobello. Although he was exhausted and rattled, Roosevelt spent many hours at the wheel of the yacht, steering it through fogbound waters to Campobello. The next day, under warm sunshine and sweating from working over the boat's hot engine, he slipped and fell overboard into water so cold "it seemed paralyzing." He still didn't feel right the next morning, but instead of resting he went swimming, ran, and then spent hours furiously fighting a forest fire on a nearby island.

The third morning his left leg dragged. Then his other leg declined to work. Eleanor sent for the family doctor, who said it was simply a bad cold. When FDR became paralyzed from the chest down, a specialist came to the island, decided it was a blood clot in the spinal column that would need heavy messaging, and sent a bill for $600.

It was two weeks after the fall from the boat that a Boston doctor who specialized in poliomyelitis told the thirty-nine-year-old Roosevelt that he indeed had the newly diagnosed disease. He thought it not a serious case.

Incredibly, the future president remained on his New Brunswick island for yet another two weeks, in dreadful pain, before he was smuggled on a stretcher to New York, the news still being shielded from the press and the public.

It was twelve years before he again saw the Canadian home he loved. He couldn't bear to return. When he finally did, in 1933, he was president—and wearing ten pounds of steel braces on his legs.

One of the reasons King and Roosevelt got along so well was that they were both Harvard men—though not at the same time. King was there at the end of one century and Roosevelt at the beginning of the next. Also, Mackenzie King, as an "industrial counsellor," had many U.S. connections and was a great favourite of large American corporations. In 1918, for example, he received $4,000 from Bethlehem Steel, $3,000 from General Electric, $2,000 from International Harvester, $5,000 from Great Western Sugar, $1,000 from Consolidation Coal, and $1,000 from Youngstown Sheet & Tube. With a retainer of $6,000 from the Rockefellers, he had an income of $22,000, not bad at all by 1918 standards.

King's and Roosevelt's first encounter, by letter, was not a propitious one, despite their common interests. In 1929, Roosevelt, as governor of New York, wrote the prime minister saying he would like to drop in and discuss the St. Lawrence Seaway idea. King rebuffed him, explaining that the opposition and "the conservative press" were already criticizing him on the grounds of sacrificing Canadian interests. Like, get lost.

King was defeated by R.B. Bennett in 1930, and when he

returned as prime minister in 1935, FDR was in the White House. Only one day after he was sworn in, King was at the door of the American ambassador in Ottawa, asking for an audience in Washington. That meeting, the first of the nineteen, was the beginning of a close but strange relationship.

Throughout their many meetings, King could never bring himself to call FDR by his first name. It was always "Mr. Roosevelt." FDR, for his part, called the Canadian prime minister "Mackenzie" (a name no one else ever used). At the beginning of their visits, FDR, after being assisted to the sofa by an attendant, would beckon King to sit down on his right. He always directed King to the same place. King, uncomfortable as usual and deferential, would instead move to a chair opposite the president in a more formal setting. It wasn't until near Roosevelt's death that he realized the president had only one good ear—his right one.

King also always declined the president's offer to go swimming with him. And he passed on other liquids as well. When King wouldn't take a pre-dinner drink, Roosevelt felt it necessary to explain that he drank because of his polio. He said his feet often grew cold and to keep the blood circulating his doctors had prescribed cocktails before dinner.

Despite its bizarre qualities, the relationship between the two leaders developed so well that by 1937 (Ronald Reagan was then making *Love Is on the Air* for Warner Bros.), the bachelor prime minister shared his private thoughts with the president and read to him in bed at the White House. Here is a metaphor, surely, for the contract between the two countries: a mysterious and lonely prime minister who worshipped his mother and believed in the occult, reading in bed to a tired, crippled president who ran his country from a wheelchair and was haunted by the prospect of a European war. Canada reading in bed to the United States—one could not quite imagine Trudeau doing it for Nixon, let alone Diefenbaker doing it for Kennedy—but in 1937 such was the bond between Franklin Delano Roosevelt, the aristocrat, and William Lyon Mackenzie King, who spent the years waiting to become Liberal leader working for the Rockefellers in the United States.

As their relationship grew closer, outsiders—in both politics and the press—grew increasingly frustrated at the Canadian prime minister's reluctance to share his inside knowledge about the president. The White House reporters even composed a ditty: "William Lyon Mackenzie King/Never tells us a goddamn thing."

King was in the middle of a massage in Ottawa, on the afternoon of April 12, 1945, when he was told that Roosevelt had died. At the grave site, three days later at Hyde Park in New York State, he carried a wreath among the mourners. Leaving his hat and coat with Edward Stettinius, the American secretary of state, he walked alone to the grave, dropped the flowers, and walked back. A motion-picture crew asked him to do it again because they had missed the shot. He complied. Walking slowly to the coffin once again, he picked up the flowers and put them down again and walked slowly back. Oh boy.

The King-Roosevelt interlude was followed by the period when a newly assertive Canada tried to flex its teensy muscles at the bully who had been kicking sand in Ottawa's face.

Governor General Lord Athlone told King that Roosevelt's successor, Harry Truman, was "a crook." King himself thought the new president probably wasn't a criminal, but just an inexperienced lowbrow who was unfit for the job.

King, buttering up Truman, once told him the Canadian people wanted to see him because he was courageous and fearless. Truman said, "I only try to do what is right; not to trouble about anything else." King, in a revealing confession, told Pearson one day that the secret of politics was not to do what is right but to avoid doing what is wrong. Wonderful! How Canadian!

President Eisenhower and Prime Minister Louis St. Laurent got along well together, partly because they were so similar. Both had entered politics late in life, both stayed aloof from the daily dirt of politics, and both ran their governments rather like a chairman of the board. When Ike, who chipped wedges out of the floor of the White House while practising his stroke, invited Uncle Louis to a round of golf on an Atlanta course, he courteously paired him with the club pro. The final score was never announced, and the president, the perfect host, declared that St. Laurent and the pro had won. The PM made no such claim and when he got back to Ottawa that night he confided to a reporter, "I was no worse than usual. But when I manage to break a hundred, I'll announce it myself."

John Diefenbaker irritated John Kennedy, who could not stand him. Diefenbaker thought Kennedy, whos early popularity with Canadians was wiping out the euphoria of the 1958 Dief sweep, was too young, too handsome, and too rich. Kennedy thought Diefenbaker was not only insincere but boring.

By the time John Kennedy made his visit to Ottawa in 1961, he and Dief the Chief had already decided they disliked each other thoroughly. If that hadn't been enough to discourage Kennedy from visiting Canada, the ill-fated experiences of his predecessors should have been, but JFK was not deterred. When he went to Rideau Hall for the ritual tree planting, there was already a feeling of macho competition. Kennedy was given a gleaming silver spade to plant two red oaks, and to show up his much older adversary, he shovelled in about a dozen good throws of dirt, remarking sardonically, "I wonder if this is symbolic."

It was something else. Kennedy had injured his back in the Pacific war in his famous PT-boat adventure, and a few hours after his Rideau Hall bravado, he sensed a twinge. He was in pain for months and thereafter had to retire to a rocking chair at every opportunity.

In December 1961, Kennedy had to participate in a "modified tree planting" in Bermuda, involving merely snipping a ribbon. "A very good way of doing it," he allowed. "Much easer than in Canada." Zap! (When it came Richard Nixon's turn to visit Ottawa and Rideau Hall, he too took part in a ritual tree planting. The tree died.)

The best example of the American reaction to the Canadian mouse came when Lester Pearson, as prime minister, made a celebrated speech at Temple University in Philadelphia, advocating that the United States pause in the bombing of North Vietnam. Pearson had been invited to lunch with Lyndon Johnson the next day at Camp David, and was whisked there by helicopter. No mention was made of the speech during lunch until, over coffee, Pearson asked the president, "What did you think of my speech?"

There followed one of the more remarkable of LBJ's many remarkable performances. Muttering "Awful," the host took his guest by the arm and led him to the terrace before launching into his tirade. Johnson strode the terrace in a rage, sawed the air with his arms, and made full use of his famous vocabulary. Canadian Ambassador Charles Richie and White House aide McGeorge Bundy, watching from the lunch table, finally grew embarrassed and went for a long walk through the woods. Then they returned, almost an hour later, Johnson was still at it. In near-apoplexy, he rode over every attempt Pearson made to reply. Finally he grabbed the prime minister by the lapels and shouted, "You pissed on my rug!"

When President Johnson came to Ottawa for what was supposed to be an official visit during Centennial celebrations, Pearson was annoyed to find that LBJ couldn't come to the prime minister's residence at 24 Sussex Drive for a luncheon because his security people wouldn't let him come into Ottawa. He was invited instead to the prime ministerial summer residence at Harrington Lake, that idyllic retreat in the Gatineau Hill of Quebec some fifteen miles north of Ottawa. It is one of the beauty spots of Canada; a great white house, full of French doors and ample fireplaces, it sits high on a plush lawn that dips down to a lake. The prime minister and family are the only residents and they can look up the entire length of the three-mile lake, rimmed by bottle-green hills—strangers in paradise. It makes the Sussex Drive residence seem like a cramped anteroom.

When Pearson arrived ahead of the president, he found his home overrun with Washington security people on rowboats and in the bushes with their walkie-talkies. Pearson went into his house and up the stairs to be met by a hard-faced agent who demanded: "Who are you? Where are you going?" Pearson replied, "I live here and I'm going to take a leak."

Johnson skimmed in by helicopter, had lunch, and was back in Washington by five o'clock. That was his Centennial visit to Canada.

American presidents, it must be realized, have never much been interested in the outside world. The first twenty-four presidents never once set foot outside U.S. soil. When Teddy Roosevelt finally did become the first one to venture afar, he went as far as Panama. That was in 1906. Astonishingly, Woodrow Wilson was the first American president to travel to Europe, for the Paris Peace Conference, which followed the end of the First World War. That was 142 years after the United States was founded.

American presidents can never be bothered to remember the names of Canadian prime ministers. When Lyndon Johnson invited Lester Pearson to his Texas ranch in 1965, he greeted the Nobel Prize-winner before the television cameras, and said how much he was looking forward to hosting "Mr. Wilson."

After dinner and many drinks, the voracious Johnson insisted on turning on the evening news—and the report of his own welcoming speech. When he saw himself greeting his "old friend . . . Mr. Wilson," he was at first completely bewildered and then apologized expansively. Said Pearson, "Think nothing of it, Senator Goldwater."

The pattern has been consistent. Senator Claiborne Pell from the state of Rhode Island, referred to Brian Mulroney throughout his 1986 visit to Washington as Prime Minister Muldoon. And Drew Lewis, Ronald Reagan's personal ambassador on acid rain—after a year of working closely with his Canadian equivalent, former Ontario premier Bill Davis— emerged from the White House to tell waiting reporters how much he had enjoyed working with "Bill Wilson."

"Wilson," you see, has that, well, nice mundane *Canadian* ring to it. And high American politicians, when they see someone coming across the tarmac in a sincere blue suit, white shirt, bland tie, immediately think one thing. The magic word "Commonwealth" flashes across either the left side or the right side of the brain, assuming they have both, and the memory calls up names like "Wilson" and "Muldoon." All Chinamen look alike. All post-facto colonials have the same names. It figures.

When Diefenbaker visited Dwight Eisenhower at the White House in 1960, Ike said, "Every member of this company feels a very definite sense of honour and distinction in the privilege of having with us tonight the Prime Minister of the Great Republic of Canada." No White House official noticed the goof, since the president referred to the "republic" of Canada again on the visit.

In 1949, Harry Truman had been president for four years. He called a press conference to state, along with other trivia, that he was about to host a visitor from Canada. In his two-paragraph statement, he mentioned the prime minister of Canada five times without actually saying his name. (This was at a time, recall, when Canada ranked as a leading middle power in the world.)

The White House Associated Press reporter, one Tony Vaccaro, asked, "For bulletin purposes, sir, what's his name?"

"I was very carefully trying to avoid it," said the president of the United States of America, "because I don't know how to pronounce it."

Carefully, he tried. "Louis St. Laurent. L-a-u-r-e-n-t. I don't know how to pronouce it. That's a French pronunciation. I wouldn't attempt to pronounce it. Tony, you put me on the spot."

When John Kennedy became president, Diefenbaker had already been prime minister for three years but no one in the White House had taken the trouble to find out how to pronounce his name. Kennedy obviously hadn't heard the name often enough to wrap it around his tongue. To avoid any gaffes like Truman's, he had his trusty Secretary of State Dean Rusk get it right.

Rusk, ever dutiful and ever unimaginative (could a phone call to Ottawa have sufficed?), checked with someone of German origin in his department, who decided that the proper pronunciation would have to be "Diefenbawker." When JFK told a subsequent press conference how much he was looking forward to welcoming Prime Minister "Diefenbawker" from Canada to the White House, the supersensitive Dief went into a rage, the first accidental slight that doomed the Kennedy-Diefenbaker relationship, which eventually deteriorated to the point where the Kennedys, in effect, overthrew the Tory government of Canada through varying "destabilizing" means.

Diefenbaker's sensitivity to a Germanesque pronunciation of his name went back a long way. In 1942, Conservative leader Arthur Meighen—unable to win a seat in the Commons— decided his successor would be John Bracken, the premier of Manitoba and a member of the Progressive Party. At the leadership convention, Bracken was opposed by H.H. Stevens, Murdoch MacPherson, Howard Green, and a prairie lawyer by name of John Diefenbaker.

It was no contest; the Toronto-Montreal Establishment gang had the fix on for Bracken. But, just in case, those in charge in that anti-German wartime atmosphere made sure that Dief was always referred to as "Diefenbacker." The joint chairman of the convention was H.R. Milner, QC, of Edmonton. He never lost a chance at the microphone to bark out "Diefenbacker" in a knowing way. Dief, who never forgot anything, never forgot that day. When he did become prime minister, he made sure that Milner, by that time the leading Conservative Tory in Alberta, never became a senator, or lieutenant-governor, as was expected through the usual patronage traditions. He got nothing. As for Mr. Bracken, he became leader on the condition that his new party rename itself the Progressive Conservative Party, a contradiction in terms to this day.

The Diefenbaker-Kennedy mutual dislike was so apparent that when their paths crossed in Nassau in the Bahamas, where each was to meet with British Prime Minister Harold Macmillan, a Canadian reporter boldly asked at a Diefenbaker press conference, "Is it true that the president hates your guts?" There was no reply. A protesting Kennedy was finally persuaded by Macmillan to join him and Diefenbaker at lunch; the president later told friends, "And there we sat, like three whores at a christening."

Then there was the famous Kennedy memo, which Dief somehow retrieved from a wastebasket after a Washington-Ottawa meeting on whether Canada should join the Organization of American States. Dief claimed—or didn't much discourage reporters who claimed—that JFK had scribbled a note in the margin that referred to Dief as an "SOB." Latter-day opinion tends to the belief it was a garbled reading of "OAS" but the matter was put to rest when Dief was dumped by the voters, and John Kennedy, as he had promised, invited his journalist friend Ben Bradlee to the White House to hear the true story of the celebrated SOB memo. "At that time I didn't think Diefenbaker was a son of a bitch," the president told Bradlee. "I thought he was a prick."

Bobby Kennedy told Knowlton Nash, the CBC anchorman, then a Washington correspondent, "There were only two people my brother really hated, Sukharno [the dictator of Indonesia] and Diefenbaker."

And so things advance. As president of the United States of America, Richard Nixon—the Watergate tapes revealed—referred to Pierre Trudeau, prime minister of Canada, as "that asshole."

When Trudeau was on his peace initiative, flying about the globe to save it from itself, Lawrence Eagleburger, who was then undersecretary of state for political affairs, told his dinner companions that Trudeau's conduct was "akin to pot-induced behavior by an erratic leftie." Trudeau, with his usual calm diplomacy, shouted to reporters in Washington that his American opponents were "Pentagon pipsqueaks." An undefended border indeed. (Trudeau was not in fact the author of the celebrated elephant-and-mouse metaphor that has now entered the language. In a speech at the National Press Club in Washington, he noted that, for Canadians, being so close to the United States was like sleeping with an elephant— every little twitch makes you nervous. It was a newspaper cartoonist the following day who added the mouse, and Trudeau's speech-writer, Ivan Head, feels wounded to this day.)

Earlier, Pierre Trudeau addressed the U.S. Congress, the first Canadian prime minister ever to do so. When he had finished, Clement Zablocki of Wisconsin summed it up: "Some members of Congress didn't think a Canadian could speak such good English." And so it goes.

Dief couldn't abide Kennedy. Kennedy detested Dief. Nixon thought Trudeau was a snob. Trudeau, in turn, thought Reagan was a dumbo. Only with the two smiling Irishmen, Reagan and Mulroney, two great storytellers, neither one an intellectual, both wanting desperately to be liked, did the relationship between Ennui-on-the-Rideau and Disneyland-on-the-Potomac get back to the FDR-King friendliness. But not even the Irish connection saved Mulroney from anonymity south of the border. The day after the "acid rain summit" in the spring of 1986, when Brian Mulroney felt he had pulled off a significant triumph by inducing Mr. Reagan to change his mind, the front-page headline in the *New York Times* read: PRESIDENT REAGAN, CANADIAN, SIGN ACCORD ON ACID RAIN REPORT.

8

Rocky XIII

In which it is explained why the first divorced president doesn't work very hard and why God is on the White House staff and why Reagan speaks with imprecision and why the trees wore signs and why Dr. Foth doesn't get called on at press conferences and other sad stories.

I was on a plane one day, flying from Tedium to Boring with a stop in Lassitude, when I head one American businessman talking to another about Ronald Reagan. One was saying he had read that Reagan didn't work very hard at his job. "That's right," the second chap said, approvingly. "He's like the Queen of England. He just sits up there above the battle and kind of supervises."

It is as good a description as any of the old-fashioned man who in 1984 was given an enormous vote of confidence by an American public unconcerned about his age, his casual work habits, his poor grasp of the language and of mundane facts. The voters simply liked what they saw, an uncomplicated guy with a few ideas he kept repeating over and over again. "I go in circles," Marshall McLuhan used to say, "because I'm drilling, and only by repetition can I get my message across." Reagan keeps repeating that he thinks America is great.

It is, when you look at it, completely loony. The most vigorous and energetic country on earth elected as its boss a guy who, if he makes it through his second term, will be within weeks of his seventy-ninth birthday, as old as the geriatric specimens who used to cough their way through the Kremlin. The USSR had three ailing and failing leaders in a row before the teenage Gorbachev hove on the scene.

The most amazing thing about Ronald Reagan is that at seventy-five—ten years past the recognized retirement age—he is the oldest ruler of any of the leading nations, while his nation is the youngest and most vigorous and brimming with energy of all. He is the oldest president, of course, ever to sit in the Oval Office, and he has gathered around him a clutch of senior citizens.

When his National Security Council meets, the guys who make the decisions average more than sixty-seven years of age. The pup of the group is Vice-President George Bush, a mere sixty-two.

The big decision to launch the attack on Libya and Colonel Qaddafi was made by a seventy-five-year-old president advised by seventy-three-year-old CIA director William Casey, sixty-eight-year-old Defense Secretary Caspar Weinberger, sixty-seven-year-old White House Chief of Staff Donald Regan, and sixty-five-year-old Secretary of State George Shultz. (Casey, Weinberger, and Regan are also all millionaires, with Reagan probably close.)

The American strike that killed one of Qaddafi's children and severely injured several others was defended at the United Nations by Ambassador Vernon Walters, who is sixty-nine. Special envoys Paul Nitze, seventy-nine, and Edward Rowny, sixty-nine, were sent out to calm the Allies. Troubleshooter Philip Habib, sixty-six, was already on assignment in Central America.

If you applied the normal sixty-five-and-out regulation of most corporations to the Reagan regime, not only would his foreign policy staff be wiped out, so would his cabinet. The retirement rule would toss out Health and Human Services Secretary Otis Bowen, who is sixty-eight. Agriculture Secretary Richard Lyng is the same age. Secretary of Commerce Malcolm Baldrige and Secretary of Housing and Urban Development Sam Pierce are close to the line at sixty-three.

(It is interesting—since the United States will in 1987 celebrate the two-hundredth anniversary of the Constitution—to contrast the Reaganauts with the men who wrote the Constitution in Philadelphia. George Washington was fifty-five. Charles Pinckney of South Carolina was twenty-nine. Alexander Hamilton was thirty. Rufus King of Massachusetts was thirty-two. Jonathan Dayton of New Jersey was twenty-six. Gouverneur Morris of Pennsylvania, who had smooth manners and a wooden leg, was thirty-five, and James Madison of Virginia, known today as the "father of the Constitution," was just thirty-six. Old Ben Franklin, at eighty-one, shifted upward the average age of these men who created this magnificent country, but even with him the average didn't hit forty-three, which was the age of John Kennedy when he became the youngest elected president.)

The president of the Pepsi generation doesn't really like young blood; he likes the old guys. When he has a chance to change, he goes for age. Agriculture's Lyng is seventeen years older than the chap he replaced, John Block. Health Secretary Bowen is thirteen years older than Margaret Heckler, whom he replaced. Chief of Staff Regan is eleven years older than James Baker, whom he replaced. The UN's Walters is ten years older than Jeane Kirkpatrick. It's a geriatric president who likes geriatric men around him. These are the men ruling and representing the nation that is thought of around the world as the epitome of youthful thrust and verve. Fun stuff.

Reagan, however, overcomes all such doubts. He grins and he aw-shucks and he tells stories about himself that, when you check the facts, don't add up, but he makes people feel good.

He makes one segment of the population in particular feel good. It is a group that has felt rather sorry for itself of late. The 1984 election could be called the Revenge of the White Male. Getting even was what it was all about, and the ballot box was each voter's private little hit man. All the good ole boys had had it up to their beer cans with, among other things, the feminist movement. First, their wives joined consciousness-raising sessions. That was enough to rot their Adidas. Then came Germaine Greer, they would have liked to hang her in effigy. Next, the Reverend Jesse Jackson, rather too good-looking for his own good, convinced millions of blacks to register to vote for the first time. And finally, there was Geraldine Ferraro, who was going to light a fire in the women of America and save the pallid personality of Walter Mondale.

The good ole boys had had their fill. They sucked in their beer bellies and headed for the polling booths. As a result, Alabama and Mississippi and Louisiana and all those other bastions of the Deep South, on which the Roosevelt Coalition was based fifty years ago, went swimmingly for the Republican Reagan. The Democrats had already lost part of their crucial Jewish vote because the strident Jesse Jackson was unable to explain away his "Himie-land" slurs and his companions, like the Black Muslim leader Louis Farrakhan, who offended the influential Jewish community. The charismatic

Norwegian, Walter Mondale, was thought to be too much the handmaiden of the big unions, at a time when unions did not fit the public's rightish mood. He represented something ever more outrageous to those who lived in, say, Georgia and liked watching football on Saturday afternoons at the college studium and Sunday afternoons before the tube.

The solution? The good ole boys used the ballot box to get revenge on all those quiche eaters hanging around Washington and writing in the *New York Times*. The result? Ferraro, who was supposed to make history, did not even carry her own district of Queens, which, lest we forget, is the setting for *All in the Family*, home of Archie Bunker. (The show wasn't set in Queens for nothing, duckie.)

The Americans were finally tired of the guilt they felt over the Watergate disgrace. They were tired of the open warfare they had waged with their children over Vietnam. They had been humiliated in Iran and wished they had never gotten involved in Lebanon.

Then this old geezer came along and told them to hold up their heads again, be as chauvinistic as they wanted to be at the Los Angeles Olympics and to wave, wave, wave the flag. They were tired of feeling hangdog and of being responsible for the ills of the world. Apple pie and Main Street sounded very good to them. So they gave this one to the Gipper.

Americans are not really all that desperately Republican in spirit. In 1984 the party actually lost two seats in the Senate and was not able to lessen by much the Democratic control of the House of Representatives. It was not the Democrats the public voted against, it was wimpish figures the party keeps running as candidates for the White House. Since John Kennedy was elected a quarter-century ago, Democrats have put up a succession of men none of whom fit the American ideal of leader. Even the supposedly tough Lyndon Johnson quit because he couldn't take the heat of Vietnam. Hubert Horatio Humphrey came across as a cheerleader. George McGovern was a disaster as a campaigner.

Jimmy Carter was a one-term sermonizer. And Walter Mondale, a man who spent forty years apprenticing for this role, confessed in the end that he neither liked television nor understood it, an astonishing admission considering that that simplistic medium now rules politics.

Democrats have now lost four of the past five presidential elections. Reagan, if his casual work habits preserve his health and if he is not shot by yet another madman, has a chance to be the first president since Eisenhower to complete two full terms. Kennedy was murdered. Johnson declined to run again. Nixon took it on the lam before being impeached. Ford was defeated, Carter lasted just one term. If Reagan can do it, he will be the first in twenty-eight years. The odds are not great. It's a high-risk business.

Reagan has beaten the odds before, though. There were many who said he'd never do all the things he promised, and yet unemployment is down, the inflation rate is down, the dollar is soaring, the military have all the death weapons they want, and the American public is exuberant in its home-again self-confidence. How does he do it?

Slowly the fog lifts and the truth emerges, creeping in on tiny feet. We can see now, quite clearly, why Ronald Reagan is such a tremendous success. The reason? The president has recruited God as a member of his cabinet. An extra chair has been placed at the table and God is in there faithfully voting the Republican ticket—and especially approving any new appropriations for the military.

The feminists say that, contrary to suspicion, God is *not* a woman because, if She were, She would have treated females far better than they are treated now. God, in fact, turns out to be not only an American, but a Republican. Every coin in America bears the inscription "In God We Trust" (all others pay cash). Now the deity has left the world of finance to get into global politics.

God never strays very far from Reagan's speeches. In fact He makes an appearance in almost every one of them. In February 1985, God came right out and joined those who want more nuclear arms. In a speech to a group of leading businessmen, the president reached into the Book of Luke and plucked forth a passage about a king who plans to make war, finds out he is underarmed, and has to back away from his plan. Luke, it seems, is on the side of nuclear arms. The president didn't reveal whether Matthew, Mark, and John are also on the side of nuclear madness. But surely now that the Bible has been revealed to support the Star Wars defence system, we can find some gospel urging that ploughshares be turned into swords. It's always been said that you can find something in the Bible to support anything you want, and President Reagan is proving it.

Except God has been known to change sides in the past. You

can't rely on Him. In our last big war, every German soldier went into battle with *Got mit uns*—God is with us—inscribed on his belt buckle. Now the rascal has switched camps and is working for the Americans.

To make sure God doesn't change countries again and go to a new suitor, President Reagan is heavily into prayer breakfasts. There are occasions at which the MX mixes with the Bible and the cruise missile gets entangled with Luke. A typical one was attended by some three thousand at the Washington Hilton at the dreadful hour of 7:30 A.M. (does God never sleep in?)

There were supposed to be some sixty Canadian MPS present, including one NDPer whose identity is still being pursued. Friends of mine attended and found themselves seated beside the Galloping Gourmet, Graham Kerr of TV fame past, who has given up the sauce, is born-again, and wolfed down the congealed Eggs Benedict with a passion only a true believer could have. (How does one make enough Eggs Benedict for three thousand people? One starts last Tuesday.) Prayer breakfasts were started by Eisenhower back in the 1950s, and people come from as far away as San Diego to gaze upon concrete Eggs Benedict and make sure that God's American citizenship has not lapsed.

In 1985, Mr. Reagan, having proven the Bible is on the side of the Pentagon, said, "Well, I don't think we ever want to be in a position of only being half as strong, and having to send a delegation to negotiate, under those circumstances, peace terms with the Soviet Union." God, as we can see, is also into the nuclear arms race, and we know whose side he's on, don't we?

On the same day, Reagan addressed a gathering of the National Religious Broadcasters, a sect of electronic fundamentalists who believe in the verities of the Bible. The president cited the same distorted passage from Luke, stating that "Divine Providence" was involved in the stressful arms debate. The president, naturally, did not recite the whole parable from Luke, which is about the folly of wanting to make war. It didn't matter, since God was clearly planning to vote the right way at the negotiations in Geneva.

Canadian politics is full of saints like J.S. Woodsworth and preachers like Tommy Douglas. Lester Pearson was a son of the manse. Mackenzie King was an expert on the afterlife, though it seems he was more into the occult and Ouija boards than straight religion. John Turner is a deeply religious man. But essentially God doesn't get too interested in, or intrude upon, Canadian politics. Perhaps He thinks it's too dull.

I have another theory: God can't spread Himself too thin. When He has to get up early for prayer breakfasts, it makes for a tiring day. When He has to spend all those hours poring over Caspar Weinberger's requests for increases in the Pentagon budgets and approving George Shultz's plans for the invasion of Libya, He doesn't have much time left to worry about the baby seal problem. Give the guy a break.

The one thing Ronald Reagan is famous for in Washington is demanding complete loyalty from his underlings. He supports, with nit-picking, some rather dubious companions. He even backed his attorney general, Edwin Meese III, who gave government jobs to those who helped him out of his financial problems and who seems puzzled, as the number-one law-enforcement officer of the nation, about the definition of the word *ethics*. In return for this loyalty, Reagan demands the same in exchange. It is thought that God accepts this arrangement. He is going to stick with this administration as long as required. Two more years.

Reagan's close ties with God contrast with his fuzzy and distant relationship with the English language. Just as the first casualty of war is truth, the first casualty of politics is the English language. While campaigning to become president in 1980, Ronald Reagan claimed that as governor of California he had refunded $5.7 billion in property taxes. He neglected to mention that he had raised taxes by $21 billion.

Even after it was proved to be false, he continued to state that Alaska had more oil than Saudi Arabia. He claimed that General Motors had to employ 23,000 full-time employees to comply with government-required paperwork. GM stated it had 4,900 bodies to do all its paperwork. The result of all this? Mr. Reagan's popularity doubled in his second presidential election.

One would think it would be linguists who change the English language. One would expect those who preside over new words and new meanings, nuances, and interpretations to be musty old professors in worn tweed suits with dandruff on their collars, their teeth stained from sucking on pipes.

One would be wrong. The people who change words are politicians. Because they command the front pages and the boob tube, they are considered arbiters of the way in which we communicate. If you do not believe it, remember John Dean, that slimy stool pigeon of Watergate fame who placed into the lingua franca the execrable phrase "at this point in time." It means "now," but every Rotarian worth his tonsils has adopted it. It infects our lives, like acne and crabgrass, never to be eradicted.

Our latest mangler comes with the highest credentials possible: he works out of the office of the president of the United States of America. His name is Larry Speakes, spokesman for the most powerful person on earth. Mr. Reagan, who finds some difficulty with the language unless it is on cue cards, allowed journalists from four Soviet news outlets into the Oval Office for an interview—the first such occasion since John Kennedy sat down with Nikita Khrushchev's reporter/son-in-law a quarter-century ago. It was an attempt to catch up with Mr. Gorbachev, who had gained public-relations points by letting the editors of *Time* into his enclave on the way to the Geneva summit.

The problem is that Mr. Reagan, unless his handlers have a secure lariat on his tongue, tends to wander all over the linguistic map. He told his Soviet guests that he wouldn't put his fanciful Star Wars nuclear shield into place until everybody had dismantled all their nuclear missiles—an explanation that sent American reporters, when they saw the transcipt, racing to their telephones.

After the spit hit the fan, Spokesman Speakes, as he always does, tried to calm the headlines by explaining everything. Spoke Speakes the spokesman: the president had spoken with "imprecision."

Ron Ziegler, a previous flack for a previous president called Nixon, introduced to the language the lovely word "misspoke" during Watergate. As in, "The president misspoke himself." What it meant was that Nixon had lied. What "imprecision" means is that Reagan doesn't know what he's talking about and gets things bass-ackwards.

This follows in the great political tradition of using the language for what it does not mean. A "government spokesman who could not be identified" means a pal close to the president or prime minister who will explain what is really going on if you promise to keep his name out of it. For some strange reason, journalism continues to go along with the subterfuge.

What does it prove? Doublespeak works. The U.S. State

Department has announced that it will no longer use the word *killing* in its official reports on the status of human rights in countries around the world. It will be replaced by the phrase "unlawful or arbitrary deprivation of life."

Good stuff. Right up there with Colonel David Opfer, a U.S. Air Force press officer in Cambodia in 1974, who told reporters, "You always write it's bombing, bombing, bombing. It's not bombing! It's air support." The chap undoubtedly perfected mumblification at the officer's mess.

In High Government Fuzzifying, facts don't matter if the lies are presented strongly enough. The Republican National Committee produced a television commercial featuring a folksy postie delivering Social Security cheques "with the 7.5 per cent cost-of-living raise that President Reagan promised." The postman went on to say, "He promised that raise and he kept his promise, in spite of those sticks-in-the-mud who tried to keep him from doing what we elected him to do."

In truth, the cost-of-living hikes had been provided automatically by law since 1975 and Reagan tried three times to roll them back or delay them, but was blocked by Congress. When confronted with the obvious untruth, one high Republican official told the Chicago *Tribune* that the ad was "inoffensive" and asked, "Since when is a commercial supposed to be accurate? Do women really smile when they clean their ovens?"

This is merely cynical, which should not be confused with sincere. Sincere is what the Pentagon was when it issued its celebrated description of the neutron bomb: "an efficient nuclear weapon that eliminates the enemy with a minimum degree of damage to friendly territory."

After the Three Mile Island accident, the nuclear-power industry developed its own sincere jargon. An explosion became "energetic disassembly." A fire became "rapid oxidation." A reactor accident is an "event," an "incident," an "abnormal evolution," a "normal aberration," or a "plant transient."

The so-called "flip flop" of Reagan's views on acid rain came about because of his early and instantly famous views that trees—because they emit oxygen—were the major cause of acid rain. This caused reporters on his campaign bus, as it travelled through the California redwoods, to break into chants of "Killer trees! Killer Trees!" Environmentalists attached signs to trees in his campaign path: "Cut me down before I kill again!"

What can you do with a man who names the new MX intercontinental ballistic missile the "Peacekeeper," who says "a vote against MX production today is a vote against arms control tomorrow," and who told the United Nations that "I suspect the future is much closer than we think"? The answer is: elect him.

The best moments in politics are when the truth finally breaks through—because of the language. A former governor of California, Pat Brown (father of later governor Jerry Brown, the space cadet and a friend of Linda Ronstadt's), is remembered for touring a calamitous flood area and announcing to the press, "This is the worst disaster in California since I was elected." Phlying Phil Gaglardi, the celebrated minister of public works in Wacky Bennett's British Columbia government, who was forever in trouble, cried out in the legislature one day, "If I tell a lie it's only because I think I'm telling the truth!" *Gotcha*.

John Diefenbaker, who knew how to play around with the language, once described his unmarried colleague Flora MacDonald, whom he did not like, as "the finest woman ever to walk the streets of Kingston."

My favourite corporate handling of the language occurred when the collective front-office genius of the Ford Motor Company decided to introduce a new car. Not only would it be the most innovative vehicle ever designed, it would have the most beautiful word in the English language on its dashboard. To ensure that, Ford hired the esteemed American poet Marianne Moore to convene a committee of linguists to select the name. After mulling over the task for close to a year, in conferences that cost Ford thousands of dollars, the language experts submitted their short list to Ford's board of directors, who couldn't agree on a choice and, as an alternative, named the car after a family member, one Edsel—a name even uglier than the car it doomed.

Pierre Trudeau finally got the attention of Canadians when he said one day in Regina, to a small boy who was tossing handfuls of wheat at his back, "You do that one more time and I'm going to kick you in the ass." Joe Clark's tenure in politics is known mainly for the funny pseudowords he employed: "specificity" and "totality." Mulroney is much more likable when he uses the vernacular of the Baie Comeau pulp mill where he worked than the unctuous pomposity that too often mars his public utterances. He should use the language of Harry Truman, not that of the senior Paul Martin.

Politicians know they are just one quote away from oblivion. Right after quick-quip Mulroney shouted to harrying reporters that because of the dreadful Liberals "Canada is bankrupt"—a great message to be sent around the world, as John Turner pointed out—it was announced the PM would be restricting his "scrum" encounters with the scribes and would hold more formal press conferences instead.

In Washington, conditions at press conferences are carefully controlled. The only thing more certain than death and taxes is a rehearsed "spontaneous" presidential press conference. Here is the packaged White House, ruled over by a veteran actor. The last thing any of the manipulators want is a bit of surprise—which might result in some news actually slipping out. Ronald Reagan, who has granted fewer press conferences than any of his four predecessors, is especially careful to control the circumstances of the live performances.

He is supposed to be grilled for thirty minutes by two hundred reporters but little is left to chance. Reagan rehearses for two days, with his aides playing the role of reporters, before stepping in front of the cameras. His officials boast that seldom does a question in a real conference catch them by surprise.

To someone watching on a television set, these conferences appear to be free-for-alls. However, an examination of who gets the presidential nod shows how highly structured these occasions are. Here is a typical press conference in the spring of 1986. It was only Reagan's thirty-fifth in five years, his first one in two months. The first question, as always, went to Helen Thomas of United Press International, who as dean of the White House press corps had the honour of opening and closing the session (Washington is very formal in its ceremonies).

Second question went to the Associated Press, the third to *USA Today*, the technicolour newspaper, Reagan familiarly calling on reporters by their first names. Fourth questioner recognized, in the first row, was NBC's Chris Wallace, son of *60 Minutes'* Mike Wallace. Fifth was CBS, followed by ABC's aggressive Sam Donaldson, who revels in his bad-boy image.

Seventh question went to an attractive young lady from Orlando, Florida, since the Reaganauts obviously had some NASA information they wanted out. Eight went to television's

Cable News. Nine went to the very attractive Patricia Wilson of Reuters. Next came the Independent TV network, then a woman from the *Wall Street Journal*.

Gerald Boyd, a black reporter from the *New York Times*, was number twelve. "Susan" from *Newsday*, a Long Island newspaper, was next. Metromedia got spot fourteen. An attractive blonde got fifteen. Reagan's (and the White House's) liking for television rather than the written press was indicated once again when he returned to NBC, featuring Andrea Mitchell, for question sixteen. For seventeen? Back to ABC, this time with a black reporter. To finish off, the eighteenth and last question, before Helen thanked the president, went to RKO Radio.

A very cleverly selected cast for the nation's eyes. Seven of the eighteen questioners given the presidential okay were women. Two were black. Just to show how tolerant the White House is, there were even three beards among those allowed their shining moment on the screen.

What there was not, of course, was any real sampling of the two hundred reporters present. Washington is the journalistic capital of the world. There are more foreign correspondents stationed there than in any city in the world, as could be expected. Nor was there any reflection of the fact in the careful selection of those chosen to ask the standard questions at the presidential press conference.

There was no indication that journalists from Germany or Japan or Mexico or Canada or Nigeria were present and curious about the president's opinion on this issue or that. But of course the handlers, apple-polishers, and mind-benders surrounding Reagan would never allow some kook from Bonn or Madrid or Ottawa to ask a question live on TV that wasn't anticipated (or rehearsed). Jack Webster would cause panic and instant ulcers in this town.

This is not, of course, a whine (harrumph) from someone who is seated well below the salt. It is just an educational reminder that it is an American spectacle, with an American president, devoted to the better and efficient distribution of American propaganda. If you happen not to see this particular hero's pudgy jowls on the screen it is because he is not (a) female; (b) black; (c) bearded; or (d) just possibly in possession of the right-coloured passport.

9
Back to the Past

*In which Dr. Foth explains what Dutch Reagan
learned as a lifeguard and why he confuses old
movies with real life and what Trivial Pursuit revealed
and how did Jack Dempsey get in here and where
the Kennedy boys learned about sex and why Nancy
chews her food so funny.*

NANCY DAVIS: *What are you going to do after the war?*

RONALD REAGAN: *I told you a hundred times.*

NANCY: *I want to hear it once more.*

RONNIE: *I'm going into the surplus business. I'm gonna buy up all the old mines and sell 'em to the man in the moon.*

NANCY: *But there's no water on the moon!*

RONNIE: *How do you know so much about the moon?*

NANCY: *I know a lot about it. I spend all my time looking at it when you're away. That's how it still is with me.*

RONNIE: *It's time for me to go now.*

   —from Hellcats of the Navy

If one wants to understand Ronald Reagan, not an easy task, one has to reach into his background. In 1926, when Ron was fifteen years old, he took a summer job that shaped his entire life and had a lasting effect on his thinking, a mental process that has changed the United States and therefore the world. In Dixon, Illinois, a town of ten thousand people about ninety miles south of Chicago, he was taken on as a lifeguard at a beach in Lowell Park. It was his summer job for the next seven years, and it not only helped build him into a big, healthy youth, it also gave him his first lesson in human nature, particularly in the area of gratitude. As a lifeguard, Reagan discovered to his surprise that people did not enjoy being rescued. Invariably, they believed they didn't need help. Having their lives saved in front of others caused them much embarrassment. They even felt a certain resentment toward their rescuer.

The lesson stuck with Reagan and has permeated his

thinking ever since. A lifeguard is like a government: help is not only not appreciated, it is somehow resented. Self-reliance is the key. People should not be encouraged to blame others for their misfortunes. Reagan's attitude toward the plight of the blacks and those at the bottom of the economic scale is influenced by this type of thinking. The government should intrude as little as possible, just as a lifeguard should intrude only when necessary. Otherwise? Otherwise, all you get for your troubles is ingratitude.

Ronald Wilson Reagan could not be more American. He is Horatio Alger, the Andy Hardy stories, and Frank Merriwell combined. The only thing missing is a log cabin. He was born on February 6, 1911, in an apartment above the store where his father worked, in Tampico, Illinois. (In early 1986, in welcoming some visitors to the White House, Reagan mused that everything comes full circle: here he was, seventy-five years later, and still "living above the store.")

Father Jack Reagan was a shoe salesman who believed one day he'd strike it rich. He never did. Though he moved from Illinois town to Illinois town, Galesburg to Monmouth to Tampico again and finally, when Ron was nine, to Dixon, which the president calls his home town. Jack Reagan's failures undoubtedly were linked to his alcoholism, which in turn affected the future president's view of drinking. He recalls, at age thirteen, coming home to find his father flat on his back, dead drunk, on the front porch. He dragged his father into bed, smelling "the sharp odour of the speakeasy" on his breath.

Reagan might have been bitter over his Catholic father's drinking had not his mother, who raised her youngest son in the Disciples of Christ church, told her two boys that the drinking was "a sickness" that deserved their compassion (a diagnosis, by the way, that has strong currency in medical circles today). Reagan will occasionally have a vodka martini, but usually drinks only a glass of wine or two. The actor William Holden, who was best man at Reagan's second wedding, recalled once going out for a drink with Reagan and another actor. When Holden and his companion called for a second round, a puzzled Reagan said, "Why would you want one when you've just had one?" Holden, the golden boy who danced with Kim Novak in *Picnic*, was in his latter days an alcoholic and died in his home, his girlfriend being away, during a heavy drinking bout when he fell, cut his head, and bled to death.

The Depression ended whatever dreams of success Jack Reagan still had. He lost his partnership in Reagan's Fashion Boot Shop and then, on Christmas Eve 1931, was sacked as a travelling salesman. Nellie Reagan went to work in a dress shop for fourteen dollars a week. Ron, who was at college, took part-time jobs to send his mother fifty dollars to enable the family to get credit at the local grocery store—without his father's knowing about it. [When Reagan made it in Hollywood, he arranged a job—handling fan mail—for his father, who then had a heart condition.)

The school was Eureka College (could you make it up?), just twenty-one miles from Peoria, the touchstone of Middle America. I am not usually a great fan of Hugh Sidey, *Time* magazine's White House columnist, who is known to his colleagues as Hugh Sidestep. But he is from the Midwest, where his brother still runs the family weekly newspaper, and in a bull session one day he explained that "if you want to understand Ronald Reagan, go out one day to Dixon, Illinois, where the farmers get up in the morning and, if it's raining, they don't plough."

Reagan, thanks to his swimming and football abilities (he couldn't play baseball because he was short-sighted), got an athletic scholarship to Eureka: $180 a year. He worked as a dishwasher at the fraternity. No Franklin Delano Roosevelt this one, no rich heir Pierre Trudeau, no William Lyon Mackenzie King coddled by the Rockefellers.

There was a certain mythic quality to Reagan's life, even back then. The heavy thumb suckers on the Washington editorial pages still seriously discuss whether the president's success has been due to luck. Luck, as my favourite lexicographer put it, can be defined as "preparation married to opportunity." In other words, you make your own luck, a proposition that your faithful agent, having been "lucky" all his life, is a prime adherent of.

As an example: when Reagan graduated from Eureka in 1932, he couldn't decide whether to pursue sports or drama— two careers linked, he has admitted, by his love of showing off. (He was a politician before he knew it.) He had dabbled in theatre at college but Broadway and Hollywood were a long way from the flat prairie of Illinois and his glib patter at sports commentary seemed a better bet.

Historians should note Reagan got his first full-time job at Davenport, Iowa's WOC—its call letters derived from World of Chiropractic, founded by Colonel B.J. Palmer of the Palmer School of Chiropractic—because his audition impressed Peter MacArthur, a gruff Scotsman who had come to America as a member of Harry Lauder's troupe of vaudevillians but, suffering from arthritis, had retreated to the Chiropractic College. (Are we getting a message here?) When MacArthur, the failed vaudevillian, demanded that Reagan show his stuff, the future leader of the Western world recalled the dramatic fourth quarter of a football game Eureka had played against Western State University and burst forth into twenty minutes of simulated description. He got the job.

"Dutch" Reagan soon progressed to bigger things on bigger Midwest stations. (He was "Dutch" from childhood because he looked like a chubby little Dutch boy, his brother was nicknamed "Moon" after Moon Mullins, the comic-strip character.) He became a master at faking "live" broadcasts of the Chicago Cubs games. With the help of the teletype and a sound man who could supply the "crack" of the bat, Reagan was able to give unknowing farm families the impression that he was actually watching the game from the press box.

He was not the first to fake it, nor was he the last. The practice continued until television came along and destroyed the myth. But it is interesting to observe that the first actor to become a politician (as opposed to vice versa, as is the usual route) started his career by faking events and, at the end of his career, really may not know the difference.

Any man who makes fifty-three movies in thirty years is bound to be profoundly affected by the experience. That's only natural. In Ronald Reagan's case, the line between the fictionalized world of the movies and real life has become blurred. Here is the president, speaking in New York to a group of Congressional Medal of Honor winners:

"A B-17 coming back across the Channel from a raid on Europe, badly shot up by anti-aircraft. The ball turret that hung underneath the belly of the plane had taken a hit. The young ball turret gunner was wounded, and they couldn't get him out of the turret while flying. But over the Channel, the plane began to lose altitude, and the commander had to order, 'Bail out.' And as the men started to leave the plane, the boy understandably knowing he was left behind to go down with the plane cried out in terror. The last man to leave the plane saw the commander sit down on the floor. He took the boy's hand and said, 'Never mind, son. We'll ride it down together.' Congressional Medal of Honor, posthumously awarded."

Great story, but there is just one thing wrong. There was no Medal of Honor awarded. Every one of the 434 medals awarded during the Second World War carries a citation that describes the circumstances for the award. There was no such incident.

Some sleuths, however, have tracked down the truth. The incident did not happen aboard an Army Air Corps bomber. It happened in a Navy TBF—a torpedo bomber with a three-man crew. It did not happen over the English Channel. It took place in the Pacific, during a dogfight with Japanese Zeroes. It wasn't a turret gunner who was wounded. It was a radio operator.

The gunner reported that the radio man had been hit. The gunner bailed out. The pilot asked the radio man, known only as Mike, if he was wounded. Mike replied through the intercom, "It's my legs, sir."

The pilot asked: "Can you move them? Mike, can you move your legs?"

Mike: "Uh-uh. We're burning back here. You'd better bail out, sir."

Pilot: "I haven't got the altitude, Mike. We'll take this ride together."

As the pilot and Mike plunged to their deaths in the Pacific, Dana Andrews shouted at them from another plane, "... Join up, join up. Do you hear me?"

That's right, Dana Andrews. The whole scene was from the movie *Wing and a Prayer*, made in 1944 by 20th Century–Fox, directed by Henry Hathaway and immediately flown to the Pacific to boost the morale of American servicemen.

Reagan to this day insists he read the medal citation while he was serving with an air-corps unit in Hollywood during the war. He has used the anecdote throughout his political career and undoubtedly will use it again. At one point in *Wing and a Prayer*, Dana Andrews reprimands a glory-seeking young pilot with the words, "This isn't Hollywood." President Reagan forgets where Hollywood ends and where life begins.

There's a professor in California, Reagan's home ground, who has made a study of this phenomenon: a president of the most powerful nation in the history of civilization who lives in a rather fuzzy dreamland. The professor is Michael Rogin, from the University of California at Berkeley, and in 1985 he presented a paper called "Ronald Reagan: The Movie" to the annual meeting of the American Political Science Association.

In support of his claim that Reagan confuses movies with real life, he shows that the president often speaks movie lines. Here is Reagan: "I have my veto pen drawn and ready for any tax increase that Congress might even think of sending up. And I have only one thing to say to the tax increases. 'Go ahead; make my day.'" (Clint Eastwood as Dirty Harry in *Sudden Impact*: "Go ahead; make my day.")

Reagan: "In the spirit of *Rambo*, let me tell you, we're going to win this time." Sylvester Stallone, in *Rambo*: "Do we get to win this time?"

Reagan's favourite movie role was in *King's Row*, made in 1941. When Drake McHugh (Reagan) awakens in his hospital bed to find that a perverted surgeon has deliberately amputated his legs because he doesn't want McHugh playing around with his daughter, McHugh says, "Where's the rest of me?" When Reagan wrote his autobiography in 1965, he called it *Where's the Rest of Me?*—a very odd title for a man climbing the political ladder. At his inauguration as president, he used the music from *King's Row*.

Reagan, in another instance: "It isn't about fear; it's about hope. And in that struggle, if you'll pardon my stealing a film line, 'The Force is with us.'" Dirty Harry and Rambo star in taxes. Obi-Wan Kenobi stars in defence spending.

Professor Rogin has put together a slide show for his fellow academics. When it comes to welfare and volunteerism, it seems Gary Cooper is the guide.

REAGAN: "I guess Gary Cooper did about the best job describing it in the movie *Mr. Deeds Goes to Town*. From what I can see, he said . . ."

COOPER (excerpt from movie): "No matter what system . . ."

REAGAN: ". . . of government we have . . ."

COOPER (movie excerpt): ". . . there'll always be leaders . . ."

REAGAN: ". . . and always be followers."

COOPER (movie): "It's like the road out in front of my house."

REAGAN: "It's on a steep hill."

COOPER: Every day I watch the cars climbing up."

REAGAN: "Some go lickety-split up that hill on high."

COOPER: "Some have to shift into second."

REAGAN: "And some sputter and shake and slip back to the bottom again."

COOPER: "Same car."

REAGAN: "Same gasoline."

COOPER: "Yet some make it."

REAGAN: "And some don't."

COOPER: "And I say the fellows who can make the hill on high . . ."

REAGAN: ". . . should stop once in a while and help those who can't."

In a noisy high-school gymnasium in Nashua, New Hampshire, on February 23, 1980, Reagan demonstrated his gift for the political moment when he captured a microphone and, with it, the Republican Party's nomination. "I paid for this microphone, Mr. Green," Reagan said to *Nashua Telegraph* editor Jon Breen, who was unsuccessfully trying to cut him off. The mistake in the name was typical, but Reagan's tough response got headlines. He whipped a shaken George Bush, the early Republican favourite, in the debate that night and went on to an easy victory at the party's convention.

So why shouldn't the line have worked for Reagan? It worked for Spencer Tracy in the movie *State of the Union*. ("Don't you shut me off! I'm paying for this broadcast.") He had to wait thirty-two years for the right occasion, but Reagan (who entertains his friends in the White House by replaying old movies and serving popcorn in a silver bowl) used the line to effect.

Here is Reagan in a speech: "In his book, *The Bridges of Toko-Ri*, novelist James Michener writes movingly of the heroes who fought in the Korean conflict. In the book's final scene, an admiral stands on the darkened bridge of his carrier, waiting for pilots he knows will never return from their mission; and as he waits, he asks in the silent darkness, 'Where did we get such men?' Almost a generation later, I asked that same question when our POWs were returned from savage captivity in Vietnam: 'Where did we find such men?'"

That was the first reference. The next time Reagan used it, the admiral invented by Michener became real. The president: "Many years ago in one of the four years of my lifetime, an admiral stood on the bridge of a carrier watching the planes take off and out into the darkness, bent on a night combat mission, and then found himself asking, with no one there to answer, just himself to hear his own voice, he said, 'Where do we find such men?'"

It turns out that the Michener novel was made into a movie, starring William Holden and Frederic March. It was March who said, "Where do we get such men?"

On March 30, 1981, just two months after being sworn into office, Reagan narrowly escaped death from a bullet fired by John W. Hinckley, Jr., a bullet that lodged within an inch of his heart. On his way into the operating room, he quipped to Nancy Reagan, "Honey, I forgot to duck." His wit under stress endeared him to the nation. The line actually was stolen from the crestfallen Jack Dempsey, who said the same thing to his wife after he was surprisingly defeated by Gene Tunney, the gentleman boxer who read Shakespeare, in 1926 for the world heavyweight championship.

His ability to remember lines (if not always their source) was noted early in Reagan's career. Despite his easy sports patter, Reagan wasn't considered a good announcer in his radio days, and once he switched to movies his first read throughs of scripts caused shudders among directors and fellow actors. But once he could memorize his lines, he did well. In the White House, his speech writers and aides are terrified whenever he varies from his script and ad libs instead. Too often, as foreign embassies quiver and headlines explode, his spokesmen later have to clarify the "imprecisions" in his language.

Reagan entered the movie business with the same luck and ease that got him into radio. He went to California to cover the Cubs baseball team in spring training in 1937, contacted a girl singer he knew, was introduced to an agent who took him to Warner Bros. And that was that. Warners needed a likable male actor in his mid-twenties with typical American good looks. Reagan fit the bill perfectly. The studio had just lost an actor (one Ross Alexander, who had committed suicide) and Reagan looked enough like him to take his place. Could anything be simpler? Two hundred bucks a week.

His Hollywood career began on June 1 and within days of being on the lot he was given the lead in a minor picture, *Love Is on the Air*. He played, appropriately, a rather brash radio announcer. Warner Bros., known as a "working-class" studio, was run like a well-tooled factory, and in 1938, Reagan's second year in Hollywood, he appeared in eight

movies, an astounding number, and he played everything
from leads to bit parts.

Considering the movies' titles, Laurence Olivier was not
yet in any danger. *Hollywood Hotel,* directed by the celebrated high-kick choreographer Busby Berkeley, starred Dick
Powell and the Benny Goodman Orchestra. Reagan played an
aide to gossip columnist Louella Parsons, who was playing
herself. *Swing Your Lady* featured Reagan as a glib-tongued
sportswriter. It was about a slick promoter down on his luck
in a small Kentucky town who tries to promote a bout
between a dim hulk of a wrestler and a lady blacksmith. The
promoter was Humphrey Bogart, who considered the film
among his worst.

Sergeant Murphy, which was about a U.S. Army horse
whose ears were too sensitive to artillery and who was
smuggled into England to enter the Grand National steeple-
chase, had been bought by Warners as a vehicle for James
Cagney, but the shrewd star turned it down after reading the
script. In *Accidents Will Happen,* Reagan was a naïve insurance adjuster whose life is brightened by the love of a
cigar-stand girl, Gloria Blondell.

The Cowboy from Brooklyn featured Pat O'Brien and Dick
Powell, the city dude with a great fear of animals—even
chickens and gophers. *Boy Meets Girl* was valuable mainly
because it gave Reagan a chance to become friends with its
stars, James Cagney and Pat O'Brien, in what became a
lifelong Irish Mafia linkage (the other two are now dead, and
the president supposedly retains the same Emerald Isle
relationship with Brian Mulroney). In *Girls on Probation,*
where Reagan played a bright young lawyer, the most interesting aspect was the casting of Susan Hayward in her first
substantial role.

Moving right along, we have *Brother Rat,* the tale of a
military academy (the title comes from the name the cadets
called each other), where Eddie Albert stole the show and
Reagan romanced the commandant's daughter, Jane Wyman,
who two years later became his first wife.

In 1939, Reagan again appeared in eight movies. *Going
Places,* featuring Dick Powell again and Anita Louise, was
memorable only because it included the song "Jeepers Creep-
ers," sung to a horse of that name by its groom, played by
Louis Armstrong.

And so it went. His retentive memory and his willingness

to take direction (both still apparent in the White House) were suited to the "B"-pictures assembly-line style of movie production at Warners, where he continued making movies for some years, working with all their famed players: Bette Davis, Errol Flynn, Olivia de Havilland, Humphrey Bogart, Dick Powell, James Cagney, Pat O'Brien.

Reagan and Jane Wyman, after appearing together in *Brother Rat*, were married in 1940. The engagement was first announced by Louella Parsons, the gossip columnist, who pronounced them the ideal American couple and gave the wedding reception in her home. The ideal couple was formally separated in 1948.

Reagan was inducted into the U.S. Army in 1942 but because of his poor eyesight was barred from combat duty. He spent the war making Air Force training films only ten miles from the Warner Bros. studios, to which he occasionally returned to make patriotic war films. When he entered the army, he was making $3,000 a week. When he returned full-time to Hollywood in 1945 and began making big-time money, he learned that he couldn't average his income— spread it out over the years—and his tax rates reached 90 percent. That experience formed the basis for his celebrated aversion to the very idea of taxes.

He "loathes taxes," says a former aide. The deficit goes up and up (it has doubled while he's been in office) but he refuses to raise taxes. His aversion to taxes is the rock upon which he has built his church. Logic and common sense play no part in it. Defence spending goes up, the deficit increases to finance it, but he won't raise taxes. Government, he insists, is too big and too wasteful (the number of government employees has actually increased under his tenure).

Jane Wyman complained that as an amateur politician her husband was becoming a bore. Reagan had been a loyal supporter of Franklin Roosevelt since Depression days, but as president of the Screen Actors Guild he began to drift to the right and supported the infamous House Un-American Activities Committee, which investigated communist influences in the film industry.

About this time his screen career started going downhill, but one pleasing prospect was that he met Nancy Davis, an obscure but attractive actress who in her biog. sheet for MGM had confessed her "greatest ambition" was to have a "successful, happy marriage."

Ron and Nancy met when a "Nancy Davis"—another actress by that name—turned up on a list of communist sympathizers. Reagan was called in to clear up the confusion. They were married on March 4, 1952, and Patricia Ann Reagan was born on October 22. (When Trivial Pursuit, the board game that made millionaires out of the Montreal sportswriter and the photographer who invented it, was franchised in the United States, the one question the American promoters insisted be removed was: "How many months pregnant was Nancy Davis when she walked up the aisle with Ronald Reagan?".)

Reagan's evolution from an actor dabbling in film-industry politics into an ideologue imbued with the true faith of free enterprise began in 1954 when he signed up, for $150,000, as host of television's "General Electric Theater." His main role, however, was to tour GE's 135 plants across the country, talking to employers and their families about the role of business in national life and the dangers of overgovernment. It was on these tours that he perfected his platform style—a speech full of certitudes delivered with modest sincerity and the help of a teleprompter. His impeccable delivery came across as obvious conviction.

When the General Electric Theater series ended, he became host of another TV series, "Death Valley Days," advertising 20 Mule Team Borax. By this time, he was attracting the attention of rich Republicans in southern California who could see his platform potential. In 1962, the Roosevelt Democrat from Dixon, Illinois, switched parties and took out his Republican membership. In 1964, Reagan made a brilliant speech ("You and I have a rendezvous with destiny") on behalf of the doomed Republican presidential nominee, Senator Barry Goldwater. (The "rendezvous with destiny" line was stolen from Roosevelt and another much-admired line in the speech, describing America as "the last best hope of man on earth," was stolen from Abe Lincoln.) Within months he was being pushed as the next governor of California by the "kitchen cabinet" of reactionary Orange County millionaires— the Annenbergs and Bloomingdales and the like—who had befriended and financed him.

In 1966, Reagan became governor, beating incumbent Pat Brown by eight hundred thousand votes.

When her husband was elected governor of California, the first thing Nancy Reagan did was redecorate the governor's office. California, being California, was fascinated during her eight years in Sacramento by her penchant for elegance and fashion.

Washington, however, is not exactly Sacramento, and Nancy's habits were not as well received when she arrived in the capital. There were a few murmurs when she immediately refurbished the family quarters of the White House—with $800,000 donated by rich Republicans. (Her husband had just been elected on a platform blasting the size and cost of government.) Her inaugural wardrobe was estimated to have cost $25,000. She decided the White House china was a disgrace and spent $209,508 to replace it, nearly $1,000 a place setting. Nancy's china policy got more ink than her husband's foreign policy.

She was mocked for "The Gaze," the transfixed way she looked at her husband every time he appeared on a podium. She said she believed in the death penalty and confided that she kept a pistol under her pillow but, she explained, it was just a "tiny little gun"—as if tiny little guns didn't also kill. She unwisely confessed, in an answer to a question about how she kept so slim, that to this day she chews each morsel of food thirty-two times before swallowing—just as her adopted father, Dr. Loyal Davis, told her to do. Reporters, sitting in the press row at official dinners, took to chanting quietly to themselves "...twenty-six...twenty-seven...twenty eight..." as they amused themselves counting her every chew. Sure enough: thirty-two on the nose.

There was the small embarrassment when it came out that millionaire Alfred Bloomingdale, who among other things founded the Diners Club and was husband of one of Nancy's best friends, Betsy Bloomingdale, had been paying $18,000 a month to his mistress, twenty-seven-year-old Vicki Morgan, since she was seventeen, and whose assigned tasks included his being tied up and whipped.

In all, things did not go well for Nancy among the Washington social elite, who were mainly Democrats and who very much looked down on *arrivistes*, especially from such a vulgar locale as California, wherever that is. (The same social arbiters had ridiculed the down-home manners of Jimmy Carter's gang from Georgia.)

Nancy was taken into a luncheon group to meet Washington's leading ladies, the idea being to get her involved more in the community. The group included Evangeline Bruce, widow of the former ambassador to Britain, David Bruce; Susan Mary Alsop, formerly married to the noted columnist Joe Alsop; Oatsie Charles, Polly Fritchey, and one or two others. The lunches did not work out. Nancy Reagan did not pass muster (she is known not to much like women). It was this very same bunch who took a liking to Sondra Gotlieb and became regulars at her dinner parties. They made her into a Washington star and gave her their imprimatur, the air kiss that starts out so affectionate and never makes contact for fear of mussing the makeup (H.L. Mencken said that whenever he saw two women kissing it reminded him of boxers shaking hands).

So Nancy was not happy. And Washington—at least the elite of Washington—was not happy with Nancy. (This is a very small town, especially among the social/journalistic elite, since, because the black population is so predominant, the effective white population of the city is some two hundred thousand. It's like living in London, Ontario.) The Reagans' friends tended to be wealthy Californians, like the Bloomingdales or like the Walter Annenbergs (who have a sign on the gate of their Palm Springs estate: INTRUDERS WILL BE SHOT), or Mary Jane and Charles Wick.

Wick is probably Reagan's closest Washington buddy. He comes out of Hollywood, where his name used to be Charles Zwick. He changed it to Charles Z. Wick. He used to be an arranger for Tommy Dorsey. Then he was an agent, his main client being the singer Frances Langford who married Ralph Evinrude, as in Evinrude Motors. Wick and Evinrude went into the nursing-home business and Wick made a pile of dough. He is now Reagan's man in charge of the U.S. Information Agency and runs the Voice of America and is disliked by the Washington press.

So we had this Nancy problem. Enter Michael Deaver, the California public-relations man who once worked his way around the world playing piano on cruise ships and in bars. ("If you can hum it," he boasts, "I can play it.") He had been close to Nancy since the Sacramento days, and he now set out to change the Washington press's perception and therefore the nation's perception of the First Lady.

The first stroke was brilliant. The occasion was the 1982 dinner of the Gridiron club, the most exclusive ticket in town in that it includes only senior journalists and their guests— always high-level government and business figures. Nancy

Reagan, coached by Deaver, used the dinner to prick the image that she was interested only in fashion and fancy china. She flounced on the stage, dressed almost as a bag lady, and did a song-and-dance routine about "second-hand clothes" to the tune of "Second Hand Rose." It brought down the house. The people who counted in Washington appreciated Nancy's self-deprecating humour, and thus began an entirely new public perception of the lady who had been in trouble.

Next? She acquired a dog. A large floppy dog, which was often seen on TV pulling the flustered lady across the White House lawn. The prickly and stiff Dan Rather, successor to Walter Cronkite as the country's security blanket on the CBS evening news, was seen at first as not "warm" enough. His producers dressed him in a sleeveless sweater underneath his blazer. His polls went up. Deaver bought Nancy a dog. Her ratings went up.

The third and final ploy in destroying the fashion-and-china image was dutiful community work. Nancy sponsored the Foster Grandparent Program and achieved much favourable publicity by convening, in Washington, a First Ladies Conference on Drugs, which drew together some seventeen wives of presidents and prime ministers to fulminate against drug use. Even Mila Mulroney managed to keep her face straight when several Caribbean and South American ladies— including Mitsy Seaga of Jamaica—said how concerned they were about the dangers to youth. (Most everyone in the room was well aware that Seaga's constitutents made a living by smuggling drugs into the United States.) PR is PR.

Throughout Nancy's travails, her husband has remained consistent: his major political strength. The main thing you must understand, if you are to understand Ronald Reagan, is that he is essentially a simple man—simple as in uncomplicated. As Eisenhower was a simple man. Journalists used to laugh at Ike's convoluted, stumbling prose—and night-club comedians used to make a living imitating it. Through it all, he remained the most popular American president in history, until Reagan came along.

Reagan is a simplistic man who fits a simplistic nation. He has only three basic ideas (which, really, is about all anyone needs) which he has been repeating endlessly ever since he entered politics. The first is that government is too big and should get off your back. The second is that taxes are evil and obscene and somehow should be done away with. The third is that America is great.

It's hard to be unpopular when you push any one of those three propositions; impossible if you ride hard on all three. Reagan is his own icon. He preaches the values of the family and the church. He almost never sees his children. His granddaughter was eighteen months old before he bothered to see her. Despite his frequent vows about religion, he seldom goes to church, and then only on ceremonial occasions.

He talks about fiscal integrity, but uses every tax loophole he can find and does not pay much income tax. It is probably one of the reasons he is so popular: Americans admire—as the homeless in Harlem admired Reverend Adam Clayton Powell—those who have perfected the scam.

He fits his time. It is almost never mentioned, but one of the reasons Reagan is so popular is that he is the first president to be divorced. There was all the fuss in 1960 about whether the United States, which had never elected a Roman Catholic president, would or could elect John Kennedy. Now, no one mentions the subject. There hasn't been a Catholic in the White House since—not Johnson, Nixon, Ford, Carter, or Reagan—but religion is no longer an interest. A second Catholic president would not raise a single eyebrow.

The 1960 controversy over religion comes as a puzzlement to Canadians who have been long used to the fact (despite the mutters from Alberta) that their country is almost one-half Catholic. No one in Canada has taken the trouble to point out, since people seem not to care, that our last four prime ministers have been Catholic—Trudeau from Quebec, Clark from unlikely Alberta (where the Catholic portion of the population in only 18 percent), Turner from Everywhere, and Mulroney from Quebec.

In the United States, being a Catholic is a big deal. In Canada (helped a lot by the heavy Italian immigration into Toronto, which has changed that tight-assed town beyond recognition), it means nothing.

So Reagan, being the first divorced leader of his country, may be so popular because he represents the exact warp and woof of his constitutents. The national divorce rate is now approaching 50 percent of all marriages (a percentagé it has "achieved" in California, his home state), and so—if you think about it—he represents the "average" American. He's been divorced. He's "one of us."

His "ordinariness" helps him win. He has problems with all his children, as most "ordinary" Americans do. His eldest, Maureen, is strong-willed and hot-tempered. She has been married three times, first to a Washington policeman after she quit college, then to a Marine officer, and now to a man eleven years her junior. Maureen, who is forty-five, lives in Los Angeles; her husband, who lives in Sacramento, commutes on weekends.

An adopted son, Michael, got in trouble when, as a vice-president of a Burbank airplane-parts company, he wrote letters to air bases using his father's name in an attempt to gain business. He was the one who revealed that neither the president nor Nancy Reagan had bothered to see their grandchild Ashley, who was then eighteen months old.

Daughter Patti Davis, who arrived less than the ideal nine months after her parents' visit to the altar (thus making the Reagans even more in tune with real-life America), has always been rebellious. The day Reagan was to receive a national award as Father of the Year, she left a note saying she'd run away from home. A real sixties child, she opposed the Vietnam war and attended sit-ins. She's been vocal in her support of a nuclear-weapons freeze and women's right to abortion. At the age of thirty-one, she married her twenty-five-year-old yoga instructor.

Ronald Reagan, Jr., was a dancer with the second company of the Joffrey Ballet in New York. The president, sensitive to the implications about dancers, ungraciously told one interviewer that he had checked his son out and that the lad was "all boy." Which may or may not have something to do with the young man appearing on *Saturday Night Live* in several skits that quite viciously satirized his parents. In one of the sketches he cavorted before the TV cameras in pink underwear. At his next press conference the president was asked what he thought of his son appearing on network TV in his underwear, a question that qualified as the most unconscious humour of the year, since it was being asked of someone who once had, as a grown man, starred in a movie opposite a chimpanzee. Ron, Jr., married a dancer seven years his senior.

Combined with the fact that Reagan is average—i.e., is divorced and has trouble with his kids—is the obvious evidence that he is apparently, visibly, happily in love, deliriously devoted to his wife—in a nation where most people are not much interested in their mates.

Americans—who we have established, one trusts, are terribly idealistic and patriotic—have been seriously disillusioned about their leaders since journalists and authors started to tell the truth about the guys in the White House.

One day in 1962, in the Timber Club in the Hotel Vancouver, which is brilliantly designed as a stout B.C. forest, I had lunch with my favourite newspaper publisher, Stuart Keate, and a visiting academic from New York who was doing a year's sabbatical at the University of British Columbia. The academic told us, over the martinis, that John Kennedy, then president, leader of what is laughingly called the free world, would sometimes go to a major New York hotel, where his Secret Service people would man the service elevator and young ladies in procession would be escorted up to dazzle his afternoon. At that time, at that lunch, I thought to myself: typical New York cynicism, typical dumping on a president. Since then, Kennedy twenty years dead, we have learned the truth.

George Bain, the witty joy of the Toronto *Globe and Mail* in his Ottawa and Washington incarnations, has in the past few years—since it has been revealed that Jackie Kennedy complained about another woman's pantyhose being found under her pillow—confessed about his early days in Washington. As a new boy, a Canadian, he had heard the stories of Kennedy's randiness and, seeking confirmation, approached the dean of the White House correspondents, Merriman Smith of the Associated Press. (Smith would later be in the lead press car in Dallas on November 22, 1963, and was the first to see someone, being Lee Harvey Oswald, from the Texas School Books Depository, fire the shot that blew the top off the head of John Kennedy, which Jackie Kennedy, scrambling to the back of the convertible, tried to retrieve.) "This guy," Smith replied to Bain, the new boy, "is going to do for fucking what Eisenhower did for golf."

Since that time, the press has suffered from a guilt complex. Now the Washington reporters and biographers have started to tell what they always knew. We are told (as Canadians were told years later by those who knew that Mackenzie King used to invite in young ladies of the street so as to repair them, and used to talk to his dog and his dead mother) that the paraplegic Franklin Roosevelt carried on an affair with a secretary, that Dwight Eisenhower had a long love affair with the woman who was his jeep driver in

Europe, and that Lyndon Johnson had a notorious wandering eye.

Johnson's biographer tells the tale of the time the president, pleading a heavy work schedule, ordered an attractive White House secretary to come down to his Texas ranch for a working weekend. After taking non-stop dictation all Saturday, she fell exhausted into bed, only to wake startled in the middle of the night by the presence of a man approaching her bed. She was about to scream, when she heard an unmistakable drawl: "Move over, honey, this is yore president."

John Kennedy once told astonished British Prime Minister Harold Macmillan that if he went more than a day without sex he got a headache. The American press is now so open about Teddy Kennedy's loose sex life, partly to compensate for remaining so reticent at the time about Jack Kennedy's activities. *Esquire* magazine, in an article about the Aspen, Colorado, ski resort that it called the sex-and-drugs capital of the world, described Teddy Kennedy's habit, while addressing a group, of simply casting his eye about and selecting a particularly attractive young lady. Later in the evening the unknowing damsel would be approached by one of his aides with the message that Senator Kennedy would like to see her in his room. After a night of dalliance, one Aspen maiden wakened to find Kennedy packed and gone, but his reading glasses still on the bedside table. Concerned, she contacted one of his aides to return the glasses, only to be told that the senator bought his reading glasses "by the gross."

It is given wisdom in Washington that the reason Ted Kennedy keeps backing away from running for the presidency is his realization that the minute he officially enters the race there would be an enormous rehash in the press of Chappaquiddick and his other escapades. He was given a taste of this in the book written by Marcia Chellis, the secretary of his ex-wife, Joan Kennedy. Among other things, she reveals that Joan first learned of the Chappaquiddick incident and the drowning death of Mary Jo Kopechne when she accidentally picked up an extension phone and heard her husband giving the details to his current girlfriend, one Helga.

The Kennedy boys inherited their sexual habits legitimately—that is, from their father. Garry Wills, in his book on the family, details how Joe Kennedy, the buccaneer millionaire who rose from the shanty Irish of Boston to become the

American ambassador to the Court of St. James, delighted in showing his sons by example how to seduce women. In fact, he used to steal away and bed the young girlfriends his sons brought to Hyannisport for weekend parties.

There has never been any suggestion that the sanctimonious Richard Nixon strayed from the marraige bed; his other sins were so venal as to deter any interest in his sex life. One of the reasons Jimmy Carter was regarded by his constitutents as such a naïf was his wondering confessional to *Playboy* that he actually, occasionally, "lusted in his heart" for someone other than his wife—a condition that has struck most every male in creation since Adam (possibly excluding Liberace and Billy Graham). I cannot speak, naturally, for the female sex.

In all this, the American press latterly has been much more open and honest with its readers than Canadian journalists have been. Canadian writers still grant politicians a great deal of privacy.

So the American public was tired of scandal, tired of hearing things about past presidents in their peccadilloes that they really didn't want to know. They'd had enough. Into all this marched Ronald Reagan, devoted to his wife, seen at age seventy-five walking hand in hand with her across the White House lawn to the helicopter, almost never without her at any function, still in love as he approaches his ninth decade. It plays well in Peoria.

10

Our Man
(and Wife Of)
in Washington

In which you get all the details about why the ambassador is so smart and why he does his courting in the graveyard and why there was an arranged marriage and how they broke into Georgetown and who else has received The Slap and why Connie drives a convertible.

You can get a good idea of what Canada and the United States think of one another by the ambassadors they ship each other. By their envoys shall ye know them. Their personalities, their backgrounds, obviously affect how the one country views the other. They are seen as the quintessential representatives of their nationalities. With every wiggle of the cocktail finger and with the character of their cuisine, they send signals to the opposing capital.

What do we make of it, then, when Washington in 1976 sent Tom Enders as its ambassador to Ottawa? Enders is six feet eight inches tall and, like John Kenneth Galbraith (who is the same height), looks down upon the rest of mankind not only literally but arrogantly. The brilliant product of a rich New England Republican family, a graduate of both Harvard and Yale, Enders was regarded as a future star in the State Department.

In fact, his popularity was not up to his intellectual promise. He was sent to Cambodia in 1971 as deputy U.S. ambassador and rapidly gained the favour of both Alexander Haig and Henry Kissinger for his vigour and ruthlessness in the secret bombings which the White House so sincerely denied were happening.

Kissinger was so pleased with his conduct that, when Enders returned to Washington in 1974, Kissinger nominated him to be assistant secretary for economic affairs. The promotion so infuriated the Senate Foreign Relations Committee, which recalled the attempts by the embassy in Cambodia to stonewall their 1973 investigation of the bombings, that it delayed Enders' nomination for six weeks. It then accompanied the reluctant approval with an unusual rebuke, calling Enders' description of the American embassy's role "grossly misleading" and deciding that the embassy had made "a conscious effort" to conceal its role in the bombings. Just two years later, Enders was made ambassador to Canada.

Enders, with his imposing manners, made a large dent in Rockcliffe Park social circles and quickly became friends with some of the establishment journalists. Those he had never met but who often twitted the official American line (meaning this scribe) he would seek out and attempt to set straight. He was aided greatly in his dent-making by his tiny Italian wife, Gaetana, who had more success in Ottawa than she did in Cambodia, where she set up a home for war widows. "The House of Butterflies," not knowing that in the local language "butterfly" meant whore.

The next Republican export to Ottawa—after Jimmy Carter sent Kenneth M. Curtis, a mild-mannered Democrat, the former governor of Maine, who became a friend of Governor General Ed Schreyer's—was the Big Blow from Chicago. Paul Robinson is the only bull I've ever met who carried his own china shop around with him.

Mr. Ambassador, who was then fifty-one, was a millionaire who made his fortune selling insurance. He owed his job, in the great tradition that makes U.S. diplomatic policy such a proud career, to the fact that he was the chief bagman—the chap who collects the boodle, the swag—in Illinois for Ronnie Reagan. This fellow was a gem, one of a kind. They threw away the mould.

To suggest that Ambassador Robinson was a hawk is like suggesting that Reggie Jackson has an ego. Ambassador Robinson zipped from speaking engagement to Rotarian lunch faster than a speeding malaprop. His tongue waggled at both ends, hinged in the middle. He dispensed advice as if it were Ronnie Reagan's hair rinse. We should have been grateful, because it was all free.

In Calgary, Washington's gift to Ottawa sternly criticized Canada for not spending enough money on defence. It was a lecture delivered with the assurance of a potentate from afar spanking a banana republic. The major concern in the world is the Soviet buildup of arms, quoth the diplomat, and Canada had best pull up its britches.

Demonstrating his wide knowledge of Canada and its politics, he allowed that the separatist Western Canada Concept (wcc) was no threat because it would be offset by such right-wing parties as the Social Credit party in Alberta. This was the week after the Social Credit party officially disbanded in that province. Mr. Ambassador made reference to the election of the wcc's Gordon Kessler in Saskatchewan, which wasn't bad, since he missed by only one province. He could have erred in the other direction and placed him in British Columbia.

Asked what the Reagan administration's view of Western Canadian separatism was, Mr. Ambassador replied, in that cultured tone that made him an immediate hit, that "it will be whatever I decide when I get back to Ottawa."

Asked to speak to the annual dinner meeting of the Canadian Press in Toronto during the week that Canada finally got a complete constitution from across the water, Mr. Ambassador lectured the collected editors and publishers of the nation with a jut-jawed sermon on his favourite subject, the need to build more guns. He criticized the marshmallow-spined Canadian newspapers for devoting more space to inflation than Russian arms buildup. The short-sighted editors were advised that the hope of Mr. Ambassador was that a more "reasonable approach to this serious and long-standing threat will somehow be able to get some credence from the press."

Good sound advice from Father, something that any right-thinking Canadian would be wise to ponder before snapping to attention. Mr. Ambassador, as a matter of fact, confided how proud he felt when he spotted a Canadian in Winnipeg saluting the Stars and Stripes. Winnipeg? Was that where Gordon Kessler was elected? No, we digress.

As part of the sermon, to demonstrate his insurance view of world history, he named twenty-nine countries that "have either fallen to or are under the control of Moscow." Included were Yugoslavia, proudly independent of Moscow's grip for thirty-four years, and Albania, which so hates Moscow it doesn't even maintain diplomatic relations.

The most emboldened among those offended by this sabre-rattling was one John Miller, deputy managing editor of the *Toronto Star*, largest paper in the beaver republic. When he approached Mr. Ambassador to mention that he felt somewhat insulted by the lecture, given the very week when Canada had achieved its technical independence, he was told to get wise to the Russian threat.

Mr. Miller: "Could you tell me, please, where the Russians are threatening us?"

Mr. Ambassador: "Shove off, kid."

Mr. Miller: "I beg your pardon?"

Mr. Ambassador: "Just shove off."

Mr. Miller was thirty-nine.

This was good sound stuff, badly needed in this weak-kneed nation. The world needs more straight talking. Canadians, shy introverts, will in future years be grateful to Mr. Ambassador, just as we should be grateful to Washington for sending us the bristly Enders and the blustering Robinson, just as we are thankful they sent us as their representative in the free-trade wars thirty-eight-year-old Peter Murphy, who has an inoperable brain tumour (up against our man, Simon Reisman, who has an inoperable swearing problem), and the current U.S. Ambassador in Ottawa, Thomas Niles. When the White House imposed the sudden tariff on shakes and shingles, someone got hold of Niles' message to Washington, which said that the Canadians, "as expected, panicked."

Canadians tend not to send such, uh, colourful figures to Washington in return. The American capital and London, of course, are the plums for the diplomatic service (or the "dips," as they're known on the Washington tennis courts among those of us who have a mean forehand). In the early 1960s, there was the very professional Arnold Heeney, who had to fight some of the brush-fire wars when Diefenbaker was going through his Saskatchewan angst in dealing with the toffs on the Potomac.

The Canadians in Washington couldn't stand Secretary of State John Foster Dulles, whom they thought an arrogant and pompous bore. Heeney, after once hosting Mr. and Mrs. Dulles for dinner, remarked, "Our dinner for the Dulleses was good except for the Dulleses."

Heeney was followed by the urbane and cultured Charles Ritchie, who has since published four volumes of diaries, which, frozen in aspic, give off the air of a don from the Bloomsbury Group, slightly tired of life but amused by the absurdities of it all. Diplomatic life in Washington, watching LBJ try to bully the sly Pearson, was raw meat for such a discerning eye.

The diarist was followed by Ed Ritchie, no relation, a former Rhodes Scholar, a man schooled in economics, renowned for his sound judgement and acumen. Marcel Cadieux, who was sent down in 1970, was also a career external-affairs man, which Ottawa in those days was famous for the production of. He was a most efficient administrator.

Jake Warren was the closest thing to a break with tradition, coming out of Trade and Commerce rather than the pinstripe set. He was a banker and had worked with Brascan, formerly Brazilian Traction, that famed old-boy hiding spot for Liberal favourites and politicians. Warren was succeeded by Peter Towe, another career man, who cut no glide path through Washington at all, leaving a quiet vacuum for the arrival in 1981 of—ta da!—Allan Gotlieb.

Allan Gotlieb has about him the air of someone perpetually puzzled by life. His owlish, quizzical look is emphasized by small wire-framed glasses that give him the appearance of a chemist in a small English town. With his shoulders hunched and his head bent forward he resembles an impatient cormorant in search of small fish to spear.

He has a brilliant mind, as one would expect from a Rhodes Scholar, the pick of Manitoba. He was at Oxford, as a matter of fact, at the same time John Turner was there representing British Columbia. (Turner, curiously, quotes the celebrated definition of a Rhodes Scholar as "someone whose future is behind him." It may apply to Turner, a Hamlet-like figure—and his quoting the phrase may be his admission of it—but it does not apply to Gotlieb. One can never imagine him using the quote, though he is of course conversant with it—as he is with almost any witticism. He was the first person in Washington I ever heard explain the Young Urban Professional Persons—Yuppie—tag, almost a year before it came into common usage—and became, rather quickly, justifiably detested.)

He worships his wife and phones her three times a day. He has been arguably the hardest-working diplomat in Washington and yet he called home just to chat, to keep in touch, to provide support (that cliché term that has no substitute). He edited all her copy, offering help and, one suspects, censorship when she trod too close to the diplomatic line. He is both father and lover. He is nine years older than his bride—somewhat short of the fourteen years that separate both Brian and Mila Mulroney, and Joe Clark and Maureen McTeer, and the doomed twenty-eight years that swamped Margaret and Pierre Trudeau.

The best description of the ambassador came from a colleague who recalls an occasion when Gotlieb, mulling over a particularly serious problem, stood at an intersection, lost in thought, as the traffic lights went through three cycles. When he finally did step off the curb, it was on the red light.

He came from an elegant home in south Winnipeg, son of a merchant family. Larry Zolf, the antic spirit from north Winnipeg who is now a celebrated writer and CBC producer, recalls Gotlieb as an unlikely counsellor at a B'nai B'rith summer camp on a Manitoba lake. If a boy, Zolf being one of them, wanted to paddle a canoe or climb a tree, the last counsellor to call would be Gotlieb, who restricted his physical exercise to the chess board. "The campers could have been off drowning for all he knew," remembers Zolf. "Campers be damned! Gotlieb was off somewhere reading Schopenhauer."

His awkwardness remains today. Forced to do the official face-off ceremonies when a Canadian NHL team visited the Washington Capitals, he dropped the puck on his foot. Sondra, who complains that he goes to the beach wearing executive hose, was assigned by the glossy magazine *Vanity Fair* to attend and do an article on a Florida "fat farm," as diet clinics are known by those socialites who can afford them. She claims that she followed the regimen religiously, was covered with sweat from dawn to dusk, and lost two pounds over the week while Allan—who is never without a tie, Saturday or Sunday—sat in the library the whole time reading and lost ten pounds.

None of the weight comes off his ego. He says, "I honestly don't have any doubts I can rise to the occasion. I'm a pretty articulate fellow. I'm a man of strong opinion and I'm not particularly timid." He doesn't have to be. A graduate of the University of California at Berkeley, he stood first in his Harvard law school class, where he was also editor of the *Harvard Law Review*.

While at Oxford, he began buying the spare, austere prints of Tissot, a nineteenth-century French artist. Speckled around the walls of the ambassador's beautiful residence in Washington, the grey-and-white paintings somehow typify their owner's meticulous mind. Today he has the world's largest private collection of Tissot's prints at a time when the artist is enjoying a revival. Gotlieb toyed with the idea of opening his own private gallery when he leaves the foreign service. His underlings call him "The Goat." He has talked about, on his recall from Washington, teaching at the University of Toronto or opening a law practice. He has no desire to return to Ottawa.

Sondra Gotlieb, for her part, was always an original. She is a throwback, a willful child who never grew up—as none of us wants to grow up. She succeeded. The night she won the Stephen Leacock Medal for Humour—the highest honour those of us who are amateur humorists and worshippers of Leacock can aspire to—she threw pickles and buns at Ben Wicks, the award chairman, because she didn't like Wicks' misogynist act. That's what a child is allowed to do: at a birthday party when you're bored, you throw the food around, a kindergarten version of John Belushi's *Animal House*. Wicks, whose stage act is even funnier than his cartoons, loved it. One suspects Leacock would have, too.

Sondra has great instincts. At a high point during a posh party at the ambassadorial residence on Rock Creek Drive, populated by one-quarter of the cabinet of the United States and three TV network anchormen and most anyone who counted in Canapé Washington, Sondra's husband the ambassador was in the midst of a eulogy to some high personage. She, behind her cigarette, yelled out "Bullshit!" Everyone laughed. That's Sondra. Husband of—Allan—allowed a small droll smile, loving the act, as George Burns loved Gracie Allen's carefully constructed dumb-blonde act.

Sondra Gotlieb is the last woman in the western world to be the product of an arranged marriage. And she is, well, proud of it. She is also amused by it. She won that Leacock Medal by detailing the strange circumstances in *True Confections*. She grew up chubby, indulged, and unacademic. At eighteen, she had failed her first year of university in Winnipeg and had been fired from her first job (as a park attendant; the kids locked her in the equipment shack and stole all the bats). She wanted to get out of Winnipeg. At a party in September she met a worldly twenty-six-year-old just in from Oxford. Allan Gotlieb's first words to his future bride after she interrupted his chess game by handing him a bowl of maple-walnut ice cream were: "Well, my plump little duck, let's go upstairs where it's quiet so I can learn all about you."

The courtship lasted just ten days—mostly in graveyards, she claims, since Allan has a passion for old objects and places. Then he flew back to Oxford, mumbling that he might think about getting engaged when she finished university in four years. Sondra's version is that their scheming families trapped them into marriage by way of a Winnipeg-Oxford phone call with bad connections. When she waited at the airport for him to return, she couldn't remember what he looked like. They were married at Christmas. Allan vaguely denies her version—but she got a Leacock Medal out of it, didn't she?

That was thirty years and three children ago, and Sondra has hardly changed, as few of us do. She affects an air of constant confusion but actually is watching the world with the careful eye of a social surgeon. The *Wall Street Journal* called her "the Alice Roosevelt Longworth of her time" (in reference to the legendary socialite, daughter of Teddy Roosevelt, who both scandalized and amused Washington for decades with her deadly wit), and said she "looks at Washington in the manner of an anthropologist discovering a long-lost primitive civilization." Her deadly eye saw something about Washington that the town didn't want to acknowledge. Which is the reason so many people were delighted to see her get in trouble. Ah, revenge.

She is a combination of Lucille Ball and Dorothy Parker, perpetually at sea socially, with a helpless air that always brings helpers volunteering to rescue her. Actually, she's just watching. When in Ottawa, she was a regular at a weekly gathering of women who called themselves Broads Canada. The group included writer Doris Anderson and broadcasters Elizabeth Gray, Nicole Belanger, and Pam Wallin, and was devoted to a witty dissection over lunch of the week's events, rumours, gossip, and speculation. Sondra, bumming cigarettes as usual, was a star.

When I complimented Sondra on a rave review her book, *Wife Of*, had received in the *New York Times Books Review*—a venue that any author would die for—she said, "Yes, I was thinking of sending the reviewer a token of my esteem. Do you think a small Pontiac would be too much?"

She is the author of the famous maxim defining the secret to success in Washington: "Suck above, kick below." Her celebrated "Dear Beverly" column in the *Washington Post* split the town: journalists hated it, diplomats' wives loved it. The column is populated with such caricatures as Popsie Tribble, the Washington socialite; Melvin Thistle, Jr., from the State Department; Lionel Portant, World Famous Columnist; Sonny Goldstone, the Gilded Bachelor and Social Asset; Baron Spitte, the dusty diplomat; and Joe Promisall, the city's most expensive lobbyist.

"Beverly" in fact is Beverley Rockett, Sondra's close friend, a Toronto fashion consultant and photographer, the second best-dressed woman in Canada, formerly married to Trudeau cabinet minister John Roberts. She is not quite sure if she deserves the "Beverly" notoriety. "Popsie Tribble" is another close friend, Popsy Johnston, wife of Canada's consul general in New York. She would rather that Sondra had chosen another name.

Early on, Bob Healy, Washington bureau chief of the *Boston Globe*, sent a memo to *Post* executive editor Ben Bradlee, the overseer of his paper's Watergate triumphs: "Sondra Gotlieb? You've got to be shitting me." Journalistic dismay at the fey whimsy of her cocktail-party mockery comes largely from natural jealousy. The *Washington Post* is the most readable major newspaper in the United States, its Watergate exposés boosting it to the level of the turgidly laid out and humourless *New York Times*. Sondra's twice-a-month *Post* columns were given an attractive, airy design on the paper's columnists' page—opposite the editorials—a spot that most of us would give half a leg and some of next month's salary for.

Her enemies claim Sondra assiduously courted Meg Greenfield, who is the *Post*'s editorial-page editor and unmarried, at the embassy's dinners. One can only add that anyone who can capture a column on the *Washington Post* op-ed page, assiduously or not, is better than someone who cannot. The supernationalism of Americans allows an American humorist, Art Buchwald, to make fun of Washington mores but it does not much abide a foreigner, Sondra Gotlieb, doing the same thing.

The only problem is that those who mock others for their social hypocrisy apparently must be perfect themselves. Sondra marches to her own off-beat drummer. She is almost professionally rude; amusing to those who know her and appreciate someone who has the courage to be completely frank amidst the artificial politeness and protocol, but not funny at all to strangers who don't know her act. One embassy staffer says she can be full of "cobra spit."

If bored, in a diplomatic ambience heavy in boredom, she simply walks away. "It's an impulse," says one Canadian journalist who has seen it. "She looks like a flashbulb has gone off in her face, and she's gone. No niceties, no apologies." Some Washington ladies have seen her, lacking an ashtray, drop her ashes in the salt-cellar. She is detested by most of the wives of resident Canadian journalists in Washington, because she does not defer—or remember names or faces, unless they are important. Suck above, kick below.

By and large, though, the Gotliebs' George-Burns-and-Gracie-Allen act, a description they don't like, has worked in Washington. Sondra first burst upon the front page of the *New York Times* when she was quoted as saying that whenever she mentioned Canada at a Powertown cocktail party, "people's eyes glazed over. Perhaps we should invade South Dakota to get some attention." It was her husband who pointed out later that "invading" South Dakota would have to involve paratroopers, since North Dakota would somehow have to be crossed first. There's the Burns-and-Allen effect: the supposed throwaway line, very shrewd, from Gracie; the clever follow-up from George. It's a well-honed act and Washington society, while puzzled, was intrigued by it.

Gotlieb maintains, not too convincingly, that Canada became the hot embassy in town rather by accident. "As a matter of fact," he says, "my first month here I had no idea what I was doing. I even felt ashamed for accepting money for doing nothing and was in a bit of a sulk." The State Department didn't even return his courtesy calls, he had never served in Washington, didn't know the town, and knew only two old friends from his days at Oxford.

The key was a network. Joseph Kraft, the nationally syndicated columnist (who died in early 1986), had always been a great admirer of Pierre Trudeau. Whenever he went to Ottawa to interview the prime minister, Kraft would be entertained by Richard Gwyn, then Ottawa columnist for the Liberal *Toronto Star*. The Gwyns and the Gotliebs are close friends. It was an invitation from Joe and Polly Kraft to a party that broke the logjam. The Gotliebs got to know "the Georgetown crowd"—meaning the most important network in a gossipy town built on networks.

Soon, ABC's David Brinkley was a regular at the Gotlieb soirés on Rock Creek Drive. Most crucial, so was Evangeline Bruce, considered the *grand dame* of Washington society and one of the best-dressed women in America. She is an amusing woman whose imprimatur can make or break any dining table in town. Lane Kirkland, the head of the AFL-CIO and noted for his courtly southern manners, became a fixture. William Safire of the *New York Times* became a friend. Former defence secretary Robert McNamara was usually around. (Lyndon Johnson, after viewing the Kennedy cabinet, concluded that the smartest of the best and the brightest was "the guy with the stickum on his hair.")

Gotlieb explains that the power guys in Powertown don't go to embassy parties—which stretch from horizon to horizon every sundown—to meet foreigners. They go to meet other powerful Americans. The parties are an extension of work where they can pick up relevant information and gossip. "I suppose," he mused one day, "that they find us relatively amusing—which most embassies aren't."

Mulroney got a useful illustration of this in June 1984, just a week after the Liberal leadership convention when John Turner was riding high as prime minister designate. The Gotliebs threw a party for Brian and Mila and all Washington turned out. Three Reagan cabinet members showed up (in a town where there are only twelve members of cabinet, unlike Ottawa's forty, to spread around the parties)—and this up against the competition of a White House barbecue party! The *Times'* James Reston was there, along with *Washington Post* chairman Katharine Graham, Watergate hero Ben Bradlee and his wife, Sally Quinn, Reagan confidant Michael Deaver, Senator Daniel Patrick Moynihan, and most everyone that Mulroney could recognize as important.

The ascent of the Gotlieb pad was even more remarkable since it took place during a period when the Trudeau government was highly unpopular among the reigning Reaganauts. Gotlieb thinks he was probably lucky, in that the highly popular British ambassador, Sir Nicky Henderson, had just left town and there was a bit of a vacuum among the hosts who knew how to entertain winningly.

It was at the Gotliebs' that Reagan adviser Edwin Meese, now the attorney general, first met labour leader Kirkland and to his surprise found him fascinating. One visitor to the residence tells of the night when Secretary of Defense Caspar Weinberger was at one table, loudly dumping on the reputation of Secretary of State Alexander Haig—while Haig at another table was running down Weinberger, the first indication social Washington had perceived of the growing row that ended with Haig being dumped.

The Gotliebs' move into the spotlight wasn't really as dependent on luck as it was painted, which would have been clear to anyone who had attended their parties in Rockcliffe Park in Ottawa. Their Ottawa recipe was simple. They used a Mixmaster when choosing the guest list: a smorgasbord of politicians who were witty (a scarce commodity), journalists who owned ties and did not drink out of the finger bowls, and a snippet of the swivel servants with the most interesting wives.

It was a dark and stormy night in March 1986 when the Slap happened. James Thurber made a classic out of "The Night the Bed Fell on Father." In diplomatic folklore, we now have "The Night Sondra Slugged Connie," in myth and song outranking most everything since Rep. Wilbur Mills, chairman of the House Ways and Means Committee, was found staggering out of the Tidal Basin, his five-piece suit intact, with Fanne Foxe, Washington's reigning stripper.

The problem started with the rent-a-trees. The "acid rain summit," involving Mr. Mulroney's visit to Mr. Reagan, required the largest bash ever at the Gotlieb ambassadorial residence. Allan Gotlieb, having been allowed to stay past the usual term in Washington, wanted very much to be around when the new Canadian embassy, designed by the brilliant Arthur Erickson, officially opened its doors at the end of 1987 on its unparalleled site opposite the National Gallery on Pennsylvania Avnue, under the shadow of the Capitol.

It was deemed, therefore, that the grandest Gotlieb party of all, two hundred strong, would be mounted for the Mulroneys. Only one problem: the ambassadorial mansion, grand as it was, could not accommoda^e two hundred to a sit-down banquet. (In Newfoundland, when you're invited out to dinner, you ask if it's "sit-down or crotch"—meaning formal or buffet. I digress.) It was determined that a tent would be erected in the garden, which would necessitate a false floor to cover the swimming pool. To make the austere tent more homey, a Washington firm that makes a living out of renting out trees for a night was engaged.

The night came cold and windy. We were all assembled and seated under the tent. The floor under our table shuffled ominously, causing furrows in the attractive brow of Mrs. Christopher Plummer. The winds were high, causing the tent to sway, bringing to mind the predictions of a certain colum-

nist that, if the whole thing went down, most of the brains of
western civilization would be wiped out.

It was, after all, an A-plus Gotlieb guest list. Brian Mulroney,
being a media groupie, had Barbara Walters placed beside
him. Sondra's seat was beside Secretary of State George
Shultz, who was resplendent in a white silk dinner jacket that
strangely made him look like a guest at a Marcos wedding.
Mulroney's patron, millionaire Paul Desmarais, was down
from Montreal for the affair, as was the party's bagman, David
Angus. Everybody was there, in fact, except the guest of
honour, the vice-president of the United States, George
Bush. He had been, it turned out, speaking in Pittsburgh and
was speeding apace by helicopter while the guests, casting
nervous glances upward at the swaying tent, waited patiently.

Sondra, standing on the front steps with Connie Connor,
her social secretary, wasn't so patient. She stood in the pool of
bright lights cast by the TV cameramen in the driveway.
Bush's security men stood to one side. A band of reporters—
who hadn't been among those invited but had to cover the
event from the outside—stood across the road, waiting for the
vice-president to arrive. It was the most public arena in
Washington at that moment.

Then Sondra asked Connie why another prized guest,
Deputy Treasury Secretary Richard Darman, hadn't arrived—a
crucial absence since, scheduled to arrive without his wife
and thus a valuable "extra man," it meant another table
setting screwed up. Connie, who several weeks earlier had
decided to look for another job, insisted she had told Sondra
that Darman had cancelled; Sondra insisted she hadn't been
told and unexpectedly delivered a swift chop.

Minus an earring and in tears, Connie fled down the steps,
along the driveway past the astounded press, around to the
back of the house, and through the kitchen. Within moments, the master of the house had been informed. He
arranged swift apologies, and Sondra and a slightly dishevelled Connie were posing, the latter *sans* one earring, for the
photographers. Meanwhile Mr. Bush was whisked inside to
meet Mr. Mulroney, who had the flu and felt terrible—but
not as terrible as he felt when he got home to Ottawa next
morning and saw the headlines: Sondra prominent; Brian
down the track.

Connie Connor is, in her own way, an original. She is a
woman of "a certain age," sophisticated, with a way of

dressing that gives the impression she comes from somewhere where the sun always shines. She is sunny in outlook, sunny in wardrobe, and has a rounded, pleasant face that exudes sunniness. She drives around Washington in a gold Mercedes convertible of a certain age, which indicates something, one is not quite sure what. Almost no one drives a convertible these days, partly because the monolithic Detroit dinosaurs stopped making the rag-tops, and a sunny blonde with a pleasant disposition driving around with the top down is a rare sight. The convertible sort of sums up Connie.

She is a heavy player in something called Who's Who International, which is a singles club for the middle-aged. Those in the angst of divorce or suffering mild desperation for a mate have a dignified, well-dressed alternative. It could be termed a meeting place for the muddled. Washington, being Washington, is a city of transition—diplomats coming and going, journalists transferred thus and so, civil servants going up or down the ladder. They are transient and confused.

Enter Who's Who International. It brings together, in various Washington watering holes, despairing widows from the horsey set in Virginia across the river and ageing Lotharios who once wished they were David Niven and too often have the air of Errol Flynn just before he expired. Connie is above all this, both in her optimism and her appearance, but, as the 1986 "social chairman," she seems to be both amused and very immersed in the operation.

Connie Gibson Wehrman Connor, as she bills herself in her third area of life, is also founder and publisher of *Space A* books, *Travel News*, and a newsletter, *Military Travel News*. *Space A* books are manuals telling U.S. military personnel and their families how to get around the globe on military planes that are moving from continent to continent.

She knows the ropes. She is a former Navy wife who has lived in Bangkok, Rio de Janeiro, Hawaii, Naples, Rabat, Panama City, Key West, Annapolis, Charleston, and other not-so-familiar places such as Fiskeville, Weekapaug, Lake Barcroft, Lake Winnepesaukee, Madison, and Ocean Reef.

After Sondra Gorlieb went through several social secretaries in her early time in Washington, Connie Connor—who had been a protocol officer with the State Department— joined her as the longest-staying social secretary of all.

Sondra has done her slap act before. One night at an Ottawa party she slapped her good friend Elizabeth Gray, the excellent CBC broadcaster who was so stupidly dumped as host of *As It Happens*. Slapping is so, well *Victorian* and out-of-date—I mean, no one *does* it anymore—that Mrs. Gray used to joke about it. She felt no vindictiveness toward her friend.

Washington, alas, has no such sense of humour. It was the worst scandal in Canadian-American relations since the night in 1977 when Margaret Trudeau showed up for an official White House dinner wearing—wait for it!—a midcalf-length frock. On such important things do foreign relations founder across the world's longest and most boring border.

Sondra, the successor to the scandalous Alice Roosevelt Longworth, had crossed the line from amusingly eccentric to outrageous. The Martha Mitchell of the Great White North who provided such good copy for the society writers was now unfortunately producing headlines for the guys who make up the front pages of the *Globe and Mail* (WIFE OF AMBASSADOR DELIVERS SLAP THAT REVERBERATES IN TWO CAPITALS), the *Toronto Star* (SLAP BY AMBASSADOR'S WIFE ECHOES AROUND TWO CAPITALS); and the *Toronto Sun* (THE SLAP-SHOT SUMMIT).

The *Washington Post*, home of Sondra's column, said nothing about the incident in the next day's paper, even though the dinner was attended by Katharine Graham, Ben Bradlee and wife Sally Quinn, editorial-page editor Meg Greenfield, and a social-scenes writer. The next day, the *Post* caught up, calling the incident "Sondra Gotlieb's Slap-Flap." But *People* magazine, strangely, never did report on it. The Time Inc. magazine designed for people who don't like to read prepared a four-page spread on Sondra keyed to the slap. The last the staff saw of it was a copy of the material marked for the attention of Henry Grunwald, editor-in-chief of *Time*. Both Grunwald and John Meyers, chairman of *Time*'s magazine group, were among the two hundred guests at the Slap dinner. The article never appeared.

For someone so self-assured intellectually, Allan Gotlieb is terribly sensitive to criticism of his wife. Sondra had been riding a wave of publicity in both Washington and in Canadian newspapers and magazines, particularly with the publication of her book *Wife Of*, when a Washington business magazine, *Regardie's*, checked in with the one bad notice. It was the familiar fate of celebrities who get so high on the pedestal that someone has to do some debunking. The magazine said, "Some people think that Sondra Gotlieb has become a character in her own comedy of manners" and, when the wary Gotliebs declined to pose for photographs, decorated the article with some cruel and unattractive photos of Sondra taken from the files.

Gotlieb, sensing bad news, had John Fieldhouse, an embarrassed press aide, dispatched to the magazine's offices in an attempt to get an advance look at the unflattering profile. He was laughed off the premises. Press secretary Bruce Phillips then attempted to discourage Southam News, which had bought the article, from distributing it to its fifteen Canadian papers. Southam News general manager Nicholas Hills politely told him to go fly a kite.

Gotlieb's embassy had used Gray & Company, Washington's best-known public-relations and communications concerns, to help raise the image of Canada. Between March 20 and April 25 of 1984, for example, the embassy paid Robert Keith Gray's company $74,573.65 in retainers and $12,580.11 in miscellaneous charges.

But Bob Gray, who used to be prominent at all the big Gotlieb parties, embarrassed Gotlieb when a *Post* story gave the impression that Gray's main assignment was to get the Gotliebs into the gossip columns. In reporting a lunch at Maison Blanche starring Mordecai Richler, Sondra Gotlieb, and Art Buchwald, the resident Washington satirist, the press release managed to misspell both Gotlieb and Richler. Maison Blanche is the restaurant where the elite meet to bleat, within an olive's throw of the White House, a place where the maître d's glance can freeze your unpressed trousers at fifty paces. Shortly after, the Canadian embassy took on the celebrated Michael Deaver, at $105,000 for a one year arrangement. It was not a wise move.

Deaver, of course, is gone—though still a Gotlieb friend. The Slap, however, remains, like Thurber's bed that fell on father. Washington society, formal and pompous, is also hypocritical. They liked Sondra to be eccentric, but not quite that eccentric. In the final analysis, it turned out that they were using her just as much as she was using them.

11

Dr. Foth's Guide to Washington

In which is laid out where to eat and get some jazz and who has the best backhand and a cheat sheet to those Democrats going up and those Republicans going down.

> *The happiness of every country depends*
> *upon the character of its people rather than*
> *the form of its government.* —THOMAS
> CHANDLER HALIBURTON

Once I had the proper (if misleading) credentials, I could resume my commentary of the best and worst in the political game as it is played in the city that Allan Gotlieb has called the New Rome. Here, first, is Dr. (Murray) Foth's rundown of the players:

Worst sportscaster in town: pick any one.

Best bartender in town: Bob, with the loose wrist, National Press Club.

Most glad-handing: Duke Zeibert's restaurant, Connecticut Avenue.

Most in need of a new tailor and new speech coach: Senator Bill Bradley (the American Don Johnston).

Worst street for potholes: pick any.

Most comfortable summer-lunch spot: the garden roof of the Washington Hotel, overlooking the White House grounds.

Broadcast office most broken into: CBC, seven times in six months.

Fading presidential candidate: Howard Baker.

Most boring fad, men: red ties.

Most boring fad, women: floppy blouse ties.

Most beautiful sight in town: the Lincoln Memorial, at night.

Ugliest building in town: the John F. Kennedy Center for the Performing Arts.

Best Vietnamese food: Germaine's.

Best jazz: Blues Alley.

Best pizza in Washington: Armand's Chicago Pizzeria, Wisconsin Avenue.

Dumbest idea: there are no non-stop flights from Washington to Toronto, to Montreal, or to Vancouver. The USAir Washington-Toronto flight, which should take one hour, stops at Rochester or Buffalo, making it a two-hour journey.

How to get your party guests' names in print: phone columnist Chuck Conconi of the *Washington Post*.

How to get embarrassing government leaks in print, so as to fight your cabinet enemies: phone the column-writing team of Robert (The Prince of Darkness) Novak, who works the Capitol Hill scene, and dapper Rowland Evans, who does the Georgetown party circuit.

Man most despised in Washington by politicians and press alike: David Stockman.

Worst senator: Jesse Helms from North Carolina, blusterer, bafflegabber, flack for the tobacco industry.

Highest-paid, most-talked-about columnist in town: George F. Will, friend of Nancy Reagan's, sometime speech writer for Ronald Reagan, much mocked by colleagues for pretentious style, former lecturer at the University of Toronto; he makes more than one million dollars a year from a syndicated column, ABC contracts, and speeches ($20,000 per pop), and is the inspiration for the *New Republic*'s revelations on the New Buckrakers, and Doonesbury's accurate satire.

Best columnist in town: David Broder, *Washington Post*.

Still able to grasp the mood of the nation in a graceful way: old sports hand James Reston, *New York Times*.

Hardest-working young-man-on-his-way-up: Fred Barnes, formerly of the *Baltimore Sun*, now with the *New Republic*.

Most genuine cabinet member: Commerce Secretary Malcolm Baldrige, who, at sixty-three, rides in rodeos as a hobby.

Worst cabinet member: Defense Secretary Caspar Weinberger, victim of a charisma bypass.

Most prestigious tennis club: St. Alban's, owned by a private boys' school on the grounds of the National Cathedral, no clubhouse, no towels, no lockers, clay courts, no playing on Sunday morning so as not to disturb church, no indoor courts—and a ten-year waiting list. Allie Ritzenberg, St. Alban's pro, ranks the prime players:

> *Best disciplined:* (no surprise) FBI director William Webster.

Best at analysing opponent's game: (surprise) Walter Mondale.

Best footwork: (obvious) Secretary of State George Shultz.

Best ball hawk: Zbigniew Brzezinski.

Most consistent: New Yorker correspondent Elizabeth Drew.

Most casual: Senator John Warner, who used to be one of Elizabeth Taylor's most recent husbands.

Greatest variety of shots: Senator John Heinz, heir to the ketchup fortune.

Best dressed: Katharine Graham, chairman of the *Washington Post,* who was the highest-paid woman in the United States in 1985 at $1,031,000

(Only 350 members are allowed in and each pays $625 annually. In the case of divorce—five to eight a year—couples must decide who is to retain the membership. Otherwise, with Washington's divorce rate, the boss, Allie, says it would be "a Malthusian, geometric expansion.")

Those on the downgrade for the 1988 Republican presidential nomination: Vice-President George Bush, Representative Jack Kemp, evangelist Pat Robertson.

Those on the rise for the Republican nomination: Senator Bob Dole of Kansas, and Senator Paul Laxalt of Nevada, Mr. Reagan's best political friend.

Those on the downgrade for the 1988 Democratic presidential nomination: Gary Hart, Reverend Jesse Jackson, Senator Edward Kennedy.

Those on the rise for the Democratic nomination: Senator Bill Bradley of New Jersey, Representative Richard Gephardt of Missouri, Senator Sam Nunn of Georgia, Governor Bruce Babbitt of Arizona, Governor Mario Cuomo of New York, former Virginia Governor Charles Robb, who is married to one of Lyndon Johnson's daughters (the other daughter lives in Toronto).

Most inexplicable of all: in the world's most important city, the taxis have no meters.

12

All Quiet on the Northern Front

In which it is laid out that most Canadian prime ministers come from the ruling class and that is why the Jaw That Walks Like a Man, our first working-class PM, likes the Americans so much and why he gravitates toward successful men and, also, Mila's tips for children and why there are such young wives at Sussex Drive.

Ottawa is a sub-arctic lumber-village con-
verted by royal mandate into a political
cockpit—GOLDWIN SMITH

Brian Mulroney is an unusual cat for several reasons. One is that he is the only Canadian prime minister to come from a working-class family. The Americans like to cherish the myth that any boy born in a log cabin can be president but practically all the occupants of the White House have been millionaires before entering (or, as in Mexico, certainly by the time they leave). Roosevelt and Kennedy were heirs to family wealth. Lyndon Johnson made his, by dubious means in part, in Texas wheeling and dealing. Jimmy Carter had his peanut fortune. Gerald Ford, an ordinary politician from Michigan, somehow has been transformed into a man who travels with the business and showbiz wealthy of the nation.

Eisenhower, a career soldier, was helped out by his friends, as was Reagan, a movie star and TV pitchman who thanks to his "kitchen cabinet," composed of men like Alfred Bloomingdale, has become a man of wealth. Richard Nixon easily became a millionaire, despite Watergate. (Or perhaps because of it. The fact remains that Nixon has had more votes cast for him—he ran three times—than for any president in history.)

George Bush, who wants very much to be the next president, is an oilionaire from Texas who tries to disguise his patrician New England upbringing and his Ivy League connections as a product of Yale. The knock on him is that he suffers from "terminal preppiness." Cartoonist Garry Trudeau, of Doonesbury fame, pictured Bush as "putting his manhood in a blind trust." Art Buchwald says he reminds every woman of her first husband. George F. Will, the hot columnist in

Washington, wrote that the thin, tinny sound coming from Bush "was 'Arf,' the sound of the lapdog." The camp of Jack Kemp, Bush's main opposition for the Republican nomination in 1988, immediately ordered a hundred thousand lapel buttons bearing just one word: *Arf*.

The point is that while Americans maintain the myth that their presidents come from the soil, Canadians over time have reflected their British political traditions by selecting their prime ministers from, if not the ruling, certainly the upper classes. From Laurier to King through Pearson and St. Laurent to the miserly millionaire Trudeau, Ottawa has been run by those raised to manners. R.B. Bennett ended up a lord in England.

Mulroney, who never ceases to remind us that when John Turner was dancing with a princess he was driving a truck in Baie Comeau, comes from origins that are what Americans like to think *their* leaders' backgrounds should be. His father *was* an electrician, young Brian *did* work in a pulp mill, he *did* support his widowed mother and his sisters in a Montreal apartment in his early years as a striving young lawyer.

His other distinctive feature is his U.S. connections. Not since William Lyon Mackenzie King has a Canadian prime minister been so influenced by Americans or had such close links with them. While waiting for the call from the Liberal party, King spent his interregnum in the United States working for the Rockefellers, the dominant family in the nation. As mentioned earlier, it was partly because of that experience, which resulted in a love/hate attitude toward the United States, that he later had a relationship with a president, Roosevelt—who was from another rich family—which was closer than that between any other Canadian prime minister and American president.

Brian Mulroney has been linked to the Americans since birth. Baie Comeau, far out on the lonely north shore of the St. Lawrence, was an artificial town built by the Chicago *Tribune* to supply it with newsprint. It's a trite story by now how the *Tribune*'s owner and flamboyant (and British-hating) publisher, Colonel Bertie McCormick, on his trips to the "colonials" of Baie Comeau, would pay the boy soprano Brian Mulroney $50 to stand on top of a piano and sing "Dearie." Brian Mulroney's electrician father owed his living to the fact that Baie Comeau was an American-owned town planted on Canadian soil. It is only natural that Brian would grow up thinking of Americans as friends and patrons, generous and open-hearted.

Pierre Trudeau went to Harvard, but if it had any effect on his feelings about Americans, it was in a negative direction. His studies in Paris and at the London School of Economics in London obviously were greater influences. Diefenbaker, the Western Canadian who was understandably insecure and eventually paranoid vis-à-vis Ottawa and Bay Street, was even more defensive toward Washington. Uncle Louis St. Laurent with his solid Quebec background had little interest in the United States. The worldly Pearson, with his Oxford experience, diplomatic travels, and United Nations credentials, had nothing especially against the Americans but equally did not hold them in awe or deference. Joe Clark, for all his small-town origins, was the first to point out that High River was the home of British remittance men and had actually won a world polo championship while he was growing up.

This returns us to the Life of Brian. His natural instincts make him ambitious, informal, friendly (except when crossed), and admiring of success and those who have achieved it. That's very American. There is a consistent pattern of attaching himself to personages of importance. When he was at university, he used to talk to Diefenbaker on the phone, trying to offer advice and help on how to keep Quebec in the Tory fold. He went out to Saskatchewan and became an aide for Agriculture Minister Alvin Hamilton—using that deep-dish baritone to phone in reports of Hamilton's speeches to the province's grateful radio stations. He became an acolyte of Robert Stanfield when a student at St. Francis Xavier in Antigonish, Nova Scotia.

Pierre de Bané, a former Trudeau cabinet minister who went through Laval law school with Mulroney, says as a college student Mulroney "had the maturity of a man forty-five or fifty. On the other hand, Brian missed his youth."

As a young man Mulroney became friends with two pivotal Quebec premiers, Daniel Johnson and Jean Lesage—one Union Nationale, the other Liberal. When "unknown" Pierre Trudeau entered a trendy Montreal bar in 1967 and couldn't find a seat, a shrewd stranger—Brian Mulroney—asked him to sit down at his table. Within a few months Trudeaumania hit, and Mulroney watched with amazement as fifty thousand delirious people mobbed Trudeau at Place Ville Marie. Brian then went off to lunch with an equally stunned Claude Ryan, then, as publisher of *Le Devoir*, the most powerful journalist in Quebec. Mulroney was twenty-eight.

He became very close to Robert Cliche, who once headed the Quebec NDP and was chairman of the Quebec royal commission on labour violence that first thrust Mulroney into the public spotlight. When Robert Bourassa was sent into exile and disgrace by the smashing victory of René Lévesque's alleged separatists, it was Mulroney who sent him a warm letter, encouraging him and predicting that he would rise again. Bourassa is now back in power and remains friends with the Tory he has to deal with at 24 Sussex Drive.

When Liberal cabinet minister Francis Fox had to resign after signing a phony name to procure an abortion for a lady friend, Mulroney spent hours on the phone bucking up his spirits. Paul Martin, Jr., the Montreal businessman who would like to be the next Liberal leader, was an usher at Mulroney's wedding. The prime minister wants to be liked. That is very American.

Mulroney even talks like an American. He worshipped at the shrine of Kennedy, and his stately, trying-for-posterity phrasing in his speeches and pronouncements is patterned on the phraseology perfected by Ted Sorensen, who was JFK's speech writer and wordsmith.

After he lost the 1976 Conservative leadership race to Joe Clark, Mulroney was offered the president's position at the Iron Ore Company of Canada by the outgoing boss, Bill Bennett, who was first impressed by the young man when he came around to the Bennett house to date a daughter—now married to a Liberal MP. Iron Ore was a branch-plant arm of Hanna Mining of Cleveland, and Mulroney came under the sway of the Americans once again.

He flew in the Hanna jet, he had reserved on stand-by a New York suite overlooking Central Park. His close New York business friend was Ross Johnson, a Canadian who ran Nabisco Brands, which has now been taken over by Reynolds Tobacco of Raleigh, North Carolina. Johnson's star "governmental relations" employee in New York is Ken Taylor, the hero of Tehran, whose trademark Afro cut and horn-rimmed glasses are still recognized by cabdrivers on the streets of Manhattan, whose brainy wife Pat is a top researcher on AIDS, and who would like to be the chief resident of the Canadian ambassador's pad on Rock Creek Drive in Washington.

Mulroney, on holidays, is a regular in the Palm Beach, Florida, haunts of men like Paul Desmarais and Charles Bronfman. He likes Americans. Americans like him.

Then there is Mila. The word to describe the relationship between the American political system and the Canadian political system is osmotic. We are dragged, mainly through the membrane of television, into their habits, their customs, their traditions. There is really no such thing as a "first lady" in Canadian parliamentary parlance but—because the Americans have one—an equivalent to Nancy Reagan must be found. Lily Schreyer or Jeanne Sauvé wouldn't quite do. The press and the public focus on the lady who resides at 24 Sussex Drive.

Margaret Trudeau was lots of fun, especially for the tabloids. Maryon Pearson, who was revered in private circles for her tart tongue, supposedly was the author of the apt comment that "behind every successful man stands a surprised mother-in-law." Maureen McTeer, a woman ahead of her time, was said to have lost her husband a ton of rural votes across the country by declining to take his surname. Geills Turner, who does not like scrutiny, did not last long enough to bear scrutiny.

So we are left with Mila, the Lady of the Crinkled Nose. Mila Mulroney actually loves being first lady, though she is not. She wears glitz well. Big occasions are her meat and potatoes. On the night her husband was elected prime minister, she appeared on the stage in downtown Baie Comeau wearing about her waist a huge wrap-around leather fastener that looked like the world's largest chastity belt. Voters boggled at their screens: we elected *this*? Today, as we know, every junior high-schooler wears the same thing.

Mila Pivnicki, from Sarajevo, Yugoslavia, where as we know the First World War started when Archduke Ferdinand was assassinated, is in one way similar to Nancy Reagan, in that she provides the stability for her husband's political adventures. Family is all. (In Nancy's case, husband is all.) Neither one, as Mrs. Carter did, wants to sit in on cabinet meetings. Neither one would really be capable of running off and marrying a Greek oilionaire. Each has her causes: Nancy the anti-drug crusade, Mila the cystic fibrosis cause and the Special Olympics for the handicapped.

It's strange that the youthful United States likes very much to be ruled by a man who is seventy-five with a wife whose "official" birthday indicates she is sixty-three (but whose school records suggest sixty-five). While fuddy-duddy Canada, supposedly cautious about things, has in Mila Mulroney, still in her early thirties, one of the youngest first ladies in countries where they keep count. (Is something going on here? Margaret Trudeau was twenty-two when she became the wife of a Canadian prime minister. Maureen McTeer was in her mid-twenties. Mila, at thirty-three, is the geriatric of three of our last four first ladies. It really is strange.) The United States is twice as old as Canada. At the moment, that is reflected, fairly accurately, in the ages of their two ruling families.

Despite her youth, Mila is a rock. Beneath that crinkled nose, she's tougher than Air Canada steak. Like Nancy Reagan, she probably has a stronger personality than her husband. It was undoubtedly her doing that Mulroney quit drinking. (It was his kids' nagging that convinced him to give up smoking.) Her solidity comes from her family's European professional-class roots. Her father, Dr. Dimitri Pivnicki, followed the family legal tradition by taking a law degree, then started all over again and took his degree in psychiatry.

Mila has a black belt in shopping. The joke is that her charge account at Holt Renfrew exceeds the national debt of Chad. She has just two rules for her four children: they are not allowed to say "can't" and they are not allowed to yawn at the table.

Brian Mulroney, the man who likes to be liked, sees himself in the pattern of his Irish father figure, the guy in the White House who is thirty years older. They have much in common: an infectious good humour in private, a natural desire to solve things peaceably so we can get on with the singing around the piano, a quick wit, a certain staginess, a love for the acclaim of the audience—they really like the smell of the crowd and the roar of the greasepaint.

The difference is that Reagan's personal philosophy, such as it is, is formed, set in concrete. He waffles on details, but he doesn't waffle on goals. The American public realizes that. Especially after Carter, they want a man who sets his course and sticks to it.

The Canadian public, by contrast, does not know what Mulroney is really trying to do, where he is aiming, what his goal is. There are, as it turns out, disadvantages to being so clever as to capture—without ever having run for anything in life—the leadership of a political party that obviously was about to become the government.

There are advantages, hard as it is to believe, in becoming an alderman in a municipal government, then perhaps a back-bench MP, then a junior minister, eventually a senior cabinet figure, and finally a prime minister. The advantages are that you learn that the tricks of public politics are not exactly the same as the tricks of the backroom. You learn a few things on the way up. Reagan learned a few things in his eight years as the boss of California. Mulroney has had to put in his training-bra period while sitting at 24 Sussex. It hasn't been easy. And he has a lot to learn—especially about the Americans, with whom he has so much in common.

It's Mulroney's excessive faith in American fair play that is going to get him in trouble. The Americans are bargainers. Their whole system is based on "making a deal." Because of their size and power, they usually get the better of the deal. (When they encounter something they don't like—for example, the World Court ruling against them on Nicaragua—they simply say the World Court has no jurisdiction in the matter, and they ignore it.) When Ottawa attempted to clear up the leftover anomalies in our constitutional relationship with London and make it apparent to the world that Canadians were a sovereign people, it took some twenty years of often rancorous public debate to get to the result. But the free-trade negotiations with the United States, with more profound implications for Canadians, supposedly are going to be wrapped up in two years. That is naïve nonsense.

Canada has snatched back some of its own oil and gas industry from foreigners, thanks to the flawed National Energy Policy, but Americans still have no idea of the fragile nature of Canada's cultural sovereignty. (First of all, they don't understand what cultural sovereignty means, and you can't explain it to them. When you do explain it to them, they don't understand it.) As writers and publishers, Canadians have never had more than 27 percent of the book market in their own country. In film and video distribution, 73 percent of the revenues go to foreign (U.S.) firms. In sound recording, 82 percent of the earnings are received by ten foreign firms. In television broadcasting in English, only 28 percent of all Canadian programming is Canadian in origin.

And when the Mulroney government made tentative at-

tempts to halt further takeovers in the book-publishing industry, the conglomerate Gulf & Western sent a message through
its lobbyist to Ambassador Gotlieb threatening a "scorched
earth" retaliation. God's tooth.

One suspects the "freer trade" nonsense will die in a
protracted, painful, and boring fashion—due to a combination
of American ignorance of what Canada is all about and a
growing Canadian nervousness about getting too chummy
with the elephant. In fact, some good could come out of it.
The Americans, meaning those few who are aware these
trade talks are going on, might become cognizant that the
Great White North is slightly different after all. And Canadians, the good Dr. Foth suggests, may tend to be a bit more
thoughtful about their country and aware of how it still must
be protected.

At any rate, the Mulroneyites are running in the opposite
direction to American public opinion. The mood is not expan-
sive and outward-looking; the mood is inward and isolationist.
In 1930 two veteran congressmen named Smoot and Hawley
(the former a Mormon leader, the latter a lawyer and teacher)
produced the Smoot-Hawley Act, which produced the highest
tariffs ever enacted in the United States. It touched off an
international round of retaliatory measures that dealt a severe
blow to international trade and caused unemployment and
which, many think, were at the root of the world recession.
(Both men were defeated in 1932, both died in 1941).

Reagan, who is anti-tariff, worries publicly about a repetition today because Son of Smoot is tramping through the
halls of Congress. There are some three hundred protectionist bills sitting in the hopper—most frivolous, but some
real—that reflect the American resentment at a trade deficit
that in 1984 hit $123 billion. The main anger is at Japan's
trade surplus of some $50 billion, but Canada's $20-some
billion trade surplus does not go unnoticed. Fortress America
is being constructed.

13
Uneasy Rider

In which Dr. Foth heads west and south and north and learns about the Rust Belt and the pickles in North Carolina and Kokomo and Kalamazoo and Cucamonga and why trailers travel in packs and Billy Carter's gas station and—would you believe it?—Peoria.

> *Republic. I like the sound of the word.*
> *Means people can live free—go or come—*
> *buy or sell—be drunk or sober however*
> *they choose. Some words give ya feelin'.*
> *Republic is one of those words that makes*
> *me tight in the throat.*—JOHN WAYNE as
> Davy Crockett in *The Alamo*

One cannot expect Americans to know much about anything or anyone from the country lurking on their northern border. Americans, from birth, are conditioned to think of Canada as an outpost of the Arctic. Every night, on the evening news, they are told that "a cold front is moving down from Canada" —giving the impression that everything north of Buffalo is a frigid waste, which accounts for the number of sophisticated American sportswriters who, when the Toronto Blue Jays were in the 1985 American League playoffs, phoned Canadian radio stations asking what time the sun went down, whether they would be able to exchange their money, and whether you could see Quebec from Toronto.

There is no use trying to explain that the southernmost portion of Ontario is farther south than northern California, that a place called Victoria has one of the most salubrious climates on earth, or that Vancouver, like London, has the worst weather in the world and the best climate. I have a Washington friend who is the daughter of a diplomat, writes for the *New York Times* travel section and *Town and Country*, has lived in the Philippines, Australia, and Belgium, and has asked, with a straight face, whether Canada is a very big country, whether there are hotels in Nova Scotia, and what side of the road do we drive on. There is no fighting myth. Hollywood and Nelson Eddy are incontrovertible.

Even when the facts intrude, you can't change American perceptions of Canada as a large, lonely place where someone left the refrigerator door open. Andrew Malcolm is an intelligent, curious journalist who was stationed in Toronto for four years by the *New York Times*. In fact he had Canadian parents and spent a lot of his youth in Canada. In 1985, he published *The Canadians,* based on his impressions and his experiences in Canada. The book was full of evocative examples of what Americans love when they think of Canada.

Malcolm describes a country that spans one-quarter of the world's time zones and "scattered across this area like a few specks of pepper on a huge freezer-room floor are the people." He writes of "city suburbs where bands of coyotes threaten household pets." (Seen any coyotes lately?) Of lakes and bays larger than entire U.S. states and of a forest six times the size of France.

He talks of Canada's North—one and a quarter times larger than India with fewer people than attend a New York Yankees baseball game. He tells of a country so big and so empty that it has less population density than Saudi Arabia. Of how it takes thirty-six hours of solid driving to get from Toronto to the next large city to the west, Winnipeg. (He was out by about twelve hours.)

The smallest province, Prince Edward Island, is still almost twice as large as the smallest American state, Rhode Island. Texas, the largest, would fit inside Quebec with enough room left over for Connecticut and Delaware. There is room for four Britains in British Columbia and almost three Frances in Quebec. Close to three Japans would fit into Ontario, which has fewer people than Tokyo. Our two northern territories are by themselves larger than West Germany, France, Britain, Italy, Egypt, Austria, Spain, Portugal, and all the New England and Middle Atlantic states put together. There are sixty people per square mile in the United States, as opposed to only six per square mile in Canada. And so on.

Most of it is true, of course. But false in picture. The truth is that the people scattered like specks of pepper on the freezer-room floor comprise a more urban population than the United States. It's a nice myth to think of the igloos and the traplines, but the fact is that Canadians, as a whole, live in cities. Americans, as a whole, don't. Some 29 percent of Canadians—more than one in four—live in metropolitan areas with a population of at least one million souls: Montreal,

Toronto, Vancouver. Only 8 percent of Americans—one in twelve—live in similar settings. More than half of all Canadians—56 percent—live in cities with a population of at least 100,000. Only 25 percent of Americans live in cities of that same size. (A similar myth applies to Australia, which is stuck with its "jolly swagman" Waltzing Matilda mythology—helped along by the hucksters who draw up the Qantas Airlines ads for North American consumption. Australia is even more urbanized than Canada, with 80 percent of its population huddled in a handful of cities along its shoreline.)

America is indeed a country of small towns—Norman Rockwell incarnate. As I meandered about in my car I found a country that views New York as decadent and foreign and San Francisco as wicked and Los Angeles as beyond redemption. Americans, essentially, are much closer to the soil than Canadians—most of whom can't wait to scrape it from their feet so they can move to the nearest city, be it Regina or Halifax. Check the statistics.

American towns? It comes to some of them—their fate in life—that the mere mention of the name evokes mirth. Kokomo, Indiana, knows all about that. So does Kalamazoo. And Cucamonga. The name Brooklyn used to bring sure-fire guffaws for any radio comedian. So what's it like to be a resident of Peoria, Illinois? Not very funny. How is it playing in Peoria? Not very well.

A scribe in search of the soul of America obviously must dive into the depths of the town that has symbolized the virtues of Middle America. There cannot be a more midwest city of the Midwest: sitting in the midst of a farming state two hundred miles southwest of Chicago.

It was the Watergate schemers who revived the old vaudevillian line. The Nixon tapes revealed that John Ehrlichman, the high-level presidential flunkey, predicted that the press would hate a new Nixon dodge but "it will play in Peoria." Dug out of showbiz mothballs, the slogan was part of the Watergate political strategy: to hell with the intellectuals, let's try to smoke it past the folks in the boonies.

It's a bad rap, actually, if you want to go by history. This middling burg, on the natural transportation circuit between Chicago and St. Louis, was a regular stop for national touring companies prior to the Civil War. For nearly a century, it was a thriving show town. Sarah Bernhardt, Beerbohm Tree, and Otis Skinner trod the boards here. "Will it play in Peoria?" in fact was the supreme compliment—the town was considered a tough, knowing audience.

Abraham Lincoln, from his base in Springfield just to the south, debated slavery in Peoria. (He didn't play too well in Peoria either. He lost in the local polls once by 212 votes and the second time by 190.) Now, thanks to the hand-me-down vaudeville rubric and comments of the venal Nixon schemers, weary residents of this town when asked where they are from most often reply, "Central Illinois." They're tired of the jokes.

They have another reason to be discouraged. Peoria, as the caricature of the Midwest, epitomizes the sadness that has hit the heartland of America. Industry is leaving the region; unable to pay the artificially hyped union wages or to compete in a world recession with an eager Japan, manufacturers are fleeing to a beckoning New South.

Caterpillar Tractor has its world headquarters in Peoria. In a city of 130,000, they once employed 30,000 people—before the sudden loss of its foreign markets in 1982. When the grim-faced Reaganites in Washington barred U.S. companies from bidding on the billion-dollar Soviet Union pipeline providing natural gas to Europe, Caterpillar lost a $90 million contract. Worse, the Russians, who know how to checkmate, transferred most of their bulldozer business from downtown Peoria to Komatsu of Japan. Cat had to lay off 8,000 workers immediately. Later, things got worse.

The Pabst brewery has shut down. So has the Hiram Walker distillery; it has gone to Arkansas. The pattern soon becomes apparent to an itinerant scribe who wanders the once-triumphant Midwest—now called the Rust Belt. Industry is moving south. In one year, the heartland's oil-pipe shipments dropped from 4.2 million tons to 667 tons. U.S. Steel's new $750-million seamless pipe mill is in—where else?—Fairfield, Alabama.

The mighty Midwest is a disaster. A man from Milwaukee says, in disgust, "Can you imagine! Russian tractors on our fields?" Just as former Ontario premier Buttermilk Billy Davis from Brampton used to fulminate over Russian-built Ladas on Ontario highways, this American fumes over cost-cutting Russian tractors chewing into the rich Illinois soil while Cat lays off more workers because of Reagan boycotts of Russian contracts.

The black soil of Illinois is incredibly rich, reaching as deep as twenty-five yards. The corruption in Illinois runs almost as deep. In California, the governor has some one hundred twenty patronage spots to fill. In Oregon, twelve. In Iowa, thirty-five. In Wisconsin, sixty-six. In Illinois? At least fifteen thousand patronage appointments and twice that number in the fabled Chicago ward-heeler Cook County domain of the heirs of Richard Daley.

Peoria, years ago, used to be a racy place; as a river joint it had drop-in sex parlours back in the days when it was a theatre town. John Gunther, in his classic *Inside America*, writing about municipal corruption, whisky bootlegging, and unsolved murders, called it "one of the toughest towns on earth."

Now, middle-class morality succumbs to nervousness. Alice Zook, a Peoria gym teacher for twenty years, was fired from Limestone Community High School after the school superintendent discovered that she was showing "Muscle Motion," a videotape of a Los Angeles male dance group.

The Hotel Pere Marquette is a magnificent old edifice on Main Street, completely restored after fifty years to its earlier chandeliered, deep-carpeted charm—just in time for the town to go down. "It's the workers who drink," says the discouraged woman who runs the bar. "If they don't show up, you know it's over."

Across the street the Madison Theater is "For Sale or Lease." Empty shops speckle the street. At five o'clock, the only activity is the forced exuberance of the graduating seniors of the town's Bradley University, on their traditional pub-crawl day, packing into Big Al's Saloon—advertising wet T-shirt contests and on Friday night a lone male stripper. The well-scrubbed co-eds move on in boredom, drinking beer out of the bottle because *Playboy* magazine told them to.

The Midwest, once the home of the classic halfback of our youth, Tom Harmon—the gridiron idols out of the F. Scott Fitzgerald mode—is a debilitated place. Cleveland, home of my heroes Bob Feller and Lou Boudreau, the latter the cleverest infielder of our time, is a mess, a city that despite its symphony orchestra no civilized man would enter. It is now called the Mistake by the Lake.

Detroit is a tragedy. The rich auto makers in their arrogance fled to the posh suburbs, to Grosse Pointe, to be followed by the middle-class blacks. They left a city that in 1960 was 26 percent black and became a ghetto with more than 63 percent black, dispirited and ripe for the inner-city revolution that inevitably came in 1967 with the most destructive race riot in U.S. history: 43 dead, 7,000 arrested, and $50 million in damage.

Geographer Robert M. Pierce of the State University of New York made a presentation to the Association of American Geographers in Washington, rating 277 urban areas as the best—and worst—places to live in America. (Peoria ranked twenty-second worst.)

Top of the geographer's "livability" list was Greensboro, North Carolina. The next four cities were all in the South: Knoxville, in neighbouring Tennessee; Asheville, North Carolina; Nashville, Tennessee; and Raleigh, North Carolina.

It fits in with the impressions of a foreign reporter drifting slowly by car around the United States, in search of the mood of America. One thing, as our geographer friend indicates, is clear. The South, indeed, will rise again. While the industrial North sucks its thumb in angst and pleads with the Ronald Reagan administration to set up more bars against the threatening Japanese, the New South gets on with taking advantage of its natural assets.

At the lunch counter at Woolworth's in Greensboro, North Carolina, where white businessmen sit oblivious to black labourers, there are, in a jar, kosher dill pickles the size of small salmon. There are corn muffins and ham biscuits. It's an ordinary Woolworth's lunch counter—but it's not. It was here, where the dill pickles swim, that on February 1, 1960, was launched the national drive for integrated lunch counters.

It caused a sensation then, the spark that set off the black revolution and eventually led to the many gains made by the angry minority that forms more than one-tenth of this rich and troubled nation.

In Atlanta, home of Martin Luther King and Coca-Cola, the magnificent Peach Tree Plaza boasts the world's tallest hotel, a black glass cylinder that reaches to the sky. Down the street, henna-rinsed New York matrons in purple jumpsuits roam in awe of the "lobby" of the Hyatt Regency, which is a plant-filled atrium twenty-three storeys high, featuring glass-enclosed high-speed elevators, a fifty-foot-high water fountain, and an elevated cocktail lounge with a pendulous parasol— and a parrot. The impression is rather like Buck Rogers turned loose with a Hugh Hefner budget.

Atlanta airport is the largest passenger-terminal complex in the world—so large that an automated subway moves passengers from airline to airline, instructed by an automated voice. Orwell would love it. You can't go anywhere in the South without going through this airport. The Southern joke is that "to get to hell you have to change in Atlanta."

In Nashville, home of the Grand Ole Opry, the radio stations play the Culture Club. Gone to ground outside Nashville, in the hills of Tennessee, is Senator Howard Baker, the man perceived as a future president because of his performance at the Watergate hearings. He has announced that he would not stand for reelection as senator "because if you want to run for president, you have to be unemployed" —Walter Mondale being the latest great example.

Separating Tennessee and North Carolina to the east are the Great Smoky Mountains, one of the more appropriately named terrains of our time. They are fold after fold of purple gauze; the mysterious mist enveloping the ridges gives them the appearance of a Chinese water-colour. This is the home of the moonshiners and the hot-eyed Reverend Billy Graham, golfing friend of presidents and convenient overlooker of Vietnam.

North Carolina itself is a surprising state—since colonial times "a vale of humility between two mountains of conceit," the mountains being its haughty neighbours to north and south, Virginia and South Carolina. The last census shows that it has passed, almost unnoticed, Indiana and Massachusetts to become the tenth-most-populated state, with nearly six million people living off three industries: tobacco, textiles, and furniture (thanks to the hardwoods flourishing on the moist slopes of those Smokies).

There's an incongruity here that would puzzle high-wage Canada. North Carolina has a larger percentage of its work force (35 percent) employed in manufacturing than any state— even such industrial biggies as Michigan, Illinois, and Ohio. But only 7 percent of the work force belongs to unions, the lowest share in the country.

The low wages are undoubtedly a factor encouraging industries to flee the Rust Belt for this region. Housing starts in the Southeast have risen, by percentage, more than in any region save wealthy New England. The state has been industrialized without being urbanized—one reason it is so livable. The tenth-most-populated state has no large cities. Charlotte, the largest, has perhaps 400,000 people. Greensboro has only 170,000.

"People here like to resist progress imposed from outside," says John Alexander, executive editor of the Greensboro *News & Record*. "They have their jobs in these little factories, but they like to keep a patch of tobacco on their country places and still pretend they're farmers." Eddie Knox, who was a candidate for the Democratic nomination for governor, chews 'baccy, affects a country accent, and sprinkles his speeches with references to "back home." He's a corporate lawyer in Charlotte.

The state with the hillbilly image in fact has a superb educational record with a sixteen-campus university system. Greensboro itself has five universities and colleges. One of them, North Carolina Agricultural and Technical, produced a quarterback by name of Jesse Jackson, who is still running.

The residential areas are no place for a man with hay fever. The dogwood blossoms mingle with the pink Japanese cherry trees to create a pastel scene out of *Gone with the Wind*. On the downtown streets, women actually wear skirts or dresses. It is culture shock for a visitor ODED on jeans. "It's a little dull," concedes Gina Conrad, a twenty-eight-year-old charmer who moved here from Philadelphia. "But, I'll tell you this. It's safe. Besides, where else can you still see cows from the airport?"

The South remains conservative. You couldn't buy liquor by the glass in Greensboro until 1980. The most livable city in the United States has, basically, one comfortable restaurant downtown. The state, three-to-one Democrat by registration, voted for Ronald Reagan. But the place is alive and optimistic when compared to the gloomy industrial states to the north.

The advantages go beyond jobs. The Pulitzer Prize for editorial writing, in five years, went to the *New York Times*, the *Miami Herald*, the *Wall Street Journal*, the *Washington Star*, and the *Washington Post*. The next one? To the *Georgia Gazette*, a weekly paper of three thousand circulation put out, precariously, in Savannah by thirty-five-year-old Albert Scardino. Son of a prominent Savannah doctor, he went off to the big time at Columbia University in New York, at the University of California, and at the Associated Press but decided to come home where he causes trouble and makes enemies with his tough journalism.

He is as much a reaffirmation of the New South as are the secretaries emerging from Greensboro office buildings, one white, one black, who go off to lunch together, chatting. The town that started it all a quarter-century ago and shied from the unwelcome publicity now proudly has erected a plaque, on Elm Street just off Friendly Street, commemorating the lunch counter that did it.

Farther south, on an abandoned air base outside Moultrie, Georgia, contrasting with the famous red clay of the state, sit 150 fat silver bugs, holding a convention. The fat silver bugs are sleek aluminum house trailers containing the retired rich of America who are spending their sunset years on wheels, roaming this puzzling, fascinating land.

The convention has gathered together a secret and closed society—those who can afford to own an Airstream, the Cadillac of the trailers. This is not hot-dogs-on-the-barbecue-ville. There are two-bedroom Airstreams. TV aerials sprout from the roofs. Microwaves sit inside, along with the air conditioning and the stereo tape decks.

The Airstream is known as the "land yacht." Some forty years ago its design was considered futuristic, but, like the original Volkswagen, it declined to change its bulbous aluminum styling over the decades, content in the belief that it cannot be improved upon. It's why Airstream owners, smug in their exclusivity, gather on abandoned airstrips in rallies, renewing Republican friendships and talking enthusiastically about the next rally, some months and some states far away to the north, or the west, or wherever. They travel in packs, fifteen or twenty in tandem, like automotive elephants, holding each others' tails in their trunks.

They represent the America of the mid-1980s: on the move, comfortable, and prepared to stick with what it's got—Ronnie Reagan, the "Teflon leader" to whom nothing sticks. A reporter roaming the backroads of the United States finds a population that is generally happier than its northern neighbours, works harder for less money, and is regaining its confidence.

There is chagrin over the humiliation of Lebanon and the debacle of Iran, and now there are the small fears that Reagan, who seems to get his historical facts from the *Reader's Digest,* may stumble into another Vietnam in Central America. On the whole, though, Americans seem happy with a president who appears to be cruising, foot off the pedal, through a second term.

At a confab of American newspaper publishers, I met a high-level New York fixer (i.e., consultant: the definition of a consultant is someone who knows thirty-seven positions for sexual intercourse but doesn't know any girls) and a Republican equivalent from California who steered Nixon and is now influential in the Reagan camp.

"It's very tough," conceded the Democrat, "to beat a president who has the image of being a nice guy who works hard."

"Well," laughs the Republican pro, Lyn Nofziger, "you're half right."

In Florida, where they worry about Leftists taking over the troubled government of the nearby Bahamas, a handsome steelworker named Jay says, "Reagan makes me a little nervous, but at least you know he's not going to take crap from anyone." It's the no-nonsense, simpistic approach they enjoy. Reagan is an uncomplicated man—as was Harry Truman, who has been rediscovered by Americans as a little guy from Missouri who was a giant when it came to making decisions. Reagan, however trigger-happy, is appreciated because of the contrast with the busy beaver Jimmy Carter, who cluttered his mind with arranging the schedules for the White House tennis courts and was seen eventually to be a vacillator in the humiliating Tehran hostage marathon.

The sad little town of Plains, Georgia, Carter's base then and now, reflects his sudden oblivion. It is a near ghost town, a "museum" to his peanut industry, peddling stale postcards and outdated memorabilia. Beer is sold across the counter at Billy Carter's once-famous—and still dirty—gas station. At the only café in town, Today's Special is $3.25: "Fried chicken (white meat 25 cents extra), black-eyed peas or English peas, creamed potatoes and jello." Water is served in Mason jars.

We are in the flatlands of southwest Georgia, where one is still slightly unnerved to view, in the pickup trucks ahead on the road, shotguns slung from racks in the rear windows. A visitor can only think of Peter Fonda and Dennis Hopper in *Easy Rider*, a film that defined a generation. There is a sad Faulkneresque touch to the rocking chairs and the porch swings on the verandas—filled with quiet people still watching the world go by. Great rocking-chair country.

Moultrie is farther south, close to the Florida border, the centre of hog country, which is the reason Swift's has its packing plant there, the redolent breezes wafting the nature of its business down through the pecan groves. Lloyd and Ruby Miller have been here for nineteen years, transferred down from Toronto by Swift's, on the long road from Moose Jaw, and preferring to retire here rather than repair to the offered rat race of the Chicago head office. They love it. The cheaper food prices, the climate, the lack of heating bills and oppressive winter wardrobes, the quiet charm and friendliness of the South.

The once "Solid South" has succumbed to the aw-shucks conservatism of the Teflon Man, whose aides slop in sleaze and patronage and back-scratching, but who emerges somehow clean in the public eye, the second lead who never got the girl and now never gets the blame. In Florida, in Georgia, the Carolinas, Tennessee, Virginia—the ageing movie star offers the promise of standing up to foreigners at a time when Americans (especially southern Americans who are on an economic roll) resent having to get involved in foreigners' problems.

They think—in part, thanks to his leadership—that they have whipped the recession and are coming out of it all right. They're pulling together—just like those fat silver bugs that travel in packs along the interstate freeways, content, mostly happy, and with a pride in the country they see rolling by. It's an Airstream society.

The optimism of America is striking. Outside the town of Lebanon, New Hampshire, near the Vermont border, is a roadside sign that says BLIND CHILD. It is not a makeshift sign erected by concerned parents. It is not some municipally erected warning. It is an official U.S. highway sign, as official as STOP and YIELD and BRIDGES FREEZE BEFORE HIGHWAY.

There is a blind child in the village. Therefore, motorists are warned. It signifies, as much as anything, the difference between Americans and Canadians. The difference is a generosity of spirit. The difference is an open-heartedness and a general optimism.

By contrast, Canadians remain just as inward-turning and stoically calm as they've always been. They are more gloomy economically, more dispirited, and more pessimistic than their American neighbours. As the continent claws its way out of a recession that so hurt its pride, Americans feel the worst is over. Canadians fear there may be more to come.

Americans have regained their confidence. Canadians don't seem very enthusiastic about their prospects or about any of the two or three younger alternatives available to them as eventual long-term successors to Pierre Trudeau.

What one finds in the United States is a country much farther on the road back to self-assurance than is Canada, more aware that it must lower its expectations in the new post-OPEC world and go back to its virtues—elbow grease and stubborn determination.

Arlene Chapman is vice-president of the Mascoma Savings Bank in Lebanon, a town on the banks of the Connecticut River, which along its length from Canada to Massachusetts, provides the border between New Hampshire and Vermont. With some thought, she says, "I'm with Reagan—despite his age. I don't know why anyone would want to be president until they're seventy-eight. But he really did make us feel proud to be Americans again."

It's a feeling I run into again and again. America, the land that rewards winners so profligately and punishes losers so cruelly, supposedly had never "lost" a war until Vietnam. It has never forgiven the earnest Jimmy Carter for the long agony of the Iran hostages, and then with twenty-twenty hindsight blamed him even more for his naïve boycott of the Moscow Olympics, thus spoiling their games and giving the Russians four years of delightful waiting before announcing they would boycott the Los Angeles Olympics.

Americans have strong views. While Canadian licence plates plead for wildflowers or keeping the world free from litterbugs, the New Hampshire plates state: LIVE FREE OR DIE.

New Hampshire, of course, is the land of Yankee virtues. You can have any colour house you want, as long as it is white. With green shutters. The gas-station attendants, like Calvin Coolidge from neighbouring Vermont, have a total vocabulary of six words. The most interesting history lesson of all is to discover, in the small towns on the back roads, that the cemeteries are twice as large as the towns. This is where Daniel Webster was born, outside Andover. There is now a motel named after him. (Just over the Georgia-Florida border, over the Suwannee River, is the Stephen Foster Memorial Highway. Did Stephen Foster really want a highway named after him?)

I digress. Americans love success while Canadians are suspicious of it. I lunch at the 21 Club with Ken Taylor, still the hero of Tehran to New Yorkers. During the course of the meal, no less than eight of the staff of the expense-account oasis, from manager to waiter, come over to pay obeisance to

"Ambassador Taylor," a man who in the Big Apple will forever bear that title—just as presidents forever retain the title of president and just as Canada, nervously not knowing what to do with Taylor-who-has-too-high-a-profile, instead let him sign up with an American corporation to sell and sell.

The generosity in America extends in all directions. The salesmen in Atlanta stores shout a greeting to a shopper as he enters. "Y'all come back now," drawled in a Southern pit stop by a waitress you will never see again, has an evocative ring. At the Indy 500, seventy-nine-year-old Catherine Holtsclaw has been renting out parking space on her lawn for race fans since 1932. She never sees the race, nor is she interested. Most of her yearly customers, from coast to coast, have grown old with her and she spends her time thanking her "guests" for their Christmas and birthday cards.

A nation twice as old as Canada has twice the confidence— and twice the weaknesses. The inevitable result of a losers-winners society crowds the papers every day. In Lake Worth, Florida, the leader of his Neighborhood Crime Watch program, Roy Knapp, buys a pistol at 9:00 A.M. and, apparently despondent over his impending divorce, murders his estranged wife at 9:27, drives home, and fires a bullet through his temple.

In Chicago, thirty-seven-year-old Charles Hunt, driven berserk by family problems and the loss of a job, kills his wife, two children, and two neighbours, wounds four people and fires twenty-four rounds at police before officers shoot him dead in a parking lot. It is almost daily reading to a drifter wandering by car through the richest society in history.

It is no real surprise, therefore, that the phenomenon transmitted by television crosses the border and that a confused young man invaded the Quebec legislature with a submachine-gun and could easily have killed the premier and half his cabinet had he not been so confused about the date. America dominates us, by example, and eventually we imitate its excesses.

An intelligent young man tells me that British Columbia mass murderer Clifford Olson would not even have made page one in the United States, so sated are they by excess. It is true. But just as we do not have their problems, neither do we enjoy their optimism. They think they are on the road up, niggled as they are by suspicions that no one loves them anymore. That's probably correct—the fate of all those at the top of the mountain. Canada, by reflection, sulks—unaware of its potential.

14

The Trip through Bountiful

In which our hero takes to the road in search of the American soul and finds the Indy 500 and a New York disco, the San Francisco gay parade featuring Sister Boom-Boom and the Saudi princess who wanted a nip and a tuck and a lift in Palm Springs.

*An American will tinker with anything he
can put his hands on. But how rarely can
he be persuaded to tinker with an abstract
idea.*—LELAND STOWE

The beer spray hits my bald spot as the people, two rows
above, pop open another can of Budweiser. It is 9 A.M. under
the Indiana sun. The men in front of me, with bellies like
Sumo wrestlers, have stripped off their T-shirts and are
digging into the fried chicken plucked from their coolers. As
he goes by, driving an 84 Eagle powered by a Chevy V-8, a
man by name of Steve Krisiloff tries to negotiate the first turn
at more than two hundred miles per hour and smashes into
the thick concrete wall, delighting spectators just three feet
away behind heavy wire mesh. He demolishes his leg and
spins three hundred yards up the track before coming to a
smoking rest. The automobile is the Kleenex of American
culture.

To understand that society, an outsider must come to the
ultimate disposal unit, the Indianapolis 500, where the American dream of excess comes to fruition. It is easy for a
foreigner glimpsing bits of this ghoulish pastime on television
each May to regard it as a sop for slobs, a beer-filled blowout
for those waiting to see an eight-car pile-up involving the
incredibly brave and ultimately foolish drivers who are, in
fact, astronauts of earthbound traffic.

Each year, faster and faster they go, reducing to split
seconds the allowable margin of error that spells the difference
between death and fortune. Those who watch them—on this
particular qualifying day, two hundred thousand bodies—are
there to view the incessant American desire to push beyond,
to seek the limit, to see how far the best of them can go.

178

"Them" means Americans as a whole. The car is simply a metaphor for a nation.

The Indy 500 is merely a measure of the American imagination, an extension—a foreigner realizes for the first time—of the country's daring, and an indicator of why the United States differs so much from Canada. It was Henry Ford who put a car within every American's reach. And who, it turned out, changed the nation's sexual mores by giving unmarried couples the miracle of a mobile bedroom. The car changed America's life. And so bred both contempt and worship for it.

The contempt is seen in the Kleenex concept: on the median of a Chicago freeway an expensive, chrome-laden auto has been abandoned (perhaps only out of gas) and it is now stripped of wheels and perhaps even engine, as surely as a body is stripped of flesh by piranhas. No one comes to the rescue of broken-down cars; they are like beached whales, abandoned and forgotten.

A visitor, driving through hills of sylvan bliss, suddenly has his eyeballs assaulted with the insult of a sea of sardine cans, squished vehicles once the pride of Detroit. Now we have, in the land of Henry Ford, the Ronald Reagan administration (supposedly the champion of unstructured free enterprise) imposing a quota on Japanese cars that have shamed America's pride. In Mount Clemens, Michigan, sales manager Steve Rouse of Mitchell Buick Sales is allowed some fifty-five Hondas a month—when he could sell twice as many. "I've got a file full of orders on every model, every colour, every transmission."

It's why there is all the editorial-page criticism of the boggling incomes paid to the Reagan-protected executives of Detroit, the boss of General Motors calling a press conference to explain why he was worth $1.8 million in salary and bonuses in the past year. And it's why Americans flock to the Indy 500—twenty-seven days in May that will culminate in a Sunday of glory, and quite possibly death—because it is the ultimate expression of their mobile society.

Indianapolis itself represents that. Six major highways converge on it, and the city is within a day's drive of half the population of the United States. Indiana is the ultimate conservative Midwest state: threatened in the north by mighty Chicago, in the south by Kentucky, in the west by Illinois, and in the east by Ohio. It is headquarters of the American Legion and birthplace of the John Birch Society—even though it produced both Hoagy Carmichael and Cole Porter, the latter born on the banks of, where else, the Wabash.

It is WASP culture supreme, but these people are proud of the Indy brickyard. It is their culture, not New York's culture, not San Francisco's, not New England's. The gates open (this is just for the qualifying rounds) at 7:00 A.M. and the beer is being swilled from the roofs of cars in the parking lots as the sun rises.

But it is not just the men in tattoos with the stickleback combs protruding from the rear pockets of their jeans who sit around me, pale white bellies exposed to the searing sun. At my Airport Hilton, winning Chevrolet salesmen and their wives are treated to an Indy driver after dinner. For a fee, he explains that the oversize tires must be inflated to different pressures, since the outside tire travels slightly farther over the five hundred miles of the race. Tour buses from the hotels take a collection of sixtyish executives in expensive sports garb to the track, which, one always assumed, attracted only Bunkeresque caricatures.

A lead sports page story in the *Indianapolis Star* contains paragraphs like this: "By comparison, the aluminum turbo Chevy V-6s at the Speedway use a straight through single pin to which two connecting rods are attached, and the ensuing uneven firing as the crank rotates through 360 degrees tends to create vibrational moments." It is all Chinese to me but, through the twenty-seven days of May, it is vital esoterica for those involved.

Since this is only a qualifying day, only the aforementioned two hundred thousand bodies are present to watch lone car drivers dare records and death. That is twice as many people as attend any Super Bowl or Grey Cup. On Indy Sunday, the number reaches five hundred thousand.

The steeply banked track is two and a half miles around. At two hundred miles per hour, a car takes just forty-two seconds to cover it. Your neck cannot swivel fast enough to follow the cars as they roar by. In the "Snake Pit" on the infield of the first turn where the camper trucks gather, four cops travel in a pack, looking for potential trouble. "Half of these people won't even see the race," confides the man in front of me. "They'll be that drunk. That's where you'll see the nude girls dancing on the tops of the campers. And the rest of them mooning the crowd."

Danger is catching—and enticing. The famed Mario Andretti,

who almost died in a crash several years ago just fifty yards past the starting line as the race began, watches as his twenty-two-year-old son Michael qualifies at 208.285 miles per hour. Canada's finest driver, Gilles Villeneuve, died in a European Grand Prix race when his overly adventurous style, predictably, sent his car airborne for seventy yards when he ran up the back of one of his competitors; his young brother Jacques, qualifying here at the two-hundred-plus-miles-per-hour speeds never attained by previous Indy drivers, smashes into the wall and is carted off to doctors who find him talking deliriously "in two languages." The finest sportswriter in America, Jim Murray, says the starting-line command should be: "Gentlemen, start your coffins."

The speed is a narcotic. The worst crash, deliciously delineated on the front page of the *Star*, involves blond and handsome Michael Chandler, who is unconscious for ten days while his mates race on, desperately trying to achieve the qualifying speed. He is worth millions, since his father is Otis Chandler, chairman of the *Los Angeles Times*. His father weeps and nurses cheer in his hospital room when he finally comes out of his coma and says, "Hi, Dad."

The red rescue trucks rush to each crash as moths to a flame and the blonde in the stretch top behind me screams, "That was great! We actually saw a wreck!" The Indy 500 is a metaphor for a nation that likes to push to the edge. It is at the heart of the American dream: faster, higher, more risk— the risk worth the reward.

Indiana is thought of as Rubeland, but to go to the edge of the frontier, one must go to New York. There we find the new line in the primitive, the cutting edge of the outrageous, the latest thing in simple, unadorned ideas. The most adult city of all thinks like a child. To illustrate this, we discover the number-one ticket in town, a joint called Area. The inmates like to die to gain entrance. They trade their mink slacks and their Sony Walkmans for an invitation. In New York, there is room for only one focus point and Area occupies that field— for the moment.

Area, hidden down on the tip of Manhattan past SoHo, is a disco disguised as a "nightspot." I thought the word nightspot went out with the Copacabana (as a matter of fact, I thought discos went out with Studio 54) but apparently not; I must have nodded off. What makes Area the hot ticket is that the club is redesigned regularly. Every month the place is tarted up with a new theme, new performers, audiovisual displays, and something called dioramas.

Partners Darius Azari, Shawn Hausman, Christopher Goode, and Eric Goode have hit upon the perfect formula for the Kleenex Society: disposable environment. The world is too much with us, late and soon. The solution is to throw it out with the garbage. All is possible once you own a garburator.

Late at night the mobs are gathered, slavering, outside the door of Area, beseeching the security guards to let them enter the forbidden territory, the cachet that will make them heroes at the office water cooler next morning. The doorman, like some feudal lord guarding the moat, gazes disdainfully over those beneath the salt, admitting only favoured customers, celebrities, and perhaps a Boy George look-alike or two. Inside, the ladies must sign receipts for their fur coats at the cloakroom for fear imposters will memorize the ticket numbers and make off with the loot.

The place looks as if someone has gone berserk with a Styrofoam gun. We are, one takes it, into a space theme. The most innovative nightspot in the world looks like the face of the moon or Sudbury, Ontario. I don't know what other theme months look like, but this one comes out as dried hair gel. The cacophonous music pounds out, threatening the stability of the Styrofoam as bodies of all possible sexes, most of them dressed in what looks like what a chic person would wear while sleeping on a park bench, writhe on the dance floor.

People who spend their days and earn substantial incomes in the communications capital of the world want nothing more than to retreat to a converted warehouse where it is useless to utter a word. This is called trashing your daytime environment. Some dance, but most watch and roam about, satisfied just to be there. In other years, it was the aforementioned Studio 54, where Bianca and Margaret and Andy hung out. Then it was Elaine's, where Woody Allen ate and where people who liked to watch Woody Allen eat came to watch, while pretending to eat.

In one room of the Area, on a raised mound, is a young lady all done up in a plastic and cellophane space costume, leaving a lot of room for ventilation. Her curly white spun-candy hair falls to her waist. She shoots customers with a blinking laser gun. Her lips are painted purple. She chews gum. (One would think it impossible to hire for this job anyone who did not chew gum.)

She resembles, whether intentionally or not, the bimbo played by Jane Fonda in *Barbarella*, the movie in which she is made love to by a robot. This was before Jane became a feminist, but we did not stay around long enough to determine if Area carried on the imitation. Once one has seen enough successful New Yorkers trying to look like punk rockers, one grows philosophical and feels a need for Chinese food.

Area offers an entire new approach to life. If you don't like your surroundings, simply simulate new ones. We already have those instant-tan parlours, where pallid city dwellers can take a long weekend and return to the office with what looks like a Caribbean-bronze physique. Political parties do this all the time. The Liberals are already talking behind the curtain about replacing John Turner, as if that would repair the intellectual sloth that has enveloped the party over the past two decades.

There are a few places left that have never heard of Area, abhorring even skin-deep simulation. Buckingham Palace is one, where every week or so another little Victoria or Albert is produced, completely togged for touring New Zealand.

Much of the rest of the world is an Area. One can see the day when an enterprising firm, following Azari and Goode, will arrange to save a failing marriage by coming in and doing a whirlwind redesign of the apartment that is providing all the angst; busy little men with spray guns and plastic props doing it while you're at the supermarket. Area, being in Manhattan, is on the frontier. The Kleenex Society marches on.

Everybody misunderstands Andy Warhol (for which you can be forgiven). He did not say that everyone in the world eventually will be famous for fifteen minutes. What he did say, and there's a difference, is that everyone should be famous for fifteen minutes. It was an empathetic statement. As one who has tasted the bitch goddess Fame, who has seen its good side, Warhol was saying that it would be nice if the cleaning woman and the bus driver could be famous for just a quarter-hour. Like, share the wealth. He has too much fame to bear, so why not lay off the action a little? Spread it around, like a layer of peanut butter.

Bernhard Hugo Goetz instinctively recognized the theorem. Goetz automatically qualified as the first fifteen-minute famous person of 1985 when he calmly plucked a silver-plated revolver from wherever one conceals silver-plated revolvers and plugged four young black men on a New York subway. He was the instant hero of the post-Orwellian year. To make it complete, he actually did the deed three days before Christmas (a Scrooge with a Saturday Night Special?), but his fame expanded on the exponential scale as 1985 advanced.

Bernhard Goetz filled a yawning vacuum in American fifteen-minute-celebrity time. The genre began with Lee Harvey Oswald and continued on down the line with the demented young men who gunned down Bobby Kennedy and John Lennon and who almost got Ronald Reagan.

One of them, I believe his name is Hinckley, still makes the papers every few weeks with his incessant and boring complaints from prison about his human rights and his demands to get back into the Warhol Law. One supposes we could go back to John Wilkes Booth, the mediocre actor who couldn't cut it on the stage and therefore achieved immortality by killing Abe Lincoln.

Goetz filled the obvious void because he became a "good" gunman. The baddy category had become crowded. He became the vigilante hero of a city terrified of crime, in a nation plagued by crime, because when the four youths approached him, supposedly demanding money, he methodically shot each of them, paralyzing one of them. Money poured in for the Goetz defence fund, graffiti sang his praise, and editorials analysed him.

Goetz was sent to one of the most expensive private boarding schools in Switzerland, near Lake Constance. In a *Sound of Music* setting of equestrian and ski trails and flower-decked homes in an old cathedral town, Bernhard spent his high-school years, at $12,000 in fees per annum. His father made a fortune in Florida real estate. Young Goetz became an electronics specialist, his company's president and sole employee, a man who had received top-secret CIA clearance because of his work with nuclear operations, a "genius" according to one of his clients. According to the camp followers of the media who wanted all the entrails on this reverse hero, he was the gunman who done good.

One niggle remains. What would a successful thirty-seven-year-old man be doing riding the New York subway, domain of all the lower species of mankind? The answer, probably, goes back to 1981 when Goetz was mugged in a subway station while carrying a thousand dollars worth of electronics equipment. The suspect, a sixteen-year-old, was kept in criminal court for two and a half hours. Goetz was detained for six hours. Three weeks later he spotted on the street the youth who mugged *him* mugging another couple, aided by a companion.

Something obviously snapped. Has this well-fixed young bachelor—kind to his neighbours and his neighbours' children, according to his neighbours—been stalking through the subways ever since, waiting his chance to apply the Warhol Law? One would think so. One of the young layabouts (who is nineteen, oldest of five children, all but two of whom were fathered by different men, a ninth-grade dropout, a cocaine addict, father of a child by a mother he no longer lives with) claims the sharpened screwdrivers with which he and his companions were found were merely for breaking into video machines—their daily living—and that they had only asked Goetz for five dollars as panhandlers so they could plug into the machines.

Other witnesses say these products of a subhuman South Bronx housing project that looks like bombed-out Beirut were already running away when Goetz took aim with his stubby handgun and carefully shot them all. It little matters, in the age of Warhol.

Celebritydom is both precious and trivial. Warhol and, say, Frank Sinatra can testify to the latter. They have more than they can handle, would willingly farm out some of their fame to the marshmallow salesman who makes it into the record books by punching out Billy Martin in a bar some forgotten night. Sinatra is one who has had more fame as a person and a womanizer and a puncher-of-photographers than he really needs, when all that was required was the deserved acclaim for his tonsils.

There are some—Michael Jackson, Carl Lewis, Madonna— that fame kills off before they can really establish their right to it. Before they become immortal, they become bores. Joe Clark was famous for nine months, an extended state of euphoria that will haunt him the rest of his life. Jimmy Carter has never recovered from his brief moment in the sun, rendered that brief partly because of the intrusion of a Warhol example even more tragic: Billy Carter and his beer

can and his contract with Libya. History is very sloppy—and
very unforgiving. Bernhard Goetz is one month's Warholism—
throwaway fame.

No one in New York understands San Francisco—or vice
versa. The first time the Democratic party held a convention
in San Francisco was in 1920, and it was a memorable
occasion. Prohibition had come in five months earlier, and
despondent delegates arrived fearing the worst. As H.L.
Mencken explained in a celebrated essay, the wholesale booze
sellers of the nation usually used these events (much as the
hookers of the Pacific Northwest headed to "Sexpo 86" in
Vancouver) to ship in the dregs of their cellars—"rye whisky
in which rats have drowned, bourbon contaminated with
arsenic and ptomaines, corn fresh from the still, gin that is
three-fourths turpentine and rum rejected by the West Indian
embalmers."

Instead, they were stunned to find that San Francisco
Mayor James Rolph, Jr., had laid in carloads of the finest aged
bourbon and provided it, gratis, to the delighted visitors.
There followed, in Mencken's words, "a series of days so
sunshiny and caressing, so cool and exhilarating that living
through them was rolling in meads of asphodel."

Reporters Ring Lardner and Irvin S. Cobb got so swacked
on the brew that they nominated each other from the floor
and actually got a few votes. When the band leader swung
into "The Sidewalks of New York," someone in the gallery
began to sing and suddenly the whole audience was bellowing
out the familiar words. The band leader switched to "Little
Annie Rooney," and someone started to dance. For a solid
hour the band danced through "The Bowery" and "A Bicycle
Built for Two" and the rest while the entire convention
waltzed in the aisles, halting all proceedings until a young
man named Franklin Delano Roosevelt could nominate Al
Smith.

Dear dead days, several eons in ambience away from the
artificial staging in an underground TV studio that masquerad-
ed in a summer sixty-four years later as a political convention.
We know that these events are staged mainly for the folks at
home, but San Francisco proved indeed that this was Orwell's
1984. Moscone Center, scene of the non-event, resembles a
subway tunnel with both ends blocked. It is built into the
ground like a root cellar, constructed in the belief that it

could withstand a California earthquake. The main floor is a
city block long, and the ceiling is only thirty-seven feet high,
giving the impression you are living in the crawl space of
your basement.

The solution, for the TV networks—since the affair is run by
them—was to turn this dismal exhibition hall into a TV studio.
Since boxing matches are now held in tiny arenas of obscure
towns (the audience required only as a backdrop for the
camera work), Moscone Center had to be converted into a
suitable setting for Dan Rather, Tom Brokaw, and the classy
Peter Jennings with the sweating delegates as filler material.
Walter Mondale is only a politician; in a society that keeps
score by salary, the TV announcers are the true stars.

CBS's Rather is the $6-million anchorman, and ABC forces
some $900,000 annually on Jennings, the Ottawa high-school
drop-out. At the parties the fighting is to see Gloria Steinem
kiss Bella Abzug, Walter Cronkite chortling with Art Buchwald,
Mike Royko taking on Roger Mudd. Steinem, who recently
celebrated her fiftieth birthday, looks almost forty. Abzug is
passing out cigars labelled "It's a girl!" in honour of Mondale's
vice-presidential pick. Buchwald says, "If I make fun of
Ferraro, I'm a sexist. If I make fun of Jackson, I'm a racist. If
I make fun of Mondale, no one will read me."

There is a reason delegates dash to the curb when the
limousines of the media celebrities rush by. These particular
Democrats, representing the party that is supposed to help
the oppressed and the hungry, are fascinated with material
success. Just as John Turner required the votes of fewer than
two thousand Canadians at the leadership convention to
become prime minister in 1984, there are fewer than four
thousand voting delegates to pick their presidential nominee.

Twenty-three percent of them are college graduates (compared with 8 percent of Democrats nationwide), and an
astonishing 49 percent of those went to graduate school. At
the 1980 convention, 26 percent of the delegates had an
income of more than $50,000. Here in San Francisco 42
percent top $50,000—compared with 5 percent of Democrats
across the country. These people paying $165 a night for a
pullout bed at the Hilton are not exactly your basic scrabbling
Americans.

Perhaps God in Her wisdom is trying to punish them.
Their choice got down to a ministerial three: Mondale was
the child of a preacher, as was his wife; the mercurial Jesse

Jackson is a minister of the cloth; Gary Hart is a product of
Yale divinity school. You could sense all the salvation was
beginning to grate. The stars of the show turned out to be the
earthy New York governor, Mario Cuomo, and Geraldine
Ferraro, the housewife from Queens who recalled in wonder
that eleven years ago she was spreading peanut butter for her
children.

With 12,500 members of the TV industry and 5,000 scrib-
blers from the pencil press overshadowing 4,000 delegates,
San Francisco had to display its own spectacular vulgarity. On
Sunday afternoon there was a one-and-a-half-mile-long parade of 100,000 gays and lesbians, including the transvestite
Sister Boom-Boom and her Order of Perpetual Indulgence—
men dressed as nuns. Missing, however, was the local lesbian
motorcycle group that bills itself as Dykes on Bikes.

On the final night, as Senator Teddy Kennedy introduced
Mondale—on the same platform from which his son, who lost
a leg to cancer, gave a fine speech the day before—there was
at the same time in the parking lot outside the convention a
"Rock Against Reagan" concert featuring a group called the
Dead Kennedys. Not a mead of asphodel could be found.

There is nothing San Francisco abhors so much as the tacky
people straight south. In the Sweat Suit Society all the world
becomes a gym. One cannot venture out on the street unless
clad in the technicolour garb that football players used to
wear to practice. Hostesses at swish parties clothe themselves
in formless athletic outfits with monograms initialled above
the heart.

The Sweat Suit Society is southern California, the leader of
the globe in the avant-garde, and a visitor dressed in *passé*
shirt and trousers feels like someone from another planet, an
intruder wearing a period-piece costume. In the land of
leisure, sweats are the fashion, and the streets resemble the
universe's largest schoolgirl pyjama party.

In Japan, custom dictates that two segments of society are
pampered and spoiled. The first is the children, who are
treated like exquisite, impeccably attired dolls. The second is
the old, who are considered to have paid their dues and are
allowed eccentricities denied the rest of a disciplined society.
The back streets of Tokyo and other Japanese cities are
speckled with old people in their pyjamas, wandering
undisturbed since they feel more comfortable that way.

Southern California has now taken this admirable custom one step further: the entire population is permitted to jog the byways and to entertain in sweat suits, garments that were invented for a weight lifter. So the world progresses.

In Palm Springs, the golf and pastel-Fortrel capital of the globe, all the talk is of the Saudi princess who decided on a facelift from one of the reigning cosmetologists in what is the resort's fastest-growing cottage industry. No dummy, she first arranged a little market testing. To ensure the finished results she shipped over two ladies-in-waiting to have *their* nips and tucks and lifts and repair work done so she could examine and evaluate the finished product. Such is the sacrifice of a lady-in-waiting.

There are the ubiquitous "walkers" who walk neither dogs nor horses but are so labelled for their profession of escorting ageing, wealthy, and lonely ladies to the spas, dining holes, and parties that enliven the desert and irrigate it with money. To be a walker is an honourable calling—the only requirement of the youngish male is that he can perform some of the dances of yesteryear, back to the minuet if possible, and divest himself of the sweat suit for the evening and replace it with a tie and preferably not Hush Puppies.

There is encountered in La Jolla, the upper-class enclave attached to San Diego's balmy shore, a happily married lady, holder of a master's degree in theatre, who decided to pick up some spare change by establishing herself as "Mrs. Clean Jeans"—a toney cleaning woman for the high-rent set. She was inundated with offers, the only problem being that there was nothing to clean, the homes of her clients being impeccable when she arrived.

What her clients wanted was a sympathetic ear, and so she set out on her rounds each week, never lifting a finger but listening with empathy to the problems and woes of those left home to vacuum their credit cards. She is the first known example of a char to practise as a shrink.

An explorer bent on research into the mores of the advanced civilization discovers Puppy Playschool, which is an apprenticeship for those canines headed for dog obedience school. One can't take it all in one leap. This is a prep school for the fire-hydrant set. In the same vein—or perhaps a larger one—there is therapy for those missing a green thumb. It is a place where one takes one's plants when leaving on a trip, where one is taught how to restore ailing plants, how to talk to plants, and to coach them back into verdant life. The name of the institution: Plant Parenthood. So the world progresses.

There are the doggie psychiatrists. There are the caterers who now, offering to arm a party with food and firewater, also supply on request a clutch of as many as thirty psychics, who will then take on guests one-on-one, leaving them by midnight with their futures mapped, their souls cleansed, and their body rhythms corrected. With your canapés comes your karma.

There is, at Rancho Mirage near Palm Springs, to the embarrassment of the Bob Hopes and Frank Sinatras, the world's largest gay resort. For those of bent persuasion, the Lost World Resort is a secure haven, attracting disciples from east and west, north and south.

There is the chagrin of the local matrons that the annual Frank Sinatra charity concert just before Valentine's Day costs a mere $1,000 a plate. A year earlier, the foray by Ol' Blue Eyes, who has had more farewell concerts than Harry Lauder, rang the bell at $10,000 a couple. The disgraceful comedown this time round indicates that the black-tie and long-gown economy is definitely in trouble.

There are the Snowbirds, some twenty thousand Canadians who flee to the forty-five golf courses of the California desert over the year-end holiday period, listening each day to a radio broadcast from Medicine Hat, Alberta, which lays out the horrific temperatures back home. There is nothing like viewing misery from afar.

Someone who spends as much time of his life as he can snuggled down in the bottle-green mountains of British Columbia, covered with a lush rug of Douglas fir and cedar, at first finds the mountains that encircle the playpen of Palm Springs rather starkers and uninteresting. The Santa Rosa mountains, which provide a protective barrier against the smog of Los Angeles, a hundred miles away on the ocean, and the San Gorgonio range, which slopes away to the east, are bereft of trees, naked as a jaybird.

After awhile, watching the slant of the sun throughout the day—a major project for a man whose brain is idling in neutral—one begins to understand the ever-changing beauty of this desert oasis and the advantages of having mountains that are undressed. Because they do not have that deep-pile carpet of foliage, the solid angular rocky crust beneath absorbs and plays with all the shadows and angles of the boring sun, modulating each hour and changing the face of the slopes from pink to mauve to purple, a wall-to-wall mural that changes from dawn to sundown.

Amazingly, an expert on mountains realizes that nude can be more interesting than clothed. I will always, hereafter, think of B.C. mountains as shy brutes afraid to come out of the closet and brandish their skeletons.

Luckily, Palm Springs itself suffers no such inhibition. As a collector of esoterica, a chap who always envisages himself as a startled visitor from Mars alighting among strange earthlings, I find this the mother lode. Here is *Homo sapiens* in self-caricature, an old black-and-white 1940s movie walking around in technicolour, where the colours don't quite match and one must wear sunglasses even at midnight—not because of the lights but because of fear of cornea damage from the hand-painted ties of the male guests.

Bob Hope's home is a giant dome that somewhat resembles a curdled pancake that droops at the edges. It hovers high on a nearby two-thousand-foot mountain, and is proudly pointed out by the locals to gawking tourists, as proof, one supposes, that Hope's architectural tastes are as antediluvian as his telegraphed jokes.

There is in Palm Springs a Bob Hope Drive, a Frank Sinatra Drive, and a Fred Waring Drive. Gerald Ford, the president who fell down a lot (an achievement surpassed only by his public pardon of Richard Milhous "I am not a crook" Nixon, the well-known crook), wanted a drive named after him since he hits people on the head with golf balls at the Thunderbird Country Club, but local sentiment squelched the idea. When Fred Waring has a lock on the white-shoe generation, mere ex-presidents finish down the track.

Tony Riccio, a restaurateur buddy of Sinatra's, holds superb private dinner parties for the Palm Springs glitterati, all of whom are legends in their own minds. His lady, devastatingly cleavaged, bejangled, begowned, and blonde-blonde, is Jeannine Monique Levitt, who in a previous incarnation was married to one of the gillionaires who built Levittown on Long Island, the model for all American suburbia.

Jeannine, Mr. Levitt having expired, hit Palm Springs like a female version of Maurice Chevalier. (Like Chevalier, like Laurier LaPierre, like Jack Webster, she shrewdly discovered that a sexy, slightly incomprehensible accent affords one a great advantage among local yokels. Her listeners are left to breathe deeply, ingesting the perfume from the cleavage—which is not only better than cocaine but cheaper—and nod dreamily.)

Jeannine Levitt, who was raised in a convent in France and graduated to a New York tycoon, soon had Palm Springs at her feet and decided to run for mayor—the first time this refuge of pastel had ventured the dangerous prospect of actually electing—as opposed to appointing—its chief magistrate. Like a visionary from a nunnery, she appeared among these Philistines in Lacoste tennis shirts. Her main platform was a proposal for moving sidewalks, an obvious head start for those attempting to make their way home from the golf club after an afternoon with deadly margaritas, which have claimed more victims than rattlesnakes in this parched mecca. Alas, she became the victim of vicious gossip, which strokes this community as crabgrass strikes more mundane locales, and tearfully withdrew. The first democratically elected mayor in Palm Springs' peroxide history turned out to be cowboy-hatted Frank Bogert (could you make it up?), beating out one John Weston, who takes the society photographs.

Oh, it is all so vile. There is the tacky, disgraceful lawsuit between the two prime plastic surgeons, Dr. Mohammad Reza Mazaheri and Dr. Borko Djordjevic, as to who *actually* did Betty Ford's facelift. There are those disgraceful four-colour ads taken out in *Palm Springs Life* by the swinging dentist Dr. Charles Block, with all that chest hair and all those gold chains, inviting all affluent widows in for deep breathing. One observes and one sees the future of Western civilization.

As an antidote, there is a trendy afternoon tearoom in Los Angeles called Trumps. On a Saturday afternoon it is filled to the corners with a sweet-sixteen party, prematurely aged teenagers down from the Beverly Hills hot tubs, dressed according to *Vogue*'s latest advice on how to look like twenty-two-year-old miniskirted hookers. Dripping tweed and envy, the stage mothers, overseers of two dozen incipient Brooke Shields, hover nearby. One looks into the tea and weeps. Listen to California. California is your future.

15

The Good, the Sad and the Ugly

In which are examined those who are thrust into the headlines and who happen to include a kind journalist and a dead teachernaut and a crooked president and a crooked lawyer and an idealist and an ego masquerading as a businessman.

Look, you have to have a little faith in people.—MARIEL HEMINGWAY *in Manhattan*

The dominant players in American life dominate the continent as well. Pierre Trudeau, in explaining why it was hard to resolve an American-Canadian treaty over fishing borders, said, "Fish swim." American personalities also "swim" across the unprotected and unprotectable border. In whatever field, their clout and fame leap that border. There is no defence. Their celebrities are exportable.

Joseph Kraft, friend and admirer of Trudeau, was the most respected Washington columnist of his era, the only heir to the mantle of Walter Lippmann, a fixture in many Canadian papers. Christa McAuliffe captured the imagination of a nation, both before and after her death. Ralph Nader invented consumer activism and became an international symbol. Richard Nixon invented high-level crime, a beacon for all small-time crooks. Lee Iacocca, in saving Chrysler, saved Canadian jobs—but mostly his own ego. Roy Cohn, a Joe McCarthy aide, helped pave the way for the death of Canadian diplomat Herbert Norman. These are characters that define America.

It's a cliché by now to assert that Americans worship success; Canadians are suspicious of success. Americans adore heroes. Canadians like to poke holes in them. The spotlights that attract the stars in the United States also burn them unmercifully if they falter or fail—from Nixon to Elvis and Janis and Jimi and Marilyn to some of the Kennedys. It can be a quick ride up and a quick ride down. Canadians are cautious of the escalator ride. They prefer the stairs. It's hard to imagine any of the following people existing in Canada.

The Journalist

A soft snow was falling, adding to the drama of the occasion, as the establishment of Washington conducted one of its rituals. The funeral of Joseph Kraft, the most intelligent journalist in town, was held in the Washington Navy Chapel, set among the spare trees and frosted grass in the better part of the capital—on Nebraska Avenue—well away from the White House he seldom visited. The long black limos created gridlock and the TV paparrazzi eagerly filmed the sombrely dressed guests who shuffled under the marquee, somewhat like the cops' cameramen at work at a Mafia wedding.

Those present, you see, were the well-dressed, well-blessed, well-educated Washington liberal elite—the people who are in control of this town's society but who no longer run its government.

Joe Kraft, a fine man with a fine mind, died in early 1986 because the demands of his excellence exceeded the limits of his body. Despite two heart attacks, he refused to slow his frantic schedule; he thought there was too little time to pursue the things that could never be reached. The eulogizers at his memorial service agreed he was a "driven" man. He knew it. They knew it. His family knew it. I saw him several weeks earlier at a party, cheerful—and grey—as always. He died at sixty-one.

What was so piquant, if the word can be used, about this gathering was that it represented a Washington that no longer exists. The Democrats have lost four of the past five presidential elections. The White House is now run by a Hollywood actor who is controlled and financed by Orange County real-estate millionaires and rock-ribbed reactionaries from the Sun Belt.

Joe Kraft, in contrast, was the last of the intellectuals to speckle the Washington media scene. A New York Jew who translated Japanese in the intelligence service during the war, he wanted the mantle of Walter Lippmann, the only journalist who became a world figure through his famous column and his celebrated personal contacts—and influences—with presidents and princes. By eerie coincidence, the last piece Kraft wrote before his death, which appeared that very week in the *New Republic*, was a typically thoughtful appreciation of a new volume of the selected letters of Lippmann—the man he wanted to be.

Secretary of State George Shultz, Mr. Reagan's token, sat in the first pew, left. Alexander Haig, trying for the exposure that makes a presidential candidate, could only make third row, right. Ambassador Allan Gotlieb, who declares openly that it was Joe Kraft introducing him into the "Georgetown set" that *made* the Canadian embassy in town, was one of the ten ushers (and the only foreigner), as was *Washington Post* editor Ben Bradlee.

Paul Volcker, head of the Federal Reserve Board, ambled in without a coat. The Georgetown minks coagulated. What we had was the glory of what was past. The cashmere melted with fur that melted with the Ivy League camel-hair coats, *mit* pearls, *mit* diamond-stud earrings.

The eight speakers, including *Washington Post* chairman Kay Graham, Senator Patrick Daniel Moynihan, and former White House counsel Lloyd Cutler, praised an unusual man who, as one of them said, proved that nice guys don't necessarily finish last—this nice guy finished **first**.

Joe Kraft, along with being the only successor to Lippmann, was a genuinely nice guy. At parties, he spent time with a Canadian columnist who was of no use to him. One of his stepsons said that while one of Joe's regrets was never having won the Pulitzer Prize, "equally important to him was the cancellation of *McHale's Navy* reruns." Cutler told how Richard Nixon bugged Kraft's Georgetown house to learn the names of his White House leaks—while Kraft continued to write about Nixon without animus.

New York Times columnist Anthony Lewis, who in his writing attempts to but does not succeed in emulating the Kraft erudition, said before the standing-room-only crowd of some five hundred Georgetown-based heavies that Joe "was something almost unknown in journalism, a genuine intellectual. As a rule, journalists have a short attention span. Joe was a singular exception to the rule. He brought to all his work a long vision of past and future." All true. Joe Kraft is dead. But part of the sadness apparent in the Navy Chapel, with the soft snow, was for an era that also was dead.

The Astronaut

Christa McAuliffe wasn't brilliant, graduating seventy-fifth out of 181 in her high school in a Boston suburb, but she had something special. Her new parish priest in Concord, New Hampshire, Father Dan Messier, says he looked down at his flock one Sunday and was struck by one face that was beaming and full of life. It was Christa McAuliffe, whom he had not yet met.

She was just twelve when she watched Alan Shepard become the first American in space. Two decades later she wrote to NASA: "I watched the Space Age being born and I would like to participate." That's how she became the teachernaut.

She was an all-star softball player, sang in the glee club, and played Sister Margarita in the senior class play, *The Sound of Music*. This was a girl right off a *Saturday Evening Post* cover. She married Steven McAuliffe when they were both twenty-one—they had dated since they were fifteen-year-olds in the same high school. She worked as a waitress in a Holiday Inn to put him through the prestigious Georgetown Law School. He is a former New Hampshire assistant attorney general who now is a civil-rights lawyer.

She wasn't quite the stereotype of the New England Republican. She was a union activist, and as a president of a local teachers' union, she battled loudly in a town-hall meeting to raise the teachers' minimum wage above $10,000—and won. The thirty-seven-year-old mother of two small children was among the eleven thousand U.S. teachers who applied for the space shot. In her history courses, she talked about ordinary people—"good people who lived and worked in our history and who you never hear about"—as opposed to kings and politicians and generals.

When she climbed into the Challenger space shuttle, she weighed the same (one hundred thirty pounds on five feet five inches) as she did in high school. She took on board her nine-year-old son's stuffed frog, Fleegle.

And so we have, a day later, the schoolchildren of Concord and their parents gathered in St. John the Evangelist church for a memorial mass for the woman who was going to make this "the schoolchildren's shuttle."

The lofts over the altar are jammed with TV cameras, movie cameras, still cameras, and photographers shoving and jockeying for position against the backdrop of the stained-glass windows. The aisles are alive with cameramen, peering over the shoulders of mothers looking at their prayer books. The whir of tape-recorders and the *click-click-click* of the cameras nearly drown out the struggling voice of Sister Irene Turgeon, principal of 240 children here from the St. John's parish.

Jimmy Breslin, the famed New York columnist, arrives looking rumpled and crosses himself, no doubt at the apparition before him. There are three stuffed animals below the altar.

"How'd you guys feel when it happened?" Father Messier asks of the kids in that accent made so familiar to us by John Kennedy. The sisters, prim and stark-eyed at the scene before them, attempt to shoo burly cameramen from the aisles. The tape-recorders whir.

Messier beckons from the pews a tousled blond boy with a dishevelled tie, holds him aloft, hugs him, and declares, "That's what God does, he hugs us." The cameras in the choir lofts go into a frenzy of *click-click*s. "That's the TV clip for tonight," a magazine reporter mutters.

Father Messier, in his white robes adorned with the words "God is Light/God is Love," introduces his stuffed animals: Zak, who is yellow; a homemade monkey doll, and a white rabbit. The sisters are fighting a losing battle in the aisles against the Chicago Bears linebackers disguised as cameramen. The parishioners are dismissed and leave, looking bewildered. The media mob makes a dash for the altar.

There, seated on the red carpet, looking like David Letterman, is Father Messier, dishing out interviews: "There was so much invested in Christa. When she stepped on that shuttle, Concord was stepping on that shuttle." Outside, the TV crews have commandeered the Exxon station across the street to get the best shots of the church's steep New England spire. On Main Street, the visiting TV camera and radio crews search futilely for an uninterviewed resident.

Inside St. John's, the cameraman cries to the sound man: "Get the priest!" On the red carpet of the altar, the stuffed monkey is trampled underfoot. He died, one supposes, in the same cause as Fleegle.

The Idealist

There was a mild little cheese-and-cracker party the other night at the Library of Congress. Ken Dryden, the classiest goalie ever, was there. Tom Berger, the former judge who changed forever the future of the Canadian North, was there. And Ralph Nader, who's been wearing the same shapeless black suit for twenty years, was there. The party, in fact, was in his honour, a twentieth-anniversary party.

It was not in honour of that horrible suit, but because this was the twentieth anniversary of the publication of a book that changed America—and, therefore, the world. Its name was *Unsafe at Any Speed,* and it invented the idea of the consumer as someone with some right to challenge the people who ruled commerce and who were guilty of venality and lying and cheating.

It has long been my boring contention that when the history books are written the two Americans of this era who will survive will be Rachel Carson (who in her book *The Silent Spring* alerted the world to environmental disaster) and Ralph Nader. Just as Canadian history books will recognize the seminal figures of Walter Gordon and Pierre Juneau.

There were some four hundred bodies at the modest affair, including members of Congress and past and present members of Nader's Raiders—the group of idealistic young lawyers and volunteers who have been drawn over the years to this ascetic crusader who still lives in a studio apartment and dresses as if he were in competition with the bag ladies who speckle downtown Washington.

That's why Dryden was there. While he was superbly performing his duties in the Montreal Canadiens' net and finishing his law degree, he spent some time as an ill-paid raider for Nader. Berger was there because Berger likes underdogs, and especially underdogs who become successful overdogs, which he and Nader have become.

Michael Kinsley, who once used to work for Nader and now is editor of the influential *New Republic,* says quite flatly that no living American is responsible for "more concrete improvements in the society we actually do inhabit." This bachelor recluse did more than singlehandedly invent the issue of auto safety. The book, a surprise bestseller that wiped out the kiss-and-tell memoirs of movie stars on the book lists, led to a whole run of federal safety legislation—which in turn gave rise to the era of consumer activism.

Example? One day this passenger arrived at Vancouver airport for a flight to Saskatoon on CP Air, a trip that had been booked months in advance. As it happened, CP Air (as airlines regularly do) had overbooked the flight, and they informed me I was slightly out of luck. The fact that my hosts in Prince Albert already had set out on a futile one-and-a-half-hour drive to Saskatoon to meet me didn't much concern the people at CP Air. They had overbooked.

My only alternative, it turned out, as an Air Canada flight to Regina and a four-hour drive through a snowstorm to Prince Albert. CP Air could offer nothing but its apologies. I've never flown with the airline since.

By contrast, on a USAir flight from Washington to Toronto, the airline found itself two seats overbooked, quickly arranged accommodation on another flight and—as compensation—gave me a free trip to any city on its United States routes. The difference? Ralph Nader, who has forced into American law the provision that airlines that take the risk of overbooking must provide compensation.

We wouldn't have no-smoking sections in airplanes today— separating the rude from the tasteful—if it were not for Nader. We wouldn't have such things, now regarded as common sense, as seat bealts, padded dashboards, collapsible steering wheels, and shatter-resistant glass. *Unsafe at Any Speed* altered this continent to a cynical and rapacious car industry—particularly General Motors with its rear-engine Corvair—that put chrome and profits ahead of safety and human lives.

A Senate committee long ago documented how General Motors' hired guns tried to find out dirt about Nader's private life and cast aspersions—nudge, nudge, wink, wink—on how he was a bachelor who had no girlfriends.

Nader, says his admirer Kinsley, is "the classic zealot" —paranoid and humourless. But, observes his former employee, reasonable people don't move the world. Everything comes full circle. Nader, with his narrow lapels, pointy shoes, and skinny ties—his uniform before and since he became famous—now resembles a rather seedy version of those prancing mincers on *Miami Vice*.

But it was he who alerted consumers—meaning me and thee—to our rights. He woke us up to the fact that businesses, secure in the belief that there is a sucker born every minute, thought they could turn out schlock and equipment built for planned obsolescence. Nader taught us that we did not have to take that anymore.

He established that we didn't have to buy cars that were

designed as instant coffins—the commercial equivalent of razor blades in Halloween apples—and that we could extend that thinking to everything else in the marketplace.

He's put in a good twenty years, and the GM private dicks no longer chase him. He is a nut, in the best sense, and we all should salute him. Particularly American industrialists, because by his truth he has made them more honest. They would never admit it, but the shambling guy in the bad suit has made them, in the end, more credible.

The Businessman

One of the endangered species of our time is the politician. Meaning the traditional type who makes his living at the arcane art, who goes through the apprenticeship and works his way up the system, hoping for the top job. What he sees now rather confounds him. The president of the United States, the most powerful man on earth, is not a politician at all but an amateur imported from Hollywood. No hard slogging through the committee rooms, no learning the rules of the game. Bingo, the chap vaults in at the top.

And so we have, looking forward to 1988, all the talk about Lee Iacocca, the man from Chrysler, as the next man in the White House. If an actor now, why not an auto maker next? Americans, of course, revere success (Canadians are nervous of it) and Iacocca is the hottest thing around.

His book, *Iacocca,* is the bestselling non-fiction hard-cover in history. In its first six months of publication, the book sold more copies than Chrysler sold cars. He's made more than $5 million on it already. He was paid salary and bonuses of $1 million in 1984 by Chrysler after he led it to a profit of $2.4 billion, which was more than the company made in the past sixty years put together. He gets three thousand speaking invitations a year. He does his own commercials for Chrysler. Every time he opens his mouth he is instant headlines. All he has to do is agree to run.

In addition to the fact that Americans like Iacocca—with his brash, yappy ways and his new wealth—they like the idea of reaching outside politics for their leader. Aside from Reagan, who had one brief stop in California, they have done it in recent years with Dwight Eisenhower, plucked out of his jeep and converted into a president more popular than all those practising politicians—Jack Kennedy and Lyndon Johnson and Richard Nixon and Gerald Ford and Jimmy Carter—who followed him. Ike, like Reagan, was liked because he gave the impression he wasn't really on the politicians' side; he was on the side of the people.

Canada, when you think about it, rather likes the thought also. Pierre Trudeau's appeal in 1968 was that he wasn't really a conventional politician, didn't really take politics seriously, and claimed he didn't really want the job. Brian Mulroney was picked as a future prime minister by his party before he had ever stood for office in his life. He was preferred over Joe Clark, who bored people because, like John Diefenbaker, he had only one interest in life—politics. John Turner was picked as a prime minister, however short-term, by the Liberals because it was felt eight years away from Ottawa had cleansed him.

It doesn't really matter what these popular outsiders believe in—it's their personalities that get them elected. Old Soldier Eisenhower was the first person to raise a warning about the military-industrial complex. To this day Pentagon generals and admirals award defence contracts to favoured firms like General Dynamics and Rockwell and then, on retirement, surface on the same companies' boards of directors.

Reagan, crying he would slash government spending and waste, has now run up the largest deficit in American history. Mulroney, who was going to abolish patronage, has merely perfected it.

Iacocca is the most loved businessman in the United States, hailed as the man whose smarts saved Chrysler from death. In fact, he is more than a bit of a socialist. His company was saved only because Washington bailed him out by guaranteeing $1.5 billion of Chrysler's borrowings. He's a strong advocate of government involvement in the great American free-enterprise system—an involvement that has just mucked up the whole farm economy. He put the boss of the United Auto Workers on the Chrysler board of directors.

Like Reagan, he has already done his apprenticing on television, the essential political medium that such intelligent men as Walter Mondale and John Turner, strangely, underestimate.

We don't know if he knows anything about the world outside the borders of the U.S. of A. But that didn't hurt Reagan, who on his first trip to South America remarked to his surprise that they were all individual countries. Or Nixon, who bounded down his aircraft steps to greet effusively "the people of Ireland," only to discover too late that he was in Iceland.

We will not worry about such things when the inventor of the Mustang, subject of every high-school dream, rules the White House. A mamn who knows just how much chrome will melt the consumer's heart is perfect to judge how much smarm should go into a speech and how many dollops of hypocrisy would make a budget recipe bake just right.

Reagan is essentially a salesman, a pitchman for ideas fed to him by his kitchen cabinet of bronzed millionaires in California. Iacocca is a salesman too, the perfect choice for the modern brand of telepolitics where illusion is all and the man who can't talk in thirty-second chunks is dead at the polls.

The mocking posters about Tricky Dicky Nixon, with his black jowls, used to read, "Would You Buy a Used Car from This Man?" Well, now we have a new-car salesman, a chap who made a fortune from planned obsolescence by convincing the public that it is a patriotic duty to purchase a new chariot every three years. The Gipper is going. Why not the Quipper to follow?

The Crooked President

On the tenth anniversary of Watergate I marvelled in retrospect at Richard Nixon's supreme contempt for his country. The power and the dignity of the capital meant nothing to him; he placed a "third-rate burglary" above it, and he corrupted the highest office in the land for two years while slipping and sliding in grime. He cared nothing for America. He cared only for Richard Milhous Nixon.

Well, he ain't done bad. The man who had less than $500 in his chequing account on the day of his resignation is now a millionaire. He lives in a fifteen-room, million-dollar mansion in a plush retreat in New Jersey, across the Hudson River from Manhattan. He still gets $119,000 a year in pensions and $300,000 in government expenses.

cbs paid him $500,000 for the privilege of an interview. He made a $1.5 million profit on his last real-estate move. His books are best-sellers, even though they are always self-serving, telling some of the truth about the press, some of the truth about government, but never the truth about Richard Nixon.

He was Tricky Dicky soon after he started out in politics in California, smearing an opponent with allegations about being a Red, and he never changed. That unctuous smile continued to reek of insincerity. And his insensitivity was so great that on leaving the White House by helicopter that August day in 1974, he held his fingers aloft in the victory salute. It was his own version of the finger, he was telling the American people that he was still right, that all those charges were unfair and unjust. He has never apologized to this day, never admitted he was wrong.

Instead, he is taken by limousine to lunch each day at exclusive restaurants such as the 21 Club or Le Cirque, to dine with bank presidents, the furtive Henry Kissinger, the furtive Alexander Haig. He has visited eighteen countries since his disgrace and in all but two has been welcomed by the heads of state. How soon we forget.

He was the first American president to flee office under threat of impeachment; he condoned law-breaking and then lied and covered up the crimes; a dozen of his closest aides were imprisoned. And yet he is now a terribly respectable member of American society. He is on the cover of *Newsweek* (the Democratically inclined newsmagazine got him on its cover first, presumably to zap the Republican inclined *Time* a pre-emptive strike). The national magazines print excerpts from every new book in which he passes down his vast wisdom. The Chinese still hold him in high regard since he opened Peking to Washington at last—years after Trudeau and Ottawa did, one might add. Certain foreign governments can't understand why what he did was wrong, since to them his crimes were child's play.

It's been revealed that he quietly briefed Reagan before the president went to the vital Geneva summit. The important people of America are still glad to seek his insights, to cove his anecdotes. Although the Republican establishment doesn't think it seemly that he be seen at their national conventions, they still dine with him.

Nixon believes in the Talleyrand maxim that "it is worse than a crime, it is a blunder." He maintains Watergate will be a mere "footnote" in history books. He regards it as just an error in tactics. If he had destroyed the tapes, everything would have been all right.

What he chooses to ignore is that Watergate was simply the logical extension of the Nixon personality, the belief that once in power anything is permissible—as long as you don't get caught. The secret bombings of Cambodia were okay as long as he didn't have to admit they happened. The wiretaps, initiated by the devious Kissinger, were okay, as were the break-ins, because the boys in charge were smart enough and arrogant enough to know they'd never be caught. The vile comments about Jews and Italians in the privacy of the Oval Office were okay because only the boys—and the tapes—were listening. As the late Joseph Kraft, the syndicated columnist, said, "He was a crook through and through, a complete cheat."

The feckless Gerald Ford, his head pressed firmly against the Peter Principle, pardoned Nixon after Kissinger blackmailed him by saying that Nixon was contemplating suicide. Nixon's partners in crime, after tarrying briefly in jail, are now respectable and well fixed. John Mitchell, who, when he was attorney general, the highest law officer of the land, lied and cheated like any car thief, still wears expensive suits and meets with Nixon regularly. Charles Colson is a born-again Christian and can be seen on television regularly, his pink face emanating sincerity of the same calibre that protested his Watergate innocence. Gordon Liddy, the man who used to hold his hand over a flame to prove how tough he was, still justifies the group's conclusion that Washington columnist Jack Anderson would have to be killed because of the leaks appearing in his column.

Jeb Magruder is out of jail and he too has discovered God. Ehrlichman writes books about mystery and intrigue, for which he is eminently qualified. Haldeman is back in California as a hotel president and at last account hadn't missed a meal. The slimy John Dean, who ratted on his boss and therefore earned only a short time in the slammer, is still on the college lecture circuit, clean of collar and still tacky around the edges. Dwight Chapin, Nixon's appointments secretary who supervised the "dirty tricks" sabotage projects, has been publisher of a Chicago magazine called *Success*. Beautiful!

What they don't understand—and what the slippery Tricky Dicky never understood—is the tremendous patriotic faith Americans place in government: his betrayal of that faith stunned them.

The fact that Nixon and his cohorts were practically all lawyers was the most outrageous of all. If they had been grasping businessmen—or piano movers or chiropractors—it would all have been so much more understandable. But the men trained in the law, appointed to uphold it, descended to the level of grafters and petty thugs in their desperation to save their own reputations after they had used the White House as a home for crime. That was the ultimate insult, and that is why Nixon and Watergate will always be more than a footnote in the books. The man who was given the greatest majority in U.S. political history did not take inspiration from that victory; it moved him to further contempt for those who elected him. He had even more power, so he could abuse it even more. He was a crook and remains one.

And Frank Wills, the security guard who discovered the break-in at the Watergate complex and triggered the whole thing? He was caught shoplifting a pair of running shoes in a Georgia department store four years ago, spent fourteen months in jail, and now lives with his mother. The banal continues to the end.

The Lawyer

God must **love** the common man, so goes the saying, because She made so many of them. Considering how many there are of them, it is amazing what they put up with. With their numbers, you would think they could fashion rules and laws so that the very uncommon people could not stick it to them. We had before us an example of a very uncommon chap who not only stuck it to the common folk but revelled in it, boasted about it, was completely contemptuous about the whole matter. He was a charmer, this guy, one of the most despicable men you would ever want to meet.

You remember Roy Cohn? He was one of the two nasty little lawyers who were Senator Joe McCarthy's henchmen some thirty years ago when that unprincipled unprintable was terrorizing innocent people (including Herbert Norman) with his Commie-bashing witch hunts. (Cohn's cohort was G. David Schine, a millionaire's son. Since the two of them and Senator McCarthy were all bachelors at the time, playwright Lillian Hellman dubbed them, "Bonnie, Bonnie, and Clyde.") The McCarthy hearings were televised, offering the first example of the power of the tube, and revealing to the public what a bully and headline-grabber McCarthy really was.

Lurking in the background in every shot was the intense, fanatical face of Roy Cohn.

By the 1980s, Roy Cohn had gone from the fierce young Red-hating lawyer to the social lion in New York who got his picture in all the slick magazines. When he threw parties, the limousines disgorged the likes of William F. Buckley and Calvin Klein. He wore thousand-dollar tailor-made suits from Dunhill. He wore two-thousand-dollar Cartier watches. He lived in a thirty-three-room townhouse on the Upper East Side. He had a house on Cape Cod, next door to Norman Mailer's. He had a villa in Acapulco, a condo in Miami Beach, a twenty-foot motorboat, and a forty-two-foot yacht.

There was one unusual thing about Roy. He did not pay taxes. Or his debts. He didn't really believe in democracy at all. He was a cheat, a millionaire who had hidden all his wealth, a man who was welcome at the White House at a time when President Reagan was talking about tax reform.

The latest records show that Roy Cohn owed some $3,187,381.10 to the Internal Revenue Service of the United States. That represents unpaid taxes for the years 1959 through 1970, plus 1974, 1976, 1977, and 1983. Roy tended to be forgetful. He owed $487,879.75 to New York State in unpaid taxes and interest. Plus $64,221.42 to New York City. Plus such tidbits as $258.10 to Tiffany's, dating back to 1971. Plus $5,621.84 to New Jersey Airways over an unpaid bill dating to the 1960s. In all, the man who lived the life of a Saudi sheik owed $5,220,039.34.

The way he operated is best illustrated by the Steinthal affair. Some twenty-five years ago, Martin and Augustus Steinthal decided to sell their parachute-making company to the Lionel Corporation, which makes toy trains. The deal specified that the brothers were to receive $800,000 worth of Lionel stock—which brought humongous tax benefits to Lionel and therefore its chairman, one Roy Cohn.

Roy was so enthusiastic about the deal that he guaranteed to compensate the brothers personally if the stock dropped in value. Unfortunately, however, Roy somehow never got around to registering the shares owned by the Steinthals, the Lionel stock did a nose-dive, and by the time the brothers were able to sell their holdings the shares were worth $247,000 rather than $800,000. They sued Cohn for the difference.

That was twenty-five years ago, and *Steinthal vs. Cohn* is still in the law courts. The brothers have long since died.

Their sons and heirs are still pursuing Cohn, since $631,932.85 ain't chicken feed. That's what a New York judge in 1964 ordered Cohn to pay the Steinthal family. The judgement grew over the years, with interest, and now totals $1,166,305.84.

It was back in that era, apparently, that Roy hit upon the idea of being a public pauper. As he had testified in the Steinthal case, he had no chequing account. He had no savings account, no stocks, no dividends, no safety-deposit boxes, no mortgages. He travelled in a chauffeured Rolls-Royce or Bentley. He lived in a six-storey townhouse, but you couldn't find his name on the ownership papers. The house was estimated to be worth $4 million (the *New York Times* reported in 1967 that he paid $325,000 in cash).

After a four-year battle, the state Supreme Court in Manhattan finally disbarred him for "dishonesty, fraud, deceit and misrepresentation." It found, among other things, that in 1975 Cohn had entered the Florida hospital room of dying multimillionaire Lewis Rosenstiel, founder of the Schenley Distillers empire, while the senile eighty-four-year-old man was semi-comatose and drugged, and held his hand to sign a document naming Cohn a co-executor of Rosenstiel's will after falsely telling him that the document dealt with his divorce. The signature, produced in court, "looked like a child's version of a football play."

Cohn was the senior partner in Saxe, Bacon & Bolan, which has such clients as New York Yankee owner George Steinbrenner and "Fats Tony" Salerno, but Cohn insisted he was merely a "contract employee." The law firm picked up most of his tabs. Everything was in someone else's name.

This was the man who in the 1960s was three times indicted, and three times acquitted, on such minor little charges as bribery, obstructing justice, extortion, and blackmail. This was the same man who since Reagan came to power was often seen at the right Washington black-tie dinners and balls. He was on the board of a half-dozen conservative foundations and lobby groups, which have so much power these days under the Reagan regime. When in Washington he stayed at a fashionable row house on Capitol Hill which, you guessed it, was not registered in his name.

This was the kind of man who could survive in America and who absolutely thrived under the Reagan philosophy, which has been described as free enterprise for the poor and socialism for the rich. The president had trouble early on getting support for his tax-reform plans. Little wonder, when the public saw among his White House guests such creations as Roy Cohn. In August 1986 the lifelong bachelor died at age fifty-nine. The *New York Times* reported that the death certificate listed causes of death as "dementia" and "underlying HTLV-3 infections." Scientists believe the HTLV-3 virus is the cause of AIDS.

16
Trading Faces

In which Dr. Foth exposes those who left the Great White North for the Almighty Buck and why we are better off for it and why there are so many Canadian reporters working for American TV, which needs cannon fodder, and then there is Sitting Bull and Louis Riel, to boot.

The Canadian is usually a happy man. Life sits lightly upon him; he laughs at its hardships, and soon forgets its sorrows. A lover of roving and adventure, of the frolic and the dance, he is little troubled with thoughts of the past or the future, and little plagued with avarice or ambition.—U.S. historian FRANCIS PARKMAN

Something that has bugged me since puberty (Ronald Reagan was then making *Desperate Journey*, with Errol Flynn, Raymond Massey, and Nancy Coleman) is the envious-sycophantic "Canadian-born" tag that the press of Canada has always pinned on expatriates. Let a waitress from Medicine Hat make it big in Hollywood oaters some eons later and she forever is dubbed "the Medicine Hat-born" actress.

This soul has had it up to his kaboom with "Moose Jaw-born" Art Linkletter and "Penticton-born" Alexis Smith and "Winnipeg-born" Deanna Durban. So Walter Pidgeon spent a few early days in Montreal? Who cares? So Raymond Burr was originally from New Westminster? Or Yvonne De Carlo from Vancouver, along with Jack Benny's wife? Does it really matter anymore? How long can one go on living off "once-were" tags?

So Moses Znaimer has decided to move to California? Good luck to him. So Johnny Aylesworth and Frank Peppiatt weren't appreciated at the CBC and took their sitcom talents to Los Angeles, along with Alan Hamel and the rest of them? Lorne Greene? Paul Anka? Rich Little? Well, they made a trade off—gaining sunshine and more money and giving up the considerable advantages of living in Canada. No big deal. Everyone makes his own choices in life. Just save us the to-the-death tags on where their parents stopped off in a motel briefly. Let's grow up.

John Kenneth Galbraith, now professor emeritus at Harvard, has always been a big hit in the United States, not only because at six-foot-eight he is even larger than this tall population but also because his ego is equal to his height. His line that "modesty is a highly over-rated virtue" describes his brilliant path through life. (Dizzy Dean said it another way— "It ain't bragging if you done it"—but they are soul mates.)

Galbraith, author of *The Affluent Society* and twenty-one other books, has been an American for more than forty years, after being an unlikely graduate from the Ontario Agricultural College. He once explained that "in those civilized days" it was felt by some that "responsible citizenship did not involve an exclusive commitment to the political life of Canada. Canada might be a mother, but Michigan was a mistress"—an intriguing metaphor.

Canadian elections, as he explained to his American fans, are on no fixed schedule and can come spring, summer, or fall, and occasionally even winter. "American elections, then as now, were always in November. This was after the crops were harvested in Canada and the seasonal migration to the assembly lines had begun. Accordingly, a man could vote in Canada in the summer and, by courtesy of the Detroit Democratic organization that assigned registered names, possibly from the local funeral directors, in Michigan in the autumn. No thought of corruption was involved. Men wished to have the best people in office in both countries. I have never understood why one's affections must be confined, as once with women, to a single country."

My favourite Galbraith story comes from his book *The Scotch*, which recounted his boyhood in rural Ontario. "It was summer and I was deeply in love," he wrote. "One day the object of my love, a compact golden-haired girl who lived on Willey's Sideroad, a half mile away, came over to visit my sisters. They were away and we walked together through the orchard and climbed onto a rail fence which overlooked a small field between our place and Bert McCallum's. Our cows were pastured on the second-growth clover in front of us. The hot summer afternoon lay quiet all round. With the cows was a white bull named O.A.C. Pride, for the Ontario Agricultural College where my father had bid him in an auction. As we perched there the bull served his purpose by serving a heifer which was in season. Noticing that my companion was watching with evident interest, and with some sense of my own courage, I said: 'I think it would be fun to do that.' She replied: 'Well, it's your cow.'"

When Pat Carney, Canada's next finance minister, and I were at the *Vancouver Sun* together, we once made an appointment to talk with Galbraith in a stateroom on a B.C. Ferry travelling from Vancouver to Victoria. Carney was encumbered by a large and bulky cast and explained that she had just broken her arm. "I doubt it," Galbraith instantly replied, the suggestion being that we had an elaborate tape machine hidden therein. When present at dinner parties at the Gotlieb residence in Washington, he always dominates, wiping out such considerable egos as Robertson Davies.

The Americans, and their best-seller lists, have recently discovered Davies. They like him because he seems British—in style and even more in person, the Canadian who is more British than the British themselves. They also increasingly like Margaret Atwood, because she seems tougher (i.e., stronger) than their top feminists. Especially since Gloria Steinem, once the exemplar, has become the constant companion of multimillionaire Morton Zukerman, late of Montreal, a Harvard law graduate who made a fortune in New York real estate and now wants to be a media tycoon as owner of *U.S. News and World Report,* the "third" U.S. newsmagazine. He is advised by his guru Harold Evans, the little Welshman who hit the heights as crusading editor of the London *Sunday Times,* and then came to his downfall as editor of *The Times* of London in confrontation with the Australian bully, Rupert Murdoch. Evans is married to the bright and beautiful Tina Brown, the Brit who as editor had made *Vanity Fair* into the hot magazine on the U.S. market by, among other things, explaining to boggled American readers that Prince Charles has turned into a wimp because he is "pussy-whipped" by Shy Di. I disgress.

Anthony Burgess once said, "Marshall McLuhan and John Kenneth Galbraith are the two most famous Canadians the United States has ever produced." Unlike Galbraith, McLuhan became famous without leaving the country. I once took a class from the great man, while I was attending the University of Toronto on a newspaper fellowship kindly supplied by the Southam group, for whom I did not work at the time—and in fact did not join until a good seventeen years later.

McLuhan's celebrated seminar, which he held one night a week, drew puzzled and fascinated advertising men from downtown Toronto, engineers, wordsmiths, and others who were sure they were onto a genius but not sure exactly what the-medium-is-the-message man was saying.

For the first few months, I didn't have a clue what he was talking about. One day I confessed my confusion to a chap called Easterbrook, who ran the university's political science department. "Don't bother your mind over it," he advised. He had known McLuhan since the age of seventeen in Winnipeg; they had gone through the University of Manitoba together and were lifelong friends. "Sometimes," he said, "I get on his wavelength and I think I understand it all. Then he's gone again and it's months before I can reconnect and figure out what he's saying." I felt much better, and relaxed.

It was an American, of course—Tom Wolfe in his New Journalism phase—who first made McLuhan famous, asking in a celebrated magazine article, "What if he is right? What if he is the most important thinker since Freud, Einstein and Darwin?" McLuhan, like Galbraith, liked his American celebrity but, unlike Galbraith, stuck with his Canadian roots. (Another proof of Dr. Foth's Lorne-Greene–Paul-Anka theory, which states that the one who stayed became a more influential thinker on the world scale than the one who went away.)

There is the great beef in Canada that the Yankees dominate our culture. Basically that is true; we are swamped with the junk, from *Dallas* and *Dynasty* and beyond, popular Pablum designed to numb the mind. There is, however, one factor largely overlooked. It is that Canadian faces—pristine, pure, and unsullied—are moving more and more into prime spots on American television.

The latest example was Mr. Suzanne Perry, who moved into a half-million-buck slot with a Los Angeles station that wants to make him into a superstud. Keith Morrison (also known as Teeth Morrison and described by his new L.A. boss as "Doll Face") started in February 1986 as anchorman of KNBC, the network's lucrative southern California station, which pulls in more than twelve million viewers.

As the second-ranked boob-tube show in the area, it draws more viewers an evening than The Teeth drew as part-time host opposite Barbara Frum on *The Journal*, the pride of The Holy Mother Corp. Keith Morrison, at $500,000 basic, husband of the beautiful Suzanne Perry, who along with being very intelligent used to be a press secretary for Mr. P. Trudeau, has been hired by KNBC director Tom Capra, who just happens to be the son of Frank Capra, the Hollywood director of such old classics as *It Happened One Night*. You remember?

Morrison, the son of a preacher in Saskatchewan (where all the great ones come from), is only the latest in the breed. As you watch ABC news every night, you hear the suave tailoring and classy mid-Atlantic accent of Peter Jennings, the high-school drop-out from Ottawa who started as a New York anchorman—as third in the raitings behind Dan Rather and Tom Brokaw—at a simple $900,000 per annum. Peter is by far the most accomplished journalist of the three competing anchorweights on the American networks. Dan Rather is the frenetic, continually tense "$6 million man" for CBS, that being the amount of his multi-year contract. Tom Brokaw is pleasant and mid-westernish at NBC, but one never gets any sense of depth or passion in him.

Jennings surpasses them both in reporting experience, a veteran of hot spots around the world. His father was Canada's first national newscaster when the CBC was founded in 1936 and was later its vice-president. Peter is cool and has a nice, understated crisp aura of authority about him on air. Although ABC's evening news show is normally third in the ratings behind Rather and Brokaw, in the major urban centres in the United States Jennings comes out on top.

When he was the ABC anchor in London, Jennings heard talk of this innovative new program, *The Journal*, that the CBC was thinking of establishing in Canada. He wrote the CBC, indicating he was quite interested and wouldn't mind returning to Canada after his many years abroad. A year went by without a reply.

Other Canadian pretty faces who are doing well on the American tube? Well, for example, you remember Peter Kent, who also used to be with Barbara at *The Journal*. He's now with NBC in Miami.

Free trade? Free mouth? It all boils down to a haircut.

It must be explained that the Americans, being practical, view Canadian pretty faces as cannon fodder. There are more than a few dicey countries in the world where American passports are not welcome. When things blow up, the Yanks are *verboten*. Canadians, being bland and noncontroversial on the world scene, are regarded as harmless. Their passports can get them into countries that regard Americans with, let us say, more than suspicion.

That is why Mark Phillips, the red-haired former CBC man, is now the CBS man in Jerusalem. It is why John Blackstone, the former CBC chap who wisely took the precaution of having a hair transplant is now with CBS in London. It is why, particularly why, Henry Champ—formerly of CTV's W5 and who owns through inheritance large hunks of southern Manitoba—is a prize catch of NBC.

Richard Brown, the handsome former CTC guy, is an anchorman in New York. Don McNeill of Newfoundland (who was a Rhodes Scholar from the Rock, as was Eugene Forsey), is an American network correspondent out of Jerusalem after doing Moscow. The classiest news show in Washington is the MacNeil-Lehrer Report, co-hosted by Canadian Robin MacNeil.

Brian Stewart, the familiar face on CBC hot stories overseas, has gone American, to NBC in Frankfurt. John Mackenzie, who used to be on CTV, is ABC's area chief in Boston. Nadine Berger, late of Vancouver and the CBC's Take 30 show, is now a regular out of Los Angeles television. Brian Nelson, sacked by CTV's ethnically hyper management because as a dumb guest host he read an anti-Zionist news broadcast in the Middle East, is with Ted Turner's CNN.

All this, of course, contrasts with the reverse brain drain. Everyone raves over Ann Medina's ballsy coverage of the Lebanon nonsense—American critics saying how brilliant this Canadian reporter is. In fact, she happens to be an American who moved to Canada. Hilary Brown, one of the best things on Toronto television, is a Canadian-turned-Brit-turned-New-Yorker who now has returned and brings all three nationalities to her role on the tube.

There were, hard as it is to believe, expatriates long before Peter Jennings. Louis Riel, who was twice elected as a member of parliament for the Manitoba riding of Provencher (now represented by Health Minister Jake Epp), was banished from Canada in 1875 for five years. After a brief stay in Keeseville, New York, he went to Montana where he married, became an American citizen, and settled down as a teacher.

Strangely enough, there were nervous rumours that Riel—then in the United States—might form an alliance with the famed Sioux leader Sitting Bull—then in Canada. Sitting Bull, who was permanently lame, had just dispatched the

U.S. 7th Cavalry, led by Lieutenant-Colonel George Custer, at the Battle of Little Bighorn in Montana. Custer, who had been eager to restore his eroded military prestige, fell along with 240 of his men. Sitting Bull, knowing the full weight of the U.S. Army would be mounted against him, eventually fled across the border into Canada, making camp with five thousand men in the Wood Mountain area in what is now southern Saskatchewan.

Inspector James Walsh of the North West Mounted Police rode into the camp with six men and assured Sitting Bull of protection from pursuit by the U.S. Army if the Sioux obeyed the laws of Canada and did not conduct raids across the border. Sitting Bull agreed to the terms, denounced the Americans, and declared himself a "British Indian."

In 1879, when American traders and hunters set fires along the border to keep the buffalo south, the end of the buffalo hunt on the Canadian prairies was in sight. Sitting Bull returned to the U.S. where, after formally surrendering, he toured briefly with Buffalo Bill's Wild West Show, which visited Toronto in 1885. In a skirmish with police on his reserve, he was killed. Three months after Sitting Bull's visit to Toronto, Louis Riel, who had returned to Canada, was hanged in Regina.

We have established that Americans, while they have no animus against Canadians, are not really interested in them. It is interesting, therefore, to observe the result when one talented American—forced by circumstance to earn a buck on a Canadian newspaper—turns his perceptive eye on those who are so close and yet so far from his own people. (This lad was born in Illinois.)

"There is one thing Toronto demands in clothes. That thing is conformation. That does not mean conformation in the same sense as it is applied to a horse at the Royal Winter Fair. No, far from it. It means conformation; to conform.

"Take my soft felt hat, for example. There is nothing wrong with the hat. It is a good hat. It sheds the rain and keep the sun out of my eyes. But the first time I wore it in Toronto was the last time. Nothing could induce me to wear it again."

The writer goes on as to how he mounted a Toronto streetcar wearing his hat. The conductor looked at him suspiciously, the passengers looked at him askance, two young girls started to giggle. The owner of the hat was one Ernest Hemingway, who in this 1924 piece for the *Toronto Star*, where he worked, demonstrated both his genius for observation and that Toronto essentially has not changed. He was only twenty-one.

It really doesn't matter, in the great scheme of things, that Mary Pickford was from Toronto or that William Shatner of Montreal and James Doohan of Vancouver are Captain Kirk and Flight Engineer Scottie of *Star Trek*. They are entertainment figures whose talents are exportable. Nor have we "lost" them, as the thumb-sucking magazine pieces and weekend features would have us believe when they anguish over Canada "losing" to the bright lights Ivan Reitman and Howie Mandel, Christopher Plummer and Margot Kidder, Lorne Michaels, Morley Safer, Leslie Nielsen (the more charming of the two Yukon brothers), Lloyd Bochner and Tommy Chong, Helen Shaver, Monty Hall, Alan Thicke, and so on. It's no loss. It's no more loss than a Manitoba hockey player signing up with the St. Louis Blues.

What would get me worried was if Eugene Forsey or Farley Mowat or Peter Gzowski left. They haven't and they won't; they are Canadians. This country is not hurt by those who have opted for another clime. It is stronger because of the ones who have stayed.

Canada's future, in fact—the oracle has spoken—rests on those who stay in the proud homeland. Does anyone doubt that Larry Zolf, with his antic mind, as lively as a flea, could not go off to Hollywood and invent an *Animal House*? A *Meatballs*? A *Mackenzie King Meets Frankenstein*?

Pierre Berton has more energy than Manhattan has invented. One somehow suspects that Robert Fulford could survive in the intellectual wastelands of Harvard. They'd love Peter Worthington in the right-wing think tanks now infesting Washington. Barbara Amiel?—Ayn Rand with a Joan Collins cleavage. Instant *People* magazine cover.

17

Risky Business

*In which our darling scout tells why Canada wants
to remain unhugged and what the elephant thinks of
the mouse and why Mulroney is wrong on free trade
and why Big Don Macdonald looks so surprised and
more sad tales than you ever want to hear.*

There can only be one winner, folks, but isn't that the American way?—GIG YOUNG in *They Shoot Horses, Don't They?*

The point is that we are in danger of being hugged to death. As has been delineated, Brian Mulroney is more sympathetic to America than any prime minister since Mackenzie King. In his own celebrated phrase, he is prepared to give the United States "the benefit of the doubt" in situations that would have offended or irritated his predecessors at 24 Sussex. That's fair enough. His genial Irish nature leads him in that direction, just as his labour-conciliator background leads him to seek solutions, to avoid public fights, to smooth things over.

All well and good. The only problem is that Uncle Sam's predilection is to dominate. It is undoubtedly true that the Allies could not have won the two world wars (probably not the first one, certainly not the last one) without American intervention, however late. From an American perspective, however, the United States won both wars; the early intervention of Britain and France and Canada and the others was almost a handicap, leaving it up to the serious guys to come in and mop up. It's a natural state of mind for the bully on the block. When you're big, you tend to swagger.

There is no way the mouse is ever going to win a battle with the elephant, at the bargaining table or elsewhere. Ask Finland. The genius (and the salvation) of Canada is to realize, and glory in, its apartness. You don't have to ask Mexico, which is in an analogous (i.e., dangerous) position to Canada's, because Mexico is protected by the buffer of a different language. That is her main salvation: Spanish is the chastity belt that protects her from Yankee penetration.

It is why René Lévesque was the greatest threat ever to

Canada. The protective buffer of French culture and the French language—this is officially a bilingual country, remember?—has been one of the thankful barriers separating us from the United States, benevolent but smothering as they be. If Quebec had gone into her Balkanized dream, there would have been little to keep Toronto (our most Americanized city) or Alberta (our most Americanized province) from giving up the ghost and surrendering to the easy lure of the siren to the south.

The Americans are not predatory by nature. It is just that their nature makes them predatory. Essentially, they feel, as Teddy Roosevelt did, that anybody as close to America as Canadians—sharing somewhat the same language, eh?—would be fools not to come under the umbrella that has given the world Columbo, Jerry Lewis, Fabian, Tiny Tim, Roy Cohn, Billy Carter, Madonna, and pet rocks. Mexicans they can forgive: different language, different culture. Canadians? We are looked on, when anyone bothers to look, as failed Americans, as those who didn't make the cutoff.

Canadians should not feel badly about this, about being regarded as would-be Yanks who are huddled outside the servants' entrance, waiting to get in. The Belgians do not feel that way, squashed by France. (They played each other for third place in the 1986 World Cup in Mexico. That's football. Soccer, as it is called north of Mexico.) The Finns don't feel that way. The Basques don't feel that way. Think of Canadians as the Basques of North America and you've sort of got it.

It's why Mr. Mulroney, down deep, is wrong in his flirtation with the Rhett Butlers of the White House. They already have a sure grip on the short hairs of this nation through television, through movies, through magazines, and through their branch-plant economic philosophy. It is not really necessary for us to get into bed with them.

Some 80 percent of the trade between the elephant and the mouse is already "free." Is the future well-being of the mouse really dependent on the other 20 percent? One thinks not.

The free-trade fandango is doomed anyway because each side is playing with a different deck of cards. For the Americans, the only civilized people in the world without a universal medicare system, to suggest that Canada shove its medicare plan on the negotiating table is ludicrous. It is ludicrous to discuss broadcasting policy with a nation that doesn't understand the philosophy of public broadcasting—which is that the airwaves can't be left to the merchandisers and ad-men to be run solely for profit.

The Americans, because their country is founded on different values, have no concept that the genius of the Canadian system is the public corporation. And without the CBC and Air Canada and the CNR there wouldn't be much of a Canada. (In the United States, they are even "privatizing" prisons, selling them to those who would run them for profit.)

It is one of the smug conceits of Canadians that they know America so well while Americans are so ignorant of Canada. What Canadians mean is that they know a lot about American movie stars and geography and every detail of the life of Jackie Kennedy, not to mention Pete Rose. In fact, Canadians know remarkably little about the United States. (There are more than two dozen major American universities with Canadian studies programs. In Canada there are perhaps six universities with American studies programs.) Canadians are especially ignorant about how the quite different American system of government works. This extends even to Ottawa.

Some surprising people can be naïve about the Americans. Big Don (Thumper) Macdonald, a finance minister in the Trudeau years, earned his nicknames from his big feet and from the way he treated the opposition in his stint as government House leader. He is not intellectually shy. He went to Harvard, he deals in a sophisticated ambience with high-powered foreigners, Americans among them, in his role as a diplomatic hit man for McCarthy & McCarthy, the Toronto law firm he retreated to after Ottawa and from which he has contemplated several abortive feints at the prime minister's chair.

He could not wait to finish his seemingly never-ending royal commission on everything anyone ever thought about Canada before he scooped his own report by telling Canadians they should embark on "a leap of faith" and get into bed with the Americans on free trade. He has been sort of a den mother to this cottage industry ever since, always available for most any seminar or think tank or head table discussing free trade. After all, he was the country's reigning expert on the proposed caper, having spent some $20 million to discover whatever it was he discovered.

On the day Mr. Simon Reisman, he of sulphuric vocabulary, and Mr. Peter Murphy, he of the red hair and the naïve manner, opened the trade talks, Mr. Reagan slapped a 35 percent tariff on Canadian shakes and shingles (the shakes are the thick ones that the toffs can afford, the shingles are the thin ones that the rest can afford). Mr. Macdonald was so shocked that he urged the trade talks to be called off immediately. The act of faith lasted just one day.

What shocked Macdonald and the already shaky Mulroney government was the insensitivity of Washington (not especially news) and sloppiness at the White House, which did not go through the diplomatic courtesies of informing Ottawa before the tariff was announced. (As it turned out, Premier Bennett of British Columbia had warned the prime minister's office some months previous that such an action could be in the works.)

There is little awareness among Canadians how constricted in power a president (as opposed to a prime minister) can be and how Congress can keep the White House in check. The president is against protectionism and is fighting more than three hundred protectionist bills that are at present in the congressional hopper. He threw in the shakes-and-shingles bone in an attempt to keep the isolationist wolves away from the door.

I fail to comprehend, being an obtuse sort, the whines of those Canadians who are always bleating about the Americans failing to be interested in their close neighbours. Why should they be interested? If I were an American, I would not be interested in Canadians. We are docile; we are polite. We are harmless; we pose no threat; we are a genuinely benign hunk of real estate (all of which, they assume, is perpetually frozen).

With their rather more significant problems with Moscow and the arms race, with the Philippines and its wrestling match with itself, with little New Zealand and its obstreperous act, with the Middle East continually aflame, with their friend Maggie Thatcher in peril, with South Africa on the brink of civil war—like, why would they spend much time worrying about Canada?

I'm rather a fan of the general American ignorance of Canada. I like it. It does little real harm other than to Canadian pride. Pride doesn't cost any money, or territory—or water. It's when the Americans, who have been profligate with their water resources, take a real interest in Canada's "surplus" of clean, cheap water that I get worried. It's when the United States starts to become interested in foreign countries that the trouble starts.

Ask Chile. And Mr. Allende—whatever precisely happened to him. Americans are rather ashamed about what the CIA did to "destabilize" his regime and they don't talk much about Chile today.

Ask Vietnam. The United States is still suffering the guilt pangs for their involvement in a fuzzy intervention that was going to stop communism from reaching San Diego's shores and instead bled a generation of youth and turned one generation against another, destroyed one president and confused several more. To say nothing of what the war did to Vietnam itself. (John Kennedy once asked Lester Pearson what he thought Washington should do about Vietnam. "Get out," Pearson told him. "Any fool knows that," replied an exasperated Kennedy. "The question is how." They got along rather well after that.)

Ask Iran. The insane Washington propping up of the Shah of Iran on his Peacock Throne (with the sycophantic Barbara Walters preening beside him on network shows) merely showed the insensitivity of the Americans as to what was really going on in a country that supposedly was riding high on American aid. (The United States actually backed the Shah in the bidding to be host of the Olympic Games.) In reality, of course, he merely proved to be the precursor of Ferdinand Marcos (BYE BYE FERDIE, said the final *New York Post* headline) and Imelda's shoes.

You can ask a number of other small and relatively insignificant countries about what happens when the United States takes a real interest in their welfare. Ask Grenada, not to mention Cuba. Ask Nicaragua and El Salvador. (In the meantime, the United States ignores the most tragic case of all, Mexico, a country with massive problems.)

Canadians are unwise to mumble and complain that the Americans know little about them. I say: let's keep that ignorance flying.

Instead of furrowing their brows and pouting that they are being ignored, Canadians would best reflect on the advantages they have. In all, they have a higher standard of living than the Americans, since "standard of living" means more than simply some numerical measuring put out by the World Bank. Standard of living, by the reckoning of any sane authority (meaning Dr. Foth), involves quality of life.

Quality of life means a certain lack of fear of violence—or even thinking about violence. I, a pudgy, reasonably active adult male who is hard to knock over because of my specific gravity, would not walk in large portions of Washington or New York alone in the daytime (and never at night) unless for some urgent reason. (In Detroit, for no urgent reason.) It's hard for a male to put himself in a female's mind, but I have some sense of the wariness and caution a woman must feel in every underground parking lot, in every lonely office elevator late at night—and I would put that too into a measure of the "quality of life" and therefore the standard of living.

An environment that is green, rather than asphalt and cement; the closeness of wilderness; a slightly less vulgar lifestyle; a society not so cleanly divided between "winners" who are rewarded obscenely and "losers" who are left on the trash heap: Canadians have a number of advantages over Americans. Instead of moaning about the ignorance that exists below the border, Canadians would be wise to keep their mouths shut and hope that no one notices the secrets they've got.

There can hardly have been a politically independent country that has survived semi-intact from such an onslaught of cultural dumping as the United States has unloaded on Canada: in movies, television, magazines, fads and fashions, sport and spoils. There are more Americans visiting Canada every year than the total Canadian population and they go home (mainly bearing salmon in their camper freezers and Kodak Instamatics worn to the frazzle) with the country left whole and unsullied, except for the cash registers. Rejoice, they are harmless and didn't catch anything from the water. We could have, as the cliché goes, worse neighbours. But let's keep them neighbours. At a safe distance.

Acknowledgements

This tome would not have seen life without the stubborn determination of Anna Porter, a publisher who combines grit with a sense of humour, both qualities much needed in the project. It owes much to the patience and guidance of Phyllis Bruce. The help of Barbara Keddy and Geri Savits-Fine is most appreciated. Perry Goldsmith is an invaluable ally.

I am grateful to my employer, Southam News, and to *Maclean's* magazine, under whose banner I have roamed enough to gather material that forms the basis of this sermon. I am especially grateful to Southam News General Manager Nicholas Hills, not normally a patient man, for granting the time necessary for the completion of this project.

For background material, I have drawn upon Lawrence Martin's *The Presidents and the Prime Ministers* (Doubleday, 1982); F.A. McGregor's *The Fall & Rise of Mackenzie King* (Macmillan, 1982); C.P. Stacey's *A Very Double Life* (Macmillan, 1976); Andrew Malcolm's *The Canadians* (Times Books, 1985); William Shawcross' *Sideshow: Kissinger, Nixon and the Destruction of Cambodia* (Simon & Shuster, 1979); *The Book of America*, by Neal Peirce and Jerry Hagstrom (Norton, 1983); Richard Gwyn's *The 49th Paradox* (McClelland & Stewart, 1985); Bruce Hutchison's *The Incredible Canadian* (Longman, Green, 1953); Eleanor Roosevelt's *This I Remember* (Harper & Brothers, 1949); Tony Thomas' *The Films of Ronald Reagan* (Citadel, 1980); Jack Pickersgill's *My Years with Louis St. Laurent* (University of Toronto Press, 1975); Charles Ritchie's *Storm Signals* (Macmillan, 1983); Ruth Montgomery's *Hail to the Chiefs* (Coward-McCann, 1970); John Diefenbaker's *One Canada* (Macmillan, 1976); *Mike*, Volume Three of the Pearson

230 *Allan Fotheringham*

memoirs (Toronto, 1975); John Griffiths Pedley's *Ancient Literary Sources on Sardis* (Harvard University Press, 1972); George E. Bean's *Aegean Turkey* (1966); and Will Durant's *History of Civilization*.

Dave Brubeck also helped very much.

ABOUT THE AUTHOR

Allan Fotheringham is the most talked about political columnist in Canada. Everybody reads *Maclean's* from back to front, just to see what he's up to first. He has already written two bestsellers, *Malice in Blunderland* and *Look Ma . . . No Hands*. He is a resident panelist on CBC's long-running show, *Front Page Challenge*. For the past two years, the corporate heads of Southam News have let Dr. Foth loose on an unsuspecting Washington, where he is currently living and writing.

SEAL BOOKS

Offers you a list of outstanding fiction, non-fiction and classics of
Canadian literature in paperback by Canadian authors, available
at all good bookstores throughout Canada.

The Mark of Canadian Bestsellers

CANADA'S GREATEST STORYTELLER

FARLEY MOWAT

Chronicler of man against the elements

Bestselling author, Farley Mowat, portrays true-life adventure and survival with unique passion. His courageous stories of remote lands, people, and animals have been read in over twenty languages in more than forty countries. And now, the most cherished of his stories can all be read in paperback.

01689-6	GREY SEAS UNDER	$2.95
42098-2	THE SERPENT'S COIL	$3.95
42137-7	NEVER CRY WOLF	$3.95
01736-1	THE WORLD OF FARLEY MOWAT	$3.95
42127-X	THE BOAT WHO WOULDN'T FLOAT	$3.50
42084-2	AND NO BIRDS SANG	$3.95
42128-8	THE DOG WHO WOULDN'T BE	$3.50
42078-8	THE DESPERATE PEOPLE	$3.95
42079-6	PEOPLE OF THE DEER	$3.95
42028-1	A WHALE FOR THE KILLING	$3.50
42058-3	THE SNOW WALKER	$3.95
42068-0	SEA OF SLAUGHTER	$9.95
42106-7	MY DISCOVERY OF AMERICA	$3.50

The Mark of Canadian Bestsellers

FM-6